Old Chicago Houses

Old
Chicago Houses

By JOHN DRURY

The University of Chicago Press
Chicago and London

To

Carl Sandburg

whose poems were beacons illuminating
new paths for me

THE UNIVERSITY OF CHICAGO PRESS, CHICAGO 60637
THE UNIVERSITY OF CHICAGO PRESS, LTD., LONDON

© 1941, 1975, by The University of Chicago
All rights reserved. Published 1941. Third impression 1976
Printed in the United States of America

International Standard Book Number: 0-226-16555-8

Publisher's Note

IN JANUARY and February of 1975, John Sifton, an architecture buff and friend of this press, visited all one hundred of the house sites listed by John Drury in the present volume. He found that thirty-four houses have survived the intervening decades, and he has provided the list reproduced below. The notes on the houses are Mr. Sifton's also. He points out that a few houses may have been moved from the sites listed by Drury rather than destroyed. The publishers would be glad to be informed of such unlisted survivors.

STILL-EXISTING HOUSES

Clarke (p. 4)[a, b]

Glessner (p. 44)[a, b, c]

Kimball (p. 49)[a, c]

Hoxie (p. 58)

Gates (p. 62)

Ryerson (p. 88)   Much altered.

McCormick (p. 106)   Now Chez Paul.

Nickerson (p. 115)[b, c]

Lathrop (p. 146)[a, b, c]   Balustrade along the top is gone.

Hull (p. 158)[a, c]   Restored; on University of Illinois Chicago
   Circle campus.

McCaffery (p. 162)

Ferguson (p. 189)

Sulzer (p. 233)   Porch is gone.

Work (p. 250)   At back of house at this address.

Fassett (p. 254)

Hoyt (p. 259)

Shedd (p. 289)

Iglehart (p. 298)   A gem.

Givins (p. 310)

Bellinger (p. 318)ᶜ

Stritch (p. 327)ᶜ   Residence of the Roman Catholic archbishop.

Dewes (p. 340)ᵃ

Van Natta (p. 352)   A surprise: see Drury's last sentence.

Brown (p. 368)   Much altered.

Dyniewicz (p. 384)

Raber (p. 392)   Still has the cupola.

Sandburg (p. 416)

Smith (p. 421)   The porch is gone.

Peattie (p. 426)

Warner (p. 449)

Eberhart (p. 453)

Heath (p. 480)

Charnley (p. 484)ᵃ, ᵇ, ᶜ

Robie (p. 494)ᵃ, ᵇ, ᶜ

ᵃ Listed in *National Register of Historic Places.*

ᵇ Described in *Chicago's Famous Buildings,* 2d ed., ed. Arthur Siegel (Chicago: University of Chicago Press, 1969).

ᶜ Described in *Chicago on Foot,* by Ira J. Bach (Chicago: J. Philip O'Hara, 1973).

Foreword

IN ALMOST every city, town, and village of America stand certain weather-beaten old houses that are well known for other reasons than the familiar one of possible ghostly tenancy. Usually located near central business districts where earliest settlement began, they survive today as eloquent, if anachronistic, links with the past. Some of these faded dwellings are of interest as striking examples of outmoded styles of architecture, others as the homes of early settlers, while still others stand apart as the birthplaces or one-time abodes of famous men or women.

But how many people, except for a few elderly folk, know the full stories of the outstanding residential landmarks in their midst? It is safe to say not many. This, of course, is not so true of the New England or southern states, where ancient houses have been a subject of wide interest for several generations. In the nation at large most people have been too absorbed with the present to have time for the past. There are signs, however, that more and more Americans are becoming conscious of the past life of their own communities and, as a consequence, are taking an increased interest in those old public buildings and private dwellings around them which survive from bygone eras.

If the majority of people have had little time to devote to old houses, they have nevertheless been aware of these dwellings and curious as to their histories. Who built the house? Was its builder someone of importance in the past? When was it built? What style of architecture does it represent?

vii

What events occurred in it? Were any famous persons enter-tained in it? What is its interior like? Who lives in it now? These are only a few of the questions that usually dangle in the mind of anyone used to seeing some curious old ante-bellum house or late Victorian mansion—perhaps one with an ornamental cupola on its roof and scrollwork decoration on its porch—standing in the midst of a sleek, modern neighbor-hood of "two flats," apartment houses, or hotels.

At the present time—a momentous time when our country and the rest of the world are in a transitional stage marking the end of one epoch in civilization and the beginning of an-other (whose outline is still dim but which contains a hint of the disappearance of large cities)—some record should be ob-tained, it seems to me, of those remaining old landmarks in all parts of the country, and particularly in cities, which are of historic significance locally or nationally or which effec-tively represent architectural styles or housing modes during past periods of our national life.

A commendable effort in this direction was made a few years ago by architects of the Historic American Buildings Survey, a Works Progress Administration project. But this survey concerned itself only with the making of architectural drawings of historic landmarks. It did not go into the stories of the landmarks, except for a few bare details. True enough, considerably more information on these buildings and houses has been uncovered by the W.P.A. writers' project and em-bodied in their excellent state and local guidebooks; yet here, too, the material is all too brief and sketchy. Another proj-ect (a private one)—Mrs. James Ward Thorne's miniature "period rooms"—touches on the old-house field, but in this case only interiors are shown.

The fact remains that the outstanding old houses of the nation are deserving of more comprehensive studies. I am aware, of course, that studies have been made, but these deal mostly with the Colonial dwellings of New England or with the plantation houses of the Old South. The vast major portion of the country, stretching from the Appalachians to the Rockies and beyond, and from the Mason and Dixon line to the Canadian line, has not yet been investigated by the old-house historian.

With this thought in mind, but limiting myself only to the dwellings of my native city, I began the series of newspaper articles which form the material of this book. These articles appeared weekly in the newspaper of which I am a staff member, the *Chicago Daily News*, and were started on March 17, 1939. After the series was completed in February, 1941, I began a new series on old Illinois houses, and this is appearing currently in the *Chicago Daily News*.

Although it was the scene, seventy years ago, of a great fire which destroyed its central business district and some residential territory near it, Chicago today contains many old houses well known either for their architecture or for the fame of their owners or as landmarks of the city's early days. These are located in all parts of town and range from pioneer farmhouses to magnificent mansions. Many were originally outside the metropolitan boundaries and were brought into the city when the early villages and suburbs in which they stood were annexed to Chicago. The city's great houses—its costly and imposing Gothic castles, Renaissance palaces, and Romanesque strongholds in which lived the merchant princes, steel kings, and packing magnates of Chicago's glamorous and golden past—are all located on the outskirts of the downtown area in once wealthy neighborhoods that sprang up after the fire of 1871.

In writing of Chicago's old houses, I have adhered only to facts. I have used, in each instance, a blend of historical, biographical, architectural, and social facts in an attempt to create a detailed picture of the dwelling under discussion. As to the ages of these houses, I am aware that a New Englander or a southerner might smile indulgently and call them young, or, at most, middle-aged. One must consider, however, that the last one hundred years in the history of Chicago, as well as of the entire Middle West, has encompassed in that relatively brief span the trail-blazing, pioneering, and social and industrial development that had taken much longer in older communities of the Atlantic seaboard. Thus, a house built fifty or sixty years ago in Chicago has achieved the dignity of age without great accretion of years.

To some persons the selection of the dwellings in this volume might seem arbitrary. My answer is that these houses were carefully chosen for a number of reasons, the main one of which is that (with one exception) they date from the nineteenth century. Other reasons for their selection is that they are representative examples of architecture at different periods, that they are important or conspicuous as neighborhood landmarks, and that they are well known as the one-time homes of locally or nationally famous men or women.

In selecting these houses, I also had in mind the possibility that they might serve as exhibits of domestic architectural styles in vogue throughout the United States for the last one hundred years, for I knew that Chicago contained examples of practically all the styles of residental architecture to be found in this country since the 1830's. With this in mind, I began with the Greek Revival style, touched on the Eclectic and what has been called the Parvenu periods, went through the Romanesque era, and finally came to a close shortly after the turn of the century with the style most expressive of our own age and which had its birth in Chicago—the "modern," or "International."

A project of this kind, which involves research in many fields, requires the assistance of numerous persons, particularly librarians, in the gathering of data. I have been most fortunate in receiving such assistance. One of the most helpful and patient in aiding me has been Mr. Thomas Sayers, librarian of the *Chicago Daily News*. Valuable assistance was also rendered by Mr. Herbert H. Hewitt, head reference librarian of the Chicago Public Library; by Miss Adele Rathbun, librarian of the Chicago Historical Society; and by Mrs. William T. Herzog (the former Marion Rawls), in charge of the Burnham Library of Architecture of the Art Institute of Chicago.

In the field of architecture I have had the guidance and advice, generously given, of Mr. Earl H. Reed, director of the former northern Illinois unit of the W.P.A. architects' project. Two others—Mr. J. Frank Graf, vice-president of the Chicago Title and Trust Company in charge of that company's abstract department, and Mr. Howard C. Brodman, superintendent of maps for Chicago—have also assisted me in many ways.

I have been aided, too, by Miss Helen Zatterberg, secretary-historian of the Ravenswood–Lake View Historical Society; Mrs. Gertrude I. Jenkins, secretary-historian of the West Side Historical Society; Miss Marion Barnes, librarian of the Morgan Park Historical Society; Mrs. Florence E. Richards, honorary president of the Chicago Lawn Historical Society; Miss Bernadine McLaughlin, curator of the Calumet Pioneers Society; Mrs. Viola B. Neeson, secretary-historian of the Englewood Historical Society; Miss Julia Baker, librarian of the Historical Society of Woodlawn; Miss Helen S. Babcock, secretary-historian of the South Shore Historical Society; and Miss Marie Antoinette de Roulet, librarian of the Chatham Historical Society.

Commendation is due here to the staff photographers of the *Chicago Daily News*, who, under the able supervision of Mr. Clyde Brown, displayed more than ordinary enthusiasm and co-operation in obtaining the photographs in this book. To them I am very much indebted.

I am greatly indebted, also, to the hundreds of individuals who have written me letters containing suggestions, advice, corrections, and appreciations, and to all of these I hereby extend my thanks. Furthermore, to those many persons who were kind enough to show me through their homes and who graciously recounted to me their personal recollections, I am similarly indebted. Lastly, I feel this list of those who aided me would lack a very essential name if it did not contain that of one who most willingly and enthusiastically placed her scholarship and knowledge of American manners and customs at my disposal—my wife Marion.

JOHN DRURY

CHICAGO
June 17, 1941

Acknowledgment

THE contents of this book appeared originally as a series of weekly articles in the pages of the *Chicago Daily News*. Permission was granted by the management of that newspaper for the reprinting of the articles in this form. All photographs in this book were taken by staff photographers of the *Chicago Daily News*.

Contents

CONTENTS

PART V. ON THE GOLD COAST

PART VI. WEST OF THE RIVER

PART VII. IN OLD LAKE VIEW

CONTENTS

CONTENTS

PART I
Pioneer Days

Introduction

*In the days before the railroads came, Chicago was a small fron-
tier city served by sailing vessels, prairie schooners, and stagecoaches. Most of the houses and buildings were of frame construction, although brick was beginning to appear here and there.
In spring the streets were muddy, and buggies and wagons were
often mired. The little stores and shops of the business district
stood along South Water and Lake streets—two streets that led
eastward to the log palisades of Fort Dearborn. Elms, lindens,
and cottonwoods shaded the residential avenues then, and most of
the houses in the outlying sections were white painted and were
designed after an extremely simple fashion. A little later came
more costly dwellings in the Greek Classical style fashionable
during ante-bellum days. After the railroads came, the little city
soon grew to a metropolis, its population increased rapidly, and
thousands of homes—most of them jerry-built—sprang up all
over the city and in the "suburbs." Then a great fire destroyed
most of the old, central portion. Few houses survived from the
early days—the days when Chicago was known as "the city in a
garden." Fortunately for the historian or architectural student,
however, several of these pioneer dwellings still stand, all that
remain of the era before the railroads came.*

3

The Widow Clarke's House

I N CHICAGO, where real estate values are of primary
importance and historic landmarks of little consequence,
where also a great fire once caused widespread destruction, it is something of a miracle that any houses survive at
all from earliest pioneer days. A few remain, however, and
one of the oldest of these is the dwelling at 4526 South Wabash Avenue, now known to historians as the Widow Clarke's
House.

This dwelling is believed to have been built about 1836. In
his *Biographical Sketches of Some of the Early Settlers of the
City of Chicago*, a work published in 1876, William H. Bushnell writes: "Mr. Clarke was, *de facto*, one of the old settlers.
About forty years ago he erected his [then] famous mansion,
dwarfing all others, on the South Side of the river, and
equalled only by that of William B. Ogden on the north—of
which it was a rival." Bushnell, who was personally acquainted with the subject of his biographical sketch, says the
residence cost $10,000 to build.

The man who built the house was Henry Brown Clarke, a
native of New York State who had come to Chicago about
1833 with his wife and family. Soon after his arrival he entered the hardware business with William Jones (father of
Fernando Jones, a well-known figure in later Chicago history)

4

and Jones's son-in-law, Byram King. The firm was known as King, Jones and Company. Their hardware store was on South Water Street, just east of Dearborn Street.

HENRY B. CLARKE HOUSE
4526 South Wabash Avenue

Supplying tools, building materials, and household articles to a rapidly growing pioneer community, the firm of King, Jones and Company prospered, and soon Henry B. Clarke was one of the town's leading citizens. Sometime during this period he bought land—twenty acres on the shore of the lake just south of town. Here he built a log house for temporary shelter and moved his family into it. By 1835 we find him one of the directors of the first bank to be opened in Chicago. He appears to have survived the panic of 1837.

By 1836 Henry B. Clarke was a man of means. In this year, it is believed, he replaced the log house on his country estate south of town with an imposing mansion in the Greek Revival style, an architectural manner then fashionable. It is described as a counterpart of the classic mansion erected on the North Side by William B. Ogden, the city's first mayor. Clarke's twenty-acre estate embraced the area north of what is now Eighteenth Street and Wabash Avenue, and his mansion is said to have stood in the vicinity of the present old First Regiment Armory at Sixteenth Street and Michigan Avenue.

Edwin O. Gale, in his *Reminiscences of Early Chicago*, says of Henry B. Clarke: "[He was] a typical pioneer, who could not brook the narrow confines of even a frontier village, but felt that the wide sweep of lake and prairie in the remote southern part of the town would be more congenial to his taste. There, far removed from every evidence of civilization, save when the fall fires or the winter snows leveled the luxuriant rosinweed and exposed to his view the town or the distant cabin of Dr. H. Harmon, he built his log abode, which was nearly hidden by the wild sunflowers that flecked the boundless prairies and the scrubby trees that drew their meagre sustenance from the drifting sands of the bleak lake shore."

The log cabin referred to was, as indicated above, Clarke's earliest residence in Chicago, but Gale goes on to say that "in the course of time the city found him, with his children grown up and his cabin as well; and when the vain North Siders would boast of William B. Ogden's grand white mansion with its lofty porticoes supported by massive Corinthian columns, occupying an entire block surrounded by magnificent trees, with equal pride would the South Siders point to its beautiful counterpart on Wabash Avenue and Eighteenth Street, the home of the former South Water Street hardware merchant."

Here, within the walls of his spacious frame mansion with its pillared portico and high cupola, Henry B. Clarke lived the life of a country squire. With him were his wife, Caroline, and their six children. It is believed that Henry B. Clarke's brother-in-law and cousin, Dr. Henry Clarke, also lived in the mansion with his wife.

In Andreas' *History of Chicago* we read that among "prominent citizens" who died in the cholera epidemic of 1849 was Henry B. Clarke. He was then but forty-seven years old. From the year of her husband's death until she died in 1860 at the age of fifty-four, Mrs. Caroline Palmer Clarke lived in the white mansion on the lake shore with her children, and it was during this time it acquired the name of the "Widow Clarke's House." During the 1850's the house was a favorite stopping-place for families taking buggy rides "out in the country" on Sunday afternoons.

After the Chicago Fire of 1871, the Widow Clarke's House was purchased by John Chrimes, a prominent Chicago tailor of that era. Fearing a repetition of the Chicago Fire, Chrimes moved the classic dwelling farther south outside the city limits into what was then the township of Hyde Park. Some twenty years later, this old township was annexed to Chicago, and the Widow Clarke's House once more found itself within the municipal boundaries. Standing on its present site since the great fire, this house was gradually surrounded with new homes, until today it is in the midst of a now old and somewhat run-down Negro neighborhood.

Six years after moving his residence to the Far South Side, John Chrimes died. The house subsequently became the home of his daughter, Mrs. William H. Walter, and her husband. A well-known livestock commission merchant, William Walter lived in this house until his death in 1933. His widow, who was proud of living in a historic Chicago landmark, died in 1939. The house is now occupied by her two daughters, Lydia and Laura Walter, both public-school teachers and both, like their mother, interested in the rich historical associations of their home.

Considering its great age, the house is in remarkably good condition. The portico has been removed, but the cupola, with its tall windows, remains, as does the pediment over the front entrance. It is a two-story frame dwelling with gable roof and high narrow windows. The rough-hewn oak beams which form its framework are as sound and solid today as when first set in place. Inside, the rooms are of ample proportions, separated by sliding doors, trimmed with Georgia pine, and enhanced by ornamental marble fireplaces.

The Eleven-Mile House

O UT at the south end of Chicago, where the prairies are wide and houses are few, there stands at 9150 South State Street a two-story, gable-roofed, frame dwelling with a wide porch along its front and side. Other than the fact that it seems old, there is nothing else about its appearance to suggest that this is one of Chicago's historic houses.

Students of the city's early days, however, would recognize it immediately as the Eleven-Mile House, one-time country inn that played a commendable if humble part in the making of Chicago. Although the tradition is strong that this house is more than a hundred years old, a number of local historians are reluctant to accept this age figure until there is more definite proof.

Those who contend that it really is more than a century old turn for support to a book, *The Wonders of the Dunes*, written in 1923 by the late George A. Brennan. In dealing with early roads and trails through the dunes country that led into Chicago, Brennan tells of one Jonathan Perriam, pioneer settler on the banks of the Calumet River, who said that in 1840 there were but three houses between his own and Chicago and that one of these was the Eleven-Mile House.

As further proof of its great age, Brennan, in a letter to a

9

friend, says that the edifice "is built of logs, covered with siding." The letter, written in 1927 to Gerrit Pon and printed in a booklet on the early history of Roseland, tells more of the South Side landmark.

JOHN SMITH HOME
9150 South State Street

In any case, if, as tradition has it, the tavern was built sometime in the late 1830's, it stood eleven miles outside of Chicago, as its name indicated. At that time Chicago as a city was but a few years old and was bounded on the north by what is now Chicago Avenue, on the west by what is now Halsted Street, on the south by what is now Roosevelt Road, and on the east by the lake. The population was about five thousand persons.

Today, the Eleven-Mile House stands inside the city. In

the years since it was built, Chicago has marched southward
—and westward and northward—until at present the city's
southern boundary is some ten miles beyond the old State
Street caravansary. But prairies are still in its vicinity, and
so the house stands in much the same setting as when the
first covered wagon drew up before its spacious porch in the
early days.

In an old history of the southern part of Cook County it is
stated that the Eleven-Mile House was built by John Smith,
early settler of the region, and that at first it was called
"Smith's Tavern." Here, then, in those primitive days before the coming of the railroads, road-weary travelers on
horses or in covered wagons—farmers, homesteaders, trap-
pers, fur traders—stopped to refresh themselves before making the last jump on the trek to Chicago.

If night was coming on, the dusty and tired wayfarers were
put up by the hospitable innkeeper. Horses were given plenty of hay in the big barns next to the tavern, hearty meals
were ready for the hungry travelers, and great, comfortable
beds awaited tired limbs upstairs. In those faraway days
when the Eleven-Mile House was in its prime there was too
much danger of mischievous Indians for anyone but the most
adventurous to be abroad on the lonely prairie road after
nightfall.

In the years after the tavern was built, railroads came to
Chicago, Lincoln was elected president, the Civil War was
fought, and the great Chicago Fire occurred; but all during
those eventful years the Eleven-Mile House continued in
business as a refreshment house and stopping-place. When
the township of Hyde Park was annexed to the city in 1889,
the Eleven-Mile House was at last engulfed by the city that
once had been miles away to the north.

Before all these things had happened, however, Innkeeper

Smith had passed away. It is said that he died in 1847 at the age of forty-seven and that he was buried in the old cemetery at Blue Island. Despite this, there is a legend that Smith's burial place was on the Smith property somewhere near the tavern and that it was marked by an apple tree.

When first built, the Eleven-Mile House was located across the street from where it now stands. John Smith afterward moved it to what he thought would be the opposite side of the road but which turned out to be the middle of State Street as it was laid out by surveyors. So the house was again moved, this time to its present location.

In addition to taking care of the daily guests in his hostelry, John Smith also had his hands full with a brood of five children. One of his daughters, Eunice Sophia, married Merrill Kile, or Kyle, and this event is noted in the *Chicago Daily American* of Monday, December 6, 1841, in the following words: "Married on 2nd inst. by F. A. Howe, Esq., Mr. Merrill Kyle to Miss Eunice S. Smith, daug. of John Smith, at his residence 10 miles south of Chicago."

The present owner of the old Eleven-Mile House, Alexander Fraatz, who lives quietly in it with his family, says that at one time—this must have been long after the death of John Smith—the tavern was sold at a sheriff's auction, the purchasers being one Henry Wendt, an innkeeper at Fiftieth and State streets, and two other men. These three hired a man by the name of Cosenbroh to operate it.

In 1880 the tavern came into the possession of Frederick Fraatz, father of the present owner. The elder Mr. Fraatz continued to operate it as a tavern. In those days it was a favorite gathering-place of Dutch farmers from Roseland, who stopped with their teams in the early morning on their way to South Water Street Market in the city.

A faded photograph of the Eleven-Mile House, taken some time in the 1890's, shows a flourishing public house shaded by several big maple trees. Farmers' wagons and teams are standing in front, and the horses are drinking from a long wooden water trough. A sign on one side of the entrance reads: "Wacker & Birk Lager Beer." The men standing about are adorned with whiskers or mustaches and sport high-crowned derbies.

The Sheldon House

~~~~~~

A PASSER-BY would hardly look at it twice. There is little to distinguish this dwelling from most of the other wooden cottages on the Near West Side that escaped the great fire. It appears to be only an old house in an old section—soot covered, a little down-at-heel, but still staunch and serviceable.

Yet, if the passer-by knew that plate drawings of this humble frame house, as well as detailed sketches of its interior and trim, are in the permanent files of the Library of Congress and the Burnham Architectural Library of the Art Institute, it is likely that he might stop and consider it with some curiosity. For, of the thousands of old houses in the city, this building at 723 West Congress Street was among three dwellings in Chicago deemed of sufficient historic or architectural interest to be included in the Historic American Buildings Survey undertaken by the W.P.A. federal architects' project.

"It was chosen by our advisory committee," explained Earl H. Reed of Chicago, director of the northern Illinois architect's project, "because this dwelling is probably the finest remaining example of a type of early Chicago cottage. Its exterior and interior decorative detail are in the best Greek Revival style of architecture, a style that was fashionable in America during the forties and fifties."

14

This Greek Revival influence cannot be noticed at first, quick glance. As Mr. Reed points out, "the average passer-by might easily overlook the subtle beauty of this obscure little building." But the classic touch is there. It shows itself in the simple and pleasant patterns of lintels, window frames, molding, cornice, door trim, and other woodwork.

"Though not measuring up to our modern standards of comfort, this little architectural gem can nevertheless teach us volumes about good taste in home design," said Mr. Reed. "Its virtues of simplicity, dignity, and good composition are of the sort more often encountered in Lake Forest than in the blighted areas of the city."

One might question the designation of this house as a "cottage," since it is a tall two-story edifice. But it was not always so high. At some unknown date the cottage was raised about eight feet, and a brick basement was built under it. Originally, it was a one-family dwelling.

What is the history of this lowly West Side abode that escaped the Chicago Fire and remained to become one of the city's distinctive architectural landmarks? When was it built? Who built it? Although research assistants, working under the direction of Mr. Reed, have sought answers to these questions in old records, very little definite information has been turned up.

Enough material has been gathered, however, to give it a name. The architects call it the "Sheldon House"—because it is believed to have been built by one Daniel H. Sheldon, an early resident of the city. Just when he erected it has not been determined, but it is believed to have been some time between 1844 and 1856. That this might be true is shown by the decorative detail, for the Greek Revival in American architecture was at its height in Chicago between those years.

DANIEL H. SHELDON HOUSE
723 West Congress Street

This makes the Sheldon House kin, architecturally, to the Widow Clarke's House.

It is recorded in a deed that title to the property was transferred from the estate of one John Green to Daniel H. Sheldon in 1844, the sale price being $61. This was probably for the vacant lot. It is fairly certain that Sheldon built the present dwelling on the lot soon afterward. It is further recorded that in 1856 Sheldon sold the place to John Mehegan for $5,000.

Just who Green, Sheldon, and Mehegan were, early city directories and histories do not say. In any case, it is known that John Mehegan sold the place to another person. Then followed a string of different owners, some of whom made alterations—adding a brick basement, building on a rear section, and putting in a marble fireplace of definitely mid-Victorian design.

With all these additions, the living space in the cottage has been increased so that today there is enough room to house three families. Although the dwelling may be old, the plumbing and some other interior appurtenances are modern.

On entering the hallway, one immediately notes the simple but well-designed newel post and staircase leading to the second floor. Paneled doors open to the parlor, on the east wall of which the marble fireplace offers its now cheerless welcome. The parlor and dining-room are separated by paneled sliding doors. Two bedrooms are on the second floor.

The drawings on file in the Art Institute library contain detailed sketches of the door and window frames, front entrance, transoms, and moldings, as well as full-sized profiles of the newel post, balusters, and outside cornice. The original cottage was thirty feet long by twenty feet wide, the ground floor plan shows.

Although this is an unusual house in Chicago, enjoying some little fame among historically minded architects of the city, it will probably not survive much longer, for it is certain that the Sheldon House will be torn down when Congress Street is widened into a superhighway. If this happens, the Sheldon House is at least preserved on paper for future architects to study.

"Long John"
Wentworth House

~~~~~~

IT STANDS on a rise of ground at the northeast corner of Archer and Harlem avenues, out on the western edge of the city. Old settlers say that this long, white, gable-roofed frame house has been there as far back as they can remember. And a few of these old-timers can even tell something of its interesting story—a story that goes back to the beginnings of Chicago.

Although no historical marker in front of it says so, this is the farmhouse of "Long John" Wentworth, a titan of early Chicago, one of that group of stern New Englanders who had come West, founded Chicago, built it from year to year, and who had lived to see it become a world-metropolis.

John Wentworth voted for the city form of government in 1837, was the city's first great newspaper editor, one of the earliest congressmen of this district, a friend of Lincoln, and mayor of Chicago just before the outbreak of the Civil War.

It was for this reason, and also because it is an unusual specimen of nineteenth-century Middle West farmhouse architecture, that the Wentworth House was included in the group of old Chicago buildings drawn by workers of the

19

W.P.A. architects' project as part of the American Historic Buildings Survey sponsored by the Department of Interior. As with the Widow Clarke's and the Sheldon houses, Mr. Reed and his architects went all over the venerable Wentworth House, measuring, sketching, drawing, and photographing. These drawings, too, are in the Library of Congress and the Burnham Library of Architecture in the Art Institute.

Another notable feature of this one-time Wentworth country seat is that it is located only half a mile south of what historians agree is the most significant historic spot in or adjacent to Chicago. This is the Chicago Portage, one-time connecting link between the Great Lakes and the Mississippi River which determined the founding of Chicago at the head of Lake Michigan.

When John Wentworth left his native New Hampshire at the age of twenty-one and came west to the muddy little frontier town of Chicago in 1836, it is doubtful whether he dreamed that one day he would be owner of a five-thousand-acre stock farm just outside the city of his adoption. It is known, however, that he had dreams and that these dreams were linked with the raw, uncouth town at the head of Lake Michigan.

He had vision, too, and he knew that some day Chicago would be a great city. There were other men of the time who had the same vision. Some of these were from Wentworth's native state, such as Stephen F. Gale and Justin Butterfield. Others were from Vermont—Gurdon S. Hubbard, Mark Skinner, Silas B. Cobb, Charles V. Dyer. These, together with Willian B. Ogden, who came from New York State, were the early giants of Chicago.

Shortly after his arrival here, Wentworth took over control of the *Chicago Weekly Democrat*, the city's first newspaper, and in 1840 changed it into a daily—first in the North-west. Then he was elected to Congress, where he served for twelve years, and in 1857 was first elected mayor of Chicago and re-elected in 1860.

During the years when he was a congressman in Washington, Wentworth saw the country estates of leading Ameri-

JOHN WENTWORTH HOUSE
5441 South Harlem Avenue

cans—Washington's Mount Vernon and Jefferson's Monticello—and these made an impression on him. He began to plan just such an estate for his old age. His final term in Congress finished, he came back to Chicago and began to acquire land in the vicinity of Summit, all of which was then in Lyons Township.

During his tenure of office as mayor of Chicago, Wentworth entertained the then Prince of Wales, who afterward became King Edward VII of England. Among his outstanding public acts were the destruction of "The Sands," a notorious bawdy-house and gambling district on the lake front north of the river, the prevention of the Camp Douglas plot during the Civil War, and the introduction of the first steam fire engine in the city, named the "Long John" in his honor.

A few years later he was owner of a five-thousand-acre stock farm at Summit. On the wide prairies of the tract roamed Wentworth's herd of a hundred and fifty blooded cattle and his many thoroughbred horses. And the center of life on this big estate was the spacious, two-story, sixteen-room Wentworth farmhouse—the house that is still standing today. The records show that it was built in 1868.

Two years after the house was built, it was darkened by the death of John Wentworth's wife, Roxana. Before his own death in 1883, Wentworth had lived long enough to see Chicago become the second largest city in the country.

Surviving him was his daughter, Mrs. Roxana Atwater Bowen, who died in 1936 in New York and who is survived by a daughter, Mrs. Roxana Van Rensselaer, now a resident of England. Living in Chicago today is "Long John's" grand-nephew, John Wentworth, as tall and personable as his famous forebear.

Occupying the old Wentworth farmhouse at present are Mrs. Jane Ann Parlin, widow of the late Cyrus E. Parlin, and her family. Not long after the death of Wentworth, some six hundred acres of the farm and the farmhouse came into the possession of Cyrus E. Parlin, pioneer Chicago horse-breeder and trader.

Here, then, with but three acres left of the original five-thousand, Mrs. Parlin and her daughters and their husbands and children live, occupying the many rooms of the great, white farmhouse whose floors once groaned under the three hundred pounds and the six-foot, three-inch height of "Long John" Wentworth, titan of early Chicago.

PART II
Old Prairie Avenue

Introduction

Two miles south of the Loop, paralleling the tracks of the Illinois Central Railroad, stand the decaying mansions of old Prairie Avenue. Sixty or seventy years ago, or in the period after the fire of 1871, this was the most exclusive and fashionable neighborhood of Chicago. Here lived the Fields, Armours, Pullmans, Hibbards, Blackstones, Gregorys, Highs, Glessners, Otises, Joneses, and other great families of the late Victorian era. Then it was a quiet, elegant street shaded by trees, bordered by stately residences, and trod on by the proud bays of millionaires' carriages. Today, it is only a forlorn ghost of its former self. The big, mansard-roofed or turreted mansions are deserted, cobwebs and dust curtain their leaded glass windows, and once-proud façades now present a picture of decay and ruin. Here and there, a stone mansion might still be in use—as a publisher's office or advertising agency—but most of the houses are vacant. There are only two families left now—the last of the old guard— of the many who lived on this street in years gone by. Meanwhile, over the turrets and mansards of old Prairie Avenue rise big, sleek, modern factories—a new one appearing almost each year to take the place of some famous old mansion.

A Great-Grandmother's Home

~~~~~~

ONE of the most interesting of Chicago's old houses, unusual for both its architecture and the person who dwells in it, is the quaint, two-story frame edifice at 1638 Prairie Avenue. Old fashioned, prim, and small, it stands there in strange contrast to the imposing mansions that surround it on all sides like proud, if down-at-heel, aristocrats.

Unlike the mansions, however, which are vacant and rundown, there are signs of life in and around the little frame house. It has a general air of neatness and trimness which indicate it is always occupied. Sometimes big cars piloted by liveried chauffeurs may be seen driving up to it and unloading important-looking personages who are welcomed into the unpretentious dwelling.

This is the home of Mrs. Adelaide Hibbard Gregory, one of the last survivors of that group of wealthy Chicagoans—the Pullmans, Marshall Fields, Armours, Kimballs—who once lived in the mansions on Prairie Avenue and made it the social center of the city in the 1880's and 1890's. These others are gone from Prairie Avenue now, but Mrs. Gregory remains, a link with the glamorous past of the city's first "Gold Coast."

To an architectural student the Gregory home is of interest because of the Gothic design of its exterior. The style is known as Hudson River Gothic. The arched window frames, porch pillars, railings, and scrollwork trim give the façade a churchlike appearance. In general, however, the house is plain, with a high-peaked gable roof, bay windows, and clapboarded sides.

Because Mrs. Gregory has lived in this house for more than half a century, many persons believe it was originally built for her and her late husband. This, however, is not the case. One of the first edifices to be built on Prairie Avenue, it was erected in 1870 by John G. Shortall, a leading Chicagoan of the pre-Fire era.

When John Shortall built this abode, he was Chicago's outstanding land-title expert and was head of the abstract firm of Shortall and Hoard, which he founded in 1861 and which was to become a forerunner of the present Chicago Title and Trust Company. Shortall was also a patron of the arts, a civic and religious leader, and had been president of the Illinois Humane Society and the American Humane Society.

A year before John Shortall erected his home there was built across the street a much more impressive dwelling for William G. Hibbard, head of a hardware firm which became Hibbard, Spencer, Bartlett and Company. There were six Hibbard youngsters—two sons and four daughters—and one of the daughters, Adelaide, looked on with interest as carpenters were building the frame house across the street.

She saw the house completed and saw John Shortall move into it with his family. Then came the Chicago Fire of 1871. Shortall's records were imperiled. So were those of Hibbard, as well as his stock of goods. Hibbard had three teams of horses available at the moment and offered one team to Shortall. With the team and a wagon, Shortall obtained his records and brought them to his Prairie Avenue house for safekeeping.

In the years following, while Adelaide Hibbard was growing to womanhood, more and more mansions were built on
Prairie Avenue, and the Hibbard hardware firm became one

MRS. ADELAIDE H. GREGORY HOME
1638 Prairie Avenue

of the largest in the city. Meanwhile, a young Lyon and
Healy Music Company official named Robert S. Gregory began to show an interest in Adelaide Hibbard. The interest

was mutual, and sometime afterward their engagement was announced.

When the couple were married, in 1880, they were presented with a wedding gift by the bride's father. That gift was the Shortall house across the street, which earlier had become vacant. The newly married Gregorys moved into it, spent their honeymoon there, and began entertaining many of the other prominent residents of Prairie Avenue. Later, Mr. Gregory became president of Lyon and Healy.

Here Mr. and Mrs. Gregory lived, reared their children, and eventually saw the gradual fading of the Prairie Avenue section as a social center. They decided to remain there, however. When Mr. Gregory died in 1918, his widow announced she would continue to live in her home, and has done so uninterruptedly since that time.

She is now eighty-one years old. Despite her years, however, Mrs. Gregory is as full of enthusiasm and almost as active as when she first moved into the little frame house sixty-one years ago. As recently as four years ago she presided at a debut tea for her granddaughter, Adelaide Sweetser, held in her Prairie Avenue home.

Until recent years, she made frequent trips across the Atlantic to her chalet in Switzerland, and once, on one of these trips, she flew across the English Channel. A few summers ago she went on a motor trip through New England. In addition to all these activities, Mrs. Gregory wrote a book, *A Great-Grandmother Remembers*, published in 1940 by Adolph Kroch, the bookseller.

Here, then, attended by family servants and a chauffeur, lives this "Grand Old Lady of Prairie Avenue," and when night falls and the street outside is deserted and silent and the big mansions stand dark and forlorn, the lights are still burning in the little frame house—one of the few signs of life on the once-famous street.

The Fernando Jones Mansion

~~~~~~

AMONG students of early Chicago history, the three-story, red-brick residence at 1834 Prairie Avenue, located across the street from the old Marshall Field home, has long been an object of interest. For here lived Fernando Jones, who, before his death in 1911 at the age of ninety-one, was widely known and revered as one of Chicago's earliest settlers.

Long before he achieved this fame, however, Fernando Jones had won a name for himself as an authority on Chicago land titles. The abstract firm he founded became the parent-body of the present Chicago Title and Trust Company. His services in this field were especially valuable after the great fire of 1871, when most of the county records were destroyed.

"Fernando Jones," wrote Miss Caroline McIlvaine, a Chicago historian, "began life in Chicago as a lad of fifteen. Starting in his father's log hardware store at the Forks in 1835, he experienced every step in the evolution of Chicago from a population of 2,000 to that of 2,000,000."

This log hardware store was known as King, Jones and Company, and one of the partners was Henry B. Clarke, builder of what was to become known as the Widow Clarke's House. The other members of the firm were Fernando Jones's father, William, and his brother-in-law, Byram King.

Before coming here, Jones had attended school in Buffalo. One of his teachers was Millard Fillmore, afterward president of the United States. Two years after his arrival in Chicago,

FERNANDO JONES HOME
1834 Prairie Avenue

young Fernando Jones went back East to complete his education at Canandaigua Academy, and there he met Stephen A. Douglas, another student. This meeting resulted in a life-long friendship between the two.

When Jones first stepped ashore here from a sloop in 1835, he saw a rough-and-tumble frontier hamlet crowded with land speculators, promoters, and others eager to buy tracts, for a land boom was under way then. The streets were muddy, and houses and stores were wooden shacks. The town was not yet incorporated as a city.

As Jones was an enterprising youngster with some education, he soon obtained a job as clerk in the government land office, and this marked the beginning of his career as a land and real estate expert. He also helped out in the Indian agent's office, having learned the Potawatomi language; and then, just before returning East to finish his schooling, we find him at work as a clerk in the office of the Illinois and Michigan Canal Company.

His academic education completed, Jones came back to Chicago and entered a real estate firm his father had founded. But because of ill-health he was forced to go South. He returned in 1854 and established the abstract firm of Fernando Jones and Company in association with John D. Brown. Then the firm was changed to Jones and Sellers, the new partner being Alfred H. Sellers.

While head of this company, Fernando Jones became active in affairs of the city. He served as alderman of the then Third Ward during the administrations of Mayors John C. Haines and "Long John" Wentworth, was trustee for several state institutions, supervisor of the South Town during the Civil War, and administrator of Camp Douglas until the military authorities took charge.

The firm of Jones and Sellers continued in business until after the great fire of 1871. After that, all of the abstract firms in the city were merged, and this led to the eventual founding of the Chicago Title and Trust Company. By this time Jones was a man of wealth and position, and it was not long until he built the palatial residence on Prairie Avenue.

Although not so big as the Marshall Field mansion across

the street, the Jones home is somewhat similar in architectural design. It is a square, red-brick building with mansard roof and English basement, and its front is marked by a white stone portico. The interior is typical of mansions of that day, with high ceilings, marble fireplaces, sliding doors, leaded windows, and carved banisters.

In the years after the great fire and after the World's Columbian Exposition, Fernando Jones lived here in retirement with his wife and two children. For a time Mr. and Mrs. Jones resided abroad, dividing their time between Paris and other cities. When at home on Prairie Avenue, the Joneses often entertained visiting celebrities, and their domicile became a gathering-place of early Chicago settlers who had become influential and wealthy.

The story is told that Fernando Jones often provided entertainment at yearly meetings of the Pioneers of Chicago, of which he was for a time vice-president, by talking in the Potawatomi language with another old settler, Alexander Beaubien. Incidentally, he was at one time president of another old-timers' group here, the Sons of New York.

Always interested in the history of Chicago and the preservation of relics and landmarks connected with its growth, Jones performed two outstanding services in this field, according to Miss McIlvaine. He located the "Massacre Tree" and the grave of Chicago's only Revolutionary War soldier, David Kennison.

The "Massacre Tree," near which the soldiers and civilians from Fort Dearborn were massacred by the Indians in 1812, was found to be only a stone's throw from the Jones edifice on Prairie Avenue. A monument was subsequently erected there, but later it was removed to the Chicago Historical Society.

Jones evidently knew David Kennison, the Revolutionary

War soldier and last survivor of the Boston Tea Party. It is recorded that Kennison presented to Jones a small bottle containing tea leaves from the famous "tea party" in Boston harbor.

Fernando Jones, patriotic and historically minded, valued that gift highly. It is said that he planned on sealing the bottle of tea leaves in the stairway newel post of his Prairie Avenue home. But he died before this could be done. The bottle was found later in his old-fashioned secretary. It is now on exhibition in the museum of the Chicago Historical Society.

The Palace of a Merchant Prince

〜〜〜〜〜〜〜〜〜〜〜〜〜〜〜〜〜〜〜〜〜〜〜〜〜〜〜〜〜〜〜〜〜〜

TO SOCIAL historians the old three-story, red-brick mansion at 1905 Prairie Avenue bears somewhat the same relation to Chicago's social life of the past as does the famous William K. Vanderbilt mansion to New York's aristocratic world. Both were built by businessmen who were among the wealthiest of their time, and both were the scenes of social functions that did much to make the late Victorian era glamorous and legendary. Both were designed also by the same great architect, Richard M. Hunt.

In the Chicago mansion, for almost thirty years, lived Marshall Field, founder of America's greatest mercantile firm, Marshall Field and Company. Renowned in his day as "the Merchant Prince," Marshall Field was then regarded as one of the richest men in the world. After his death in 1905, the Field estate was estimated "at about $100,-000,000," according to one authority. Much of this was in Chicago real estate, both in the Loop and in outlying sections.

If he made a fortune out of the city of his adoption, Marshall Field also gave large portions of it back to Chicago. He established the great lake-front museum named after him and was largely responsible for the founding of the Art Institute. He was also one of those who laid the groundwork for the University of Chicago and the one-time Chicago Manual Training School.

Marshall Field picked Richard Morris Hunt, a great architect of that day, to design his mansion. Mr. Field knew that Hunt was a product of Brattleboro, Vermont, and was therefore undoubtedly imbued with the New England qualities of dignity, simplicity, and common sense. He knew that Hunt could design a less grandiose if no less majestic house than the one he had planned for Vanderbilt on New York's Fifth Avenue. So Hunt received the commission.

It was just five years after the Chicago Fire of 1871 that the Field mansion was built. It is said to have cost two million dollars and was the first house in Chicago to have electric lights. Constructed of red brick with stone trim, the house is three stories high and is marked by a mansard roof. It stands on grounds surrounded by an ornate grillwork iron fence.

Here, then, the "Merchant Prince" lived, and his wife, who was the former Nannie Scott of Ironton, Ohio, ruled as social queen of Chicago. Here, the Fields reared their son, Marshall Field, Jr., and their daughter, Ethel, and here, in the years before the World's Columbian Exposition, the couple quietly entertained famous American and European personages and held notable social functions.

When Marshall Field, Jr., was seventeen years old and Ethel was fourteen, there was held in the Field mansion one of the biggest social events ever to be staged in Chicago up to that time. This was in January, 1886. It was a ball in honor of the two Field youngsters, and both young and old were invited. More than five hundred guests were present.

As Gilbert and Sullivan's operetta *Mikado* was then the

rage in the fashionable world, the Marshall Field event was a
"Mikado Ball." Youngsters and their parents, driving up in
handsome carriages, all came in colorful oriental costumes.

MARSHALL FIELD MANSION
1905 Prairie Avenue

On the night of the ball, Prairie Avenue was lighed with special calcium lights. The ball was said to have cost $75,000.
It was talked about for years afterward.

Young Field grew to manhood, but met his death in an
accident in 1905. His sister, Ethel, first became the wife of
Arthur Tree, son of a prominent Chicago judge, and then,
after the couple were divorced, she married a dashing young

British naval officer in 1901 named David Beatty—afterward Admiral Beatty, first sea lord of the British admiralty and hero of the Battle of Jutland.

Following the death of his wife in 1896, Marshall Field remained a widower in the Prairie Avenue mansion for some years, but in 1905 he married Mrs. Delia Spencer Caton, widow of a well-known Chicago attorney who had been a friend and neighbor of the Fields in the Prairie Avenue neighborhood. Mrs. Caton was a daughter of one of the founders of Hibbard, Spencer, Bartlett and Company. But their wedded life was of short duration, for, a few weeks after his son met his death, the "Merchant Prince" died of pneumonia.

Having inherited the Field mansion, Mrs. Field lived in it for many years, much of that time with her niece, Mrs. Albert J. Beveridge, widow of the Indiana senator. Several years before the first World War, however, Mrs. Field took up permanent residence in Washington and left only a caretaker and housekeeper in the mansion on Prairie Avenue. She seldom came to Chicago, and the house lapsed into obscurity.

Before her death in 1937, at the age of eighty-four, Mrs. Field deeded the house to Marshall Field III. He, in turn, deeded it to the Association of Arts and Industries, with the stipulation that it be used as an industrial art school.

This school, called the New Bauhaus, was established by L. Maholy-Nagy and carried out the aesthetic theories of the school of design founded by Dr. Walter Gropius, in Germany. After two years the school in the Field mansion closed its doors, and since then the famous residence has been vacant.

Before the Field home was remodeled for the New Bauhaus, however, it once more blazed with lights that shone on a gay party similar to the ones given long ago by the second Mrs. Field. This was in May, 1936, when the Association of

Arts and Industries lent the mansion to a group of younger society members who staged an 1885 ball there. All came in the costumes of the gaslight era.

On that memorable night the old mansion came back to life once more. Guests walked up the great circular staircase of carved wood at the end of the central hall and gazed at the big hall clock built in 1793, marveling that it only needed to be wound once a year. They conversed in the big, roomy conservatory at the south end and gazed with admiration at the high-ceilinged, ivory-and-gold drawing-room.

After that the interior was remodeled in the modernist style for the short-lived New Bauhaus.

Last of the Old Guard

LTHOUGH most of the once great mansions along
old Prairie Avenue are deserted and falling into
decay, such is not the case with the venerable red-
brick residence at No. 2021. For here lives one of the two
socially prominent Chicago families who still occupy the
same homes they moved into more than half a century ago
and who now compose the last of the avenue's old guard.
This house is also of note because of the man who built its
original portion.

At the north end of the half-mile stretch of mansions in the
center of the old Gold Coast area lives Mrs. Adelaide Hibbard Gregory, now eighty-one years old and popularly known
as "the Grand Old Lady of Prairie Avenue." At the south
end, at No. 2021, lives Major Shirley T. High,* now sixty-six
years old, and his wife, Velma. Major High and Mrs. Gregory often meet on their strolls in fine weather and recall the
past glories of their street.

When Major High, soldier, lawyer, former city fire attorney, and son of a pioneer Chicagoan, was a youngster in
short pants chasing fire engines in Thirty-first Street, there
lived at 2021 Prairie Avenue a man who was one of the city's
first grain shippers and flour manufacturers. This personage

* Since this book went to press, Major High died June 12, 1941.

was Benjamin Adams, who founded the Adams Mills here in 1852 and who, sometime in the late 1870's, erected the red-brick, three-story residence at 2021 Prairie Avenue.

In 1886, Benjamin Adams sold his house to James L. High, then a leading attorney and an author. Born in Ohio, James High had served in the Civil War and had come to Chicago in 1869. After buying the Adams house for $40,000, High had its front remodeled and made many improvements in its interior.

The Highs moved into the Prairie Avenue house in 1888. Their street was then the bon ton neighborhood of the city. Trees shaded the wide sidewalks, ladies in bustles and gentlemen in silk toppers strolled past the mansions, and the hoofs of high-stepping horses could be heard above the soft voices of Negro servants.

Installed in their big residence, the Highs were soon taking part in the social life of Prairie Avenue and entertaining their friends and neighbors. When the family moved into the house, Shirley High was fourteen years of age and his sister, Jessie Margaret, was sixteen. They grew to maturity here, saw the great personages of Prairie Avenue almost daily, and in time witnessed the decline of their neighborhood.

The master of the house died in 1898, and his widow survived him by thirteen years, remaining in the family home even when most of her neighbors had moved away. Before all this happened, however, Shirley High had been graduated from Yale University and Northwestern University Law School and had served in the old "Dandy First" Regiment during the Spanish-American War. Two years after his father died, he married Helen Raymond.

It was not until 1909 that Major High became master of the dwelling on Prairie Avenue. This was after his second marriage, his new bride being Velma Hickey, a native of

Iowa. The two have been living here since. Their two sons, James L. and Raymond H., were reared here.

"Aside from the fact that we like the old house, with its sixteen big rooms," said Major High, "we prefer to remain in

SHIRLEY T. HIGH RESIDENCE
2021 Prairie Avenue

the neighborhood because it is practically the quietest spot in Chicago."

That Major High is not without interests is evident to the visitor in this comfortable home. A fire-department enthusiast most of his life, Major High has had installed in his house a "joker stand," as firemen call the instrument board that registers fire alarms. Major High's "joker stand" is connected with the fire-alarm office, and at all hours he is able to tell the movements of fire apparatus.

Another long-time hobby of his—in fact, dating all the way to 1885—is photography. The mahogany-paneled walls of his home are hung with scores of photographs, including a prize-winning photograph of his German police dog. This picture has been exhibited in many parts of the world. In his basement are darkrooms, floodlights, enlarging apparatus, and cabinets of negatives.

Major High, since boyhood, has also been interested in carpentry and the making of mechanical things. So, in addition to photographic darkrooms, the basement of his house is outfitted with a machine and carpentry shop. At other times he reads in his library or in his den where hang the swords, insignia, and documents of his military career.

When not pursuing his hobbies, Major High may be found entertaining his friends in the fire department or in the ranks of old-time fire fans of the city. Sometimes Fire Commissioner Michael Corrigan drops in for a chat, or maybe "Father Bill," as the Reverend William J. Gorman, chaplain of the fire department, is called. And when M. P. ("Pearly") Goodwillie, veteran fire fan, comes in, the two spend many hours recalling the "four-elevens" they went to in the old days.

An Architectural Shrine

REGARDED as something of an oddity when it was built more than half a century ago, the granite residence at the southwest corner of Prairie Avenue and Eighteenth Street, now known as Glessner House, is today a world-famous architectural shrine. In increasing numbers each year students of architecture visit this unique Chicago house standing in dignified, if lonely, splendor just south of the downtown skyscrapers.

When L. Mies van der Rohe, noted German architect and city planner, arrived in Chicago, one of the first buildings he wanted to see was Glessner House. The same was true of L. Moholy-Nagy, distinguished European designer, who came here several years ago. Both visitors caused surprise by revealing that they knew more about the architectural features of Glessner House than did its present occupants.

If this outwardly somber-looking edifice is an object of devotion among architects, it is almost of equal interest to educators and an older generation of socially prominent Chicagoans. For today the house is occupied by a new institution known as the Human Engineering Laboratory. And, during the early years of the present century, it was the scene of another institution, Mrs. Glessner's famous Monday morning reading class.

What brings the architects to this old Chicago house is the fact that it is the best example of domestic design in the Romanesque style of one of America's greatest architects, Henry Hobson Richardson, of Boston. It is also of interest because this was his last work; he died in his forty-eighth year, just three weeks after completing it. Before his death, how-

JOHN J. GLESSNER RESIDENCE
1800 Prairie Avenue

ever, he had designed another famous Chicago building, the Marshall Field wholesale house, which, unfortunately, was demolished a few years ago.

Built in 1886, when the Prairie Avenue section in which it is located was the "Gold Coast" of the city, Glessner House is an eloquent demonstration of what is now known in archichecture as "Richardsonian Romanesque." This is a modification of French and Spanish Romanesque architecture adapted to American needs.

Richardson broke with the Greek and Gothic styles of architecture fashionable in America during his day. He wanted buildings that were simple, direct, solid, and tastefully designed. He believed that beauty was to be found in strength. He achieved his aim and, in so doing, created a new architectural fashion. Romanesque buildings sprang up in all parts of America.

As with most Richardsonian Romanesque structures, Glessner House is built of rough-hewn granite blocks. It looks almost like a medieval fortress. This was the way Mr. and Mrs. Glessner wanted their home, according to friends of the family. They were a conservative, quiet couple, educated and cultured, who wanted a home that would insulate them from the noise and confusion and stir of such a bustling city as Chicago. So Richardson designed just such a home. It is plain and solid on the outside—no bay windows or other unnecessary ornament—and roomy, bright, and comfortable on the inside, which looks out on a courtyard.

The interior is tastefully, if simply, designed. The walls of the reception-room are paneled with oak wainscoting, and a grand staircase leads to the second floor. There are great marble fireplaces in the library, parlor, and dining-room, and all ceilings are beamed, the beams resting on ornate wrought-iron supports. In the big kitchen are a huge range and a long marble sink. Bedrooms and a glassed-in conservatory are on the second floor.

Here, then, in this quiet, cloister-like residence, the Glessners lived after 1886 and brought up their children and sedately entertained some of the leading personages of Chicago's old society world. Mr. Glessner, one of the founders and for years a director of the International Harvester Company, died in 1936 at the age of ninety-two. His wife, Frances, died in 1932. They were social leaders of Chicago for nearly sixty years.

During his life Mr. Glessner took an active part in artistic, musical, and literary activities in Chicago and was one of the principal patrons of the Chicago Symphony Orchestra. In the house today the visitor can see Mr. Glessner's favorite room, a cork-lined room which contained etchings, prints, and oils he had gathered from all parts of the world.

It was more than forty years ago that Mrs. Glessner sponsored the first of her Monday morning reading classes. Among some of Chicago's great ladies who attended these classes in subsequent years were Mrs. Charles L. Hutchinson, Mrs. William R. Linn, Mrs. T. B. Blackstone, Mrs. E. A. Lancaster, and Mrs. W. W. Kimball, all of whom are now dead. Still living are Mrs. James Ward Thorne, Mrs. Frederick Stock, Mrs. Tracy Drake, Mrs. Robert B. Gregory, Mrs. Walter Brewster, Mrs. William O. Goodman, and Mrs. Philo Otis.

Before he died, Mr. Glessner deeded his house to the Chicago chapter of the American Institute of Architects with the stipulation that they could take possession after his own and Mrs. Glessner's deaths. The architects were to maintain the residence as a "museum, library, gallery, and educational institution, including a school of design for legitimate architectural assemblages."

As the cost of remodeling and maintaining the house was beyond their means at the time, the architects' club turned it back to Mr. Glessner's heirs—a daughter, Mrs. Frances Glessner Lee, and a widowed daughter-in-law, Mrs. John G. M. Glessner. Then, three years ago, the Human Engineering Laboratory was established in Glessner House by Armour Institute of Technology, now the Illinois Institute of Technology.

The laboratory, created originally by Dr. Johnson O'Connor at the Stevens Institute of Technology in New Jersey, is an institution for making vocational tests. Through the use of what are called "work samples," the laboratory technicians are able to determine what career an individual is best suited by nature to follow.

Although not strictly devoted to architecture, Glessner House is nonetheless dedicated to educational purposes, in keeping with the owner's will. And, in accordance with another provision of the will, there hangs in the reception room a large portrait of H. H. Richardson. It will hang there as long as the house stands—and architects say the building is as strong as the pyramids of Egypt.

A French Château

CHICAGO'S finest example of the French château style of architecture is generally considered to be the great gray-stone mansion at the southeast corner of Prairie Avenue and Eighteenth Street. It was formerly the home of W. W. Kimball, the piano manufacturer. For some years it was occupied by the Architects Club of Chicago.

Not only is the Kimball mansion architecturally of note, but it also stands today as a reminder of the glory that once was Prairie Avenue—a glory that was at its height during the World's Fair of 1893. One by one the deserted mansions are being torn down and replaced by factories or parking lots. How long the Kimball house will remain is a matter that will be decided by financial exigencies, such as property values and taxes.

In its day the Kimball abode was one of Chicago's great houses. The man who built it, W. W. Kimball, founder of a piano and organ manufacturing firm that became one of the city's leading industries, is said to have spent a million dollars on its design and construction. Looking at it today, seeing its solidity, its majestic exterior, its richly paneled halls and parlors, one is easily convinced that Kimball paid a million to build it.

When Kimball first visited Chicago in 1857, he was a traveling salesman for a Boston firm. The energetic young city made such a favorable impression on him that the following year he established his home here and set up in busi-

W. W. KIMBALL RESIDENCE
1801 Prairie Avenue

ness as a dealer in pianos and organs. In 1864 he founded the city's first wholesale piano firm, with offices in the Crosby Opera House.

Although his offices and plant were completely destroyed in the great fire of 1871, Kimball was not discouraged. Forty-eight hours after the embers of the conflagration had ceased to smolder, he had converted his private residence—an earlier house that stood in South Michigan Avenue—into a piano and organ warehouse, the billiard-room serving as an office and the coach house as a shipping office.

Kimball's business prospered, and in 1882 the W. W. Kimball company was formed. His piano and organ factories were then considered the largest in the world. They are now located at Twenty-sixth Street and California Avenue. Kimball Hall, in South Wabash Avenue, is today the center of activities on Chicago's "Music Row."

In 1865 Kimball married Evalyne M. Cone of Chicago, who eventually presided as chatelaine of the great stone mansion in Prairie Avenue. She became a discerning art patron of the city, and her large collection of paintings are now on permanent exhibition in the Kimball Gallery of the Art Institute.

When Kimball decided, in 1890, to build a magnificent residence on Prairie Avenue, then the "Gold Coast" of the city, he made up his mind to locate it across the street from the brownstone mansion of his friend, George M. Pullman. The site he chose was at the southeast corner of Eighteenth Street and Prairie Avenue, on a large lot owned by Pullman. He purchased the lot, and his next move was to select an architect.

But this was no problem for Kimball. His friend Pullman at once suggested the name of S. S. Beman, one of Chicago's famous architects at that time, and Kimball accepted the suggestion. Brought here in 1879 from New York by Pullman, Beman, as an architect, was not an innovator like Richardson or Sullivan, but he was supreme in traditional or classic fields.

It was after Beman had planned and designed the village of Pullman, said to be America's first model industrial town, and had also planned the Pullman Building, still standing at

Adams Street and Michigan Boulevard, that Kimball commissioned him to do the home on Prairie Avenue.

With almost unlimited funds at his command, Beman took up the work of designing the Kimball mansion. When it was completed in 1892, Chicagoans gazed admiringly at the sumptuous house. It is said to have been modeled after the Château de Josselin in Brittany. Its style is marked by many large and small turrets topped by spires. The Kimball house is three stories high and is built of tooled Bedford stone. The stonework over the arched entrance is highly ornamental.

The top story is characterized by numerous turrets, gables, balconies, and stone chimneys. On the roof is a cresting of ornamental ironwork. There are many windows at each floor level, some of them of curved glass and others flat. An oriel window protrudes from the north façade. Along the front of the house is a high fence of iron grillwork.

If the exterior of the Kimball house has the impressiveness of a feudal castle, the interior is no less arresting. All the apartments and halls are virtually in their original state. The ceilings are beamed and the walls are paneled in oak and mahogany. Great onyx fireplaces dominate some of the rooms. The bathrooms are tiled from floor to ceiling, and the washbowls are of onyx. A staircase with intricately carved balusters and railing leads to the second floor.

In 1924 the house was acquired by the Architects Club of Chicago and converted into headquarters for the club without any material changes in the interior. The club, under the direction of F. W. Maynard, managing director, outfitted the house with its own furniture and equipment. For a time it conducted an atelier there for young architects and also provided living quarters for some twenty architectural students.

Among the many oil paintings of famous Chicago architects which hung on the walls of the rooms was a large one of

Solon Spencer Beman, the work of Oliver Dennett Grover, noted portrait painter.

Seeing the old mansions on Prairie Avenue disappear one by one, and realizing that some day the Kimball house might disappear, too, the thoughtful observer cannot help but feel how futile it was for the millionaires of Prairie Avenue to build such costly and time-defying homes—homes which they apparently thought would stand for generations.

PART III
Millionaires' Row

Introduction

Dating from the leisurely days of broughams, victorias, rock-aways, and surreys, stand the impressive stone and brick man-sions of South Michigan Avenue—the Millionaires' Row of the 1880's and 1890's. But today there is no leisure on Million-aires' Row. Sleek, streamlined automobiles speed past the lone-ly old residences at forty and fifty miles an hour. And there is quickness and efficiency, too, in the automobile salesrooms, auto-mobile schools, and automobile repair shops that have replaced many of the huge, luxurious, aristocratic town houses of finan-ciers and industrialists, packers and steel kings, who ruled the city fifty years ago. Many mansions remain, but most of them are sadly impaired by age, by soot and smoke, and by a changing way of life. Quite a few are either boarded up or converted into rooming-houses or schools of various kinds. Here and there, among these survivors, are dwellings whose stories are worth telling, dwellings redolent of a glamorous bygone era.

A South Side Mansion

~~~~~~

A NOTEWORTHY old mansion that has come back to life as a charitable institution is the dignified edifice of cream-colored brick at 4448 South Michigan Avenue. When built almost three-quarters of a century ago, it stood outside the city limits in the village of Hyde Park. For many years, however, because of the annexation of Hyde Park to Chicago and because of a later shift in population, it stands in the center of the city's Negro community, serving as a convalescent home for crippled white children.

The man who built this house, who made it widely known in the years before the World's Fair of 1893, was John R. Hoxie, financier, railroad and traction magnate, and pioneer Chicagoan. He acquired a large personal fortune through his financial operations and investments, and it was he after whom Hoxie Avenue in South Chicago is named. He is regarded by local historians as an outstanding city builder of the 1860's and 1870's.

It was not until after his marriage in 1873 to Mary J. Hamilton, daughter of an early Chicago settler, that John Hoxie built this great house. Several years after it was erected he was elected president of the Hyde Park Village Board of Trustees, serving in that office until 1876. At that time Hyde Park was experiencing a large influx of citizens from

Chicago who wanted homes out in a "suburb" and away from the city that had but recently been largely destroyed by fire.

Before building his house in South Michigan Avenue, John Hoxie had become a successful and wealthy citizen. He had come to Chicago in 1858 as an employee of what was then the Michigan Southern Railroad, had risen rapidly to become an executive of that road, and had become vice-president of the newly organized Union Stock Yards National Bank. Soon he was investing heavily in real estate for speculative purposes.

"From the date of his location in the city to the present time [1894]," says an old reference work on notable Chicagoans, "Mr. Hoxie has been interested in cattle, stock yards, railroads and franchises. He is a large stockholder in all the street railroads on the South Side, including the elevated. He was one of the projectors of the first cable line and had the pluck to push it to completion when some of his associates were ready to abandon it."

The book goes on to say that he acquired a large tract of unimproved land on the South Side and that he developed it, thus helping to build up that section. We learn that at one time he was a member of the board of education of the town of Lake. While living in his newly built mansion on South Michigan Avenue he was also an unsuccessful candidate for Congress on the Democratic ticket.

In 1878 he bought a large tract of land in Texas, says the work referred to. "This grant embraced 10,000 acres of land in Williamson County, Texas, to which he added another purchase of 7,000 acres," the book continues, adding that "Mr. Hoxie also bought 52,000 acres of land at Midland, Texas, in the counties of Martin and Andrews, this land being used for grazing."

The story is told that after the completion of the Hoxie

residence Mrs. Hoxie decided she did not like the red brick used in its construction. Being devoted to his wife, John Hoxie soon had workmen busy covering the red-brick exterior with a veneer of cream-colored brick, which was more

JOHN R. HOXIE RESIDENCE
4448 South Michigan Avenue

to his wife's liking. As a result of this, the walls of the house are unusually thick.

Three children were born to the Hoxies in this residence. They were John R., Jr., Gilbert H., and Anna C. They were reared here and grew to maturity in the Quaker atmosphere of the Hoxie home. It is somewhat ironical that one of them, Gilbert, in later life, invented the Hoxie expanding bullet and became president of the Hoxie Ammunition Company.

After the death of her husband, Mrs. Hoxie continued to occupy the Michigan Avenue home, and there she died in 1922 at the age of seventy-five.

A man who lived in this house for many years as a member of the Hoxie family was Mrs. Hoxie's father, Polemus D. Hamilton. Coming to Chicago in 1834, Mr. Hamilton became a builder of houses and soon formed a contracting firm. After the death of his wife in 1872 he made his home with the Hoxies. His son was David G. Hamilton, prominent Chicago lawyer of the 1880's.

About 1926 the old Hoxie residence, still in good condition despite its age, was acquired by the Martha Washington Club as a home for dependent crippled children being cared for by the club. It has been so occupied since and is now known as the Martha Washington Home. An average of between thirty-five and forty youngsters, most of them victims of infantile paralysis, live at the home in the care of a nursing staff headed by Mrs. Sue B. Keller.

Although the children—some with crutches, some with braces, and some without any mechanical aids—have access to the entire house, its twenty-five rooms are remarkably well preserved and still retain their old-time grandeur. The entrance hall, reception-room, library, and dining-room on the first floor are each enhanced by great tiled or brick fireplaces and decorated with hand-carved woodwork of cherry, oak, and mahogany.

Surrounding the venerable mansion are the parklike grounds of the old Hoxie estate. Here, under the trees, the little boys and girls who can get about play baseball and other games and enjoy themselves generally. "In about three to five years they will be cured and restored to their homes as healthy children," explained Mrs. Keller.

Here Lived "Bet-a-Million" Gates

〜〜〜〜〜〜〜〜〜〜〜〜〜〜〜〜〜〜〜〜〜〜〜〜〜〜〜〜〜〜

O F THE old mansions still standing here and there among the glistening automobile salesrooms on South Michigan Avenue below Cermak Road, none housed a more spectacular Chicagoan than the large red-brick residence at No. 2944. For this was the home of John W. ("Bet-a-Million") Gates, promoter and captain of industry of the 1890's, whose daring financial exploits were nation wide in scope.

It is now the largest and most sumptuous of the group of free "'hotels" for indigent young men in Chicago conducted by the Catholic Youth Organization. The fine old house, with its luxuriantly carved woodwork, tiled fireplaces, great staircase, and big leaded bay windows, provides shelter for an average of one hundred young men who are fed, provided with sleeping quarters, and given instruction in various trades.

This venerable three-story mansion, contrary to popular belief, was not built by Gates. Proof of this can be seen in the elaborately carved stonework over the entrance. Here may be seen an imbedded medallion carrying the date the house was built—1882—and another medallion showing the initials "S. K."

These are the initials of the man who built the house, Sidney Kent. He was an eminent Chicago financier of the 1880's, who had acquired a fortune through his stock-market opera-

JOHN W. GATES MANSION
2944 South Michigan Avenue

tions. With the building of this house Kent took his place among the millionaires whose mansions lined both sides of South Michigan Avenue in the gilded days before the World's Fair of 1893. The Kent home was said to have cost $90,000. At the time Kent was living in this great house John W.

Gates was acquiring control of various wire companies supplying barbed-wire fencing to settlers in the Great West. He
was thus laying the groundwork for his greatest industrial
achievement, the founding of the American Steel and Wire
Company, which made him the "wire king" of the country
and a multimillionaire.

Born near what is now West Chicago and educated at
Naperville, Gates lost no time in coming to Chicago and getting into the business world here a few years after the great
fire of 1871. It was not long before he began roving about,
and ultimately he became salesman for a St. Louis wire company. While with this company he went to Texas and introduced barbed-wire fencing to settlers and ranchers.

He showed daring from the start. He was always willing
to take a chance. Shrewd and ambitious, he soon gained partnership with the man who owned the St. Louis wire company
and afterward became sole owner of the enterprise. This gave
him his start. He climbed rapidly upward, taking in new business territory each year.

By the time Gates had become "wire king" of the country
he was already active in the stock exchanges and was indulg-
ing in many other large-scale financial operations, in some of
which he outwitted the great J. P. Morgan. Because of his
daring and independence, Gates was feared on the stock exchange. The newspapers of the country dubbed him "Bet-a-
Million" Gates.

It is said apocryphally that in 1897 he cleared more than
twelve million dollars in Wall Street through various stock-
market manipulations. Strong evidence that this must have
been true can be gathered from the fact that in this same year
he bought from Sidney Kent the big mansion at 2944 South
Michigan Avenue and moved into it with his wife and son.

John W., hale, hearty, hospitable, and of a strong masculine type, staged gala parties and entertained lavishly. The crystal chandeliers in the great paneled rooms often burned brightly far into the night, and the porte-cochere on the north side of the house was always astir with the arrival or departure of polished carriages or coaches-and-four.

In later years Gates began to turn his thoughts eastward. He and his family subsequently moved to New York, where they were said to have maintained seventeen rooms and a private elevator in the Waldorf-Astoria Hotel. Afterward he went abroad and acquired a château near Paris. Before moving East he sold the South Michigan Avenue mansion to M. D. Spades, a millionaire from Indianapolis. Gates died in New York in 1911.

"Gates was one of the most vigorous and colorful figures in American finance," says the *Dictionary of American Biography*. "His significance may be said to lie chiefly in the application of the rough qualities of the frontier to the realm of big business."

The Indianapolis man, Spades, occupied the mansion for several years. Later, when South Michigan Avenue began to change, and automobile salesrooms replaced the stately old residences, the Gates house was closed. Then, in 1929, it was acquired by Francis J. Lewis, a Chicago manufacturer, philanthropist, and Catholic leader, who turned it over to the C.Y.O. This was shortly after that organization of Catholic youths, now nation wide in scope, was founded by the Most Reverend Bernard J. Sheil, senior auxiliary bishop of Chicago.

Now occupied by more than a hundred boys and young men, the Gates mansion is kept in good condition, and the only change in it since the days it was occupied by "Bet-a-Million" Gates is that some of the rear rooms have been transformed into dormitories. The one-time ballroom on the third floor is now a chapel, and here the director of the house, the Reverend L. V. Czyl, celebrates mass each morning.

Assisting in the operation of this C.Y.O. hotel are three brothers, members of the Clerics of St. Viator. They are Brothers Emirick, Kelly, and Hebert. All work in and out of the house is done by the young men living there. These young men are only temporary guests and leave the house when they secure jobs and can support themselves.

A Packer's Residence

S THE northbound Drexel Boulevard bus swings
into Michigan Avenue at Thirty-third Street, its
passengers may observe a great brownstone mansion to the left. Of imposing proportions, marked by a single
conical tower, arched portico, dormer windows, and other
architectural details of a more grandiose era than ours, this
mansion has been a residential landmark of Millionaires' Row
for more than half a century.

Many Chicagoans, of course, will remember it as the one-
time headquarters of the Chicago Motor Club. It was in this
ornate stone residence that the motor club set up its first
elaborate headquarters in 1919, and here the club remained
until its downtown building at 66 East South Water Street
was completed in 1928. While occupying the mansion, the
club made few alterations in the interior, and it retains much
of its old-time atmosphere.

In keeping with its architectural impressiveness, this mansion was occupied by an important Chicagoan of an ostentatious era in domestic architecture. For here lived John
Cudahy, a business titan of the 1880's and 1890's and one
of the founders of a Chicago packing firm that today is known
throughout the world. John Cudahy was at the height of his
career when he build the great brownstone residence at 3254
South Michigan. The house is said to have cost $200,000.

67

A nephew of John Cudahy was prominent in the news a year or two ago. This was John Cudahy, former American ambassador to Belgium. He is a son of Patrick Cudahy, one of the four brothers who founded the meat-packing firm.

JOHN CUDAHY MANSION
3254 South Michigan Avenue

While still children, these four brothers were brought to this country in 1849 by their parents, who were natives of Kilkenny, Ireland. The boys got their first jobs in the John Plankinton packing-house in Milwaukee.

It is said that within three years after he came to Chicago in 1876—years when the city was being rebuilt after the great fire—John Cudahy had accumulated a million dollars. This he made as a partner in the packing-house of Chapin and Company. He later acquired control of the company and changed the name to the Cudahy Packing Company. About this time he joined his brothers in founding another packing firm in Milwaukee.

After five years, according to old newspaper accounts, Cudahy had amassed a fortune estimated at more than two million dollars. It was about this time he built the big residence on "Millionaires' Row," as South Michigan Avenue was called in those days. Here he retired from active life and from then on devoted his time to the Board of Trade. He lived quietly with his family, which consisted of his wife, Margaret, daughter of an early Chicago settler, and two sons and two daughters.

"On July 31, 1893, came the great John Cudahy failure," says a newspaper account written at the time of his death. "He had attempted to corner pork and lard, and not only was his fortune, then estimated at over $4,000,000, wiped out, but there were debts aggregating $1,500,000. This failure was regarded as one of the greatest disasters ever experienced on the Board and within two hours after it was known Mr. Cudahy had gone under six other concerns smashed."

The newspaper account continues: "Then began a struggle to recuperate his losses and repay his indebtedness, and his success in this endeavor has never been paralleled in the wheat or provision trade. Going resolutely to work, luck was with him again, and by 1898 he not only had repaid every cent of his losses but had amassed another fortune."

During all this time John Cudahy continued to hold sway as master of the brownstone house in South Michigan Avenue. Here he was often visited by his brothers, as well as by other leading Chicagoans of that day, and here he and his wife reared their children. His brougham and team of horses were greatly admired as he was driven downtown each morning.

In his later years John Cudahy spent considerable time in the mild climate of California. He was on his ranch in that state when he became ill in 1915 and was brought back to Chicago. He died soon afterward in his mansion at the age of seventy-one. For some years afterward his family continued to occupy the mansion. When the neighborhood began to change, they moved to another part of the city.

His widow died in Los Angeles in 1924. When in her prime as chatelaine of the Cudahy residence, she was widely known as a hostess of rare charm and as an active philanthropist. It is said that at one time her mansion was the center of social service activity in Chicago. She served as president of the Chicago Child Society and the Big Sisters Society.

A visit to the old Cudahy house today shows its forty rooms, except for furnishings, to be in practically the same condition as when occupied by the famous packer. Here are spacious rooms and halls, most of them enhanced with elaborate tiled fireplaces and paneled in rare woods of all varieties. On the third floor is a ballroom finished in ivory. A large conservatory occupies the rear portion of the first floor.

The mansion today is known as the Graduate House of Armour Institute of Technology (now a part of Illinois Institute of Technology). A yearly average of forty engineering students live here, and the house is operated by a staff under the direction of Mrs. Amy Lindahl. An interesting slant on the builder of this abode, in connection with its present use, is that John Cudahy was a one-time protégé of P. D. Armour—founder of Armour Institute of Technology.

Where Presidents Were Guests

~~~~~~

WHEN South Michigan Avenue was at its peak half a century ago as a street of millionaires' mansions, one of the best-known dwellings on the thoroughfare was the house at No. 1826. It was designed by William Le Baron Jenney, one of the originators of the skyscraper, and it remains today on its original site—a solidly built residential landmark of Vermont granite that looks as time-defying as a medieval castle.

This house was famous as the dwelling-place of Ferdinand Wythe Peck, son of a pioneer Chicago settler and prominent citizen of the 1880's. It was Peck who sponsored and brought to completion that unique combination of hotel, opera house, and office building known as the Auditorium. The Peck home was equally noteworthy as the stopping-place of presidents of the United States, cabinet members, governors, visiting royalty, and other foreign dignitaries, as well as many celebrities who had come to the World's Columbian Exposition of 1893.

This substantial residence was built in 1889, soon after the completion of the Auditorium. Ferdinand Peck was president of the Auditorium Association and was mainly responsible for erecting the new opera house. He had been aided in this work by his attractive and capable wife, and the honor of entertaining President Benjamin Harrison, who had come to deliver the Auditorium dedicatory address, fell to Mr. and Mrs. Peck.

At that time the Pecks and their children had just moved into their new granite home on Michigan Avenue, and the interior was far from complete. But this did not deter Mrs. Peck. With only three days for preparation, she sought the assistance of several leading merchants of the city, including the family friend, Marshall Field, and all responded quickly. Furniture was moved in, draperies and curtains were hung, florists and caterers were summoned, and the house was swiftly put in shape for the presidential party.

The dinner party given by the Pecks for President Harrison marked the first time in history that a president of the United States had left Washington, together with the vice-president, during a session of Congress. President Harrison was accompanied by Vice-President Levi P. Morton, as well as by several members of his cabinet and numerous other Washington personages. Among the guests at the Peck dinner party was Adelina Patti, opera star, who sang "Home, Sweet Home" at the Auditorium dedication.

After that gala event, the thirty-room Peck residence, which now housed Ferdinand Peck's father-in-law and mother-in-law, Captain and Mrs. William Spalding, continued to attract well-known citizens of the 1890's. Here came Harlow N. Higginbotham, Mrs. Potter Palmer, and other leading men and women of Chicago who were then planning the World's Fair of 1893. Here, too, came Louis N. Sullivan, famous architect, who, with his associate, Dankmar Adler, had designed the Auditorium.

At the time of the World's Columbian Exposition, Ferdinand Peck had been offered the presidency of the exposition, but had declined it in favor of Harlow Higginbotham. He served, instead, as first vice-president and chairman of the exposition finance committee. And at this time he entertained many notable persons in his South Michigan Avenue home.

FERDINAND W. PECK RESIDENCE
1826 South Michigan Avenue

These included the Infanta Eulalia of Spain and other royal visitors.

At a later date there came to the house as a guest President William McKinley. In 1900 President McKinley appointed Commodore Peck—he was addressed as "Commodore" by his friends because of his enthusiasm for yachting and outdoor sports—American commissioner-general to the Paris exposition of that year. This appointment enlarged the circle of his friends, and in the years following many European dignitaries were visitors in the Peck residence.

Seated in his study under a collection of hunting trophies, Commodore Peck must often have thought of his boyhood in Chicago before the Civil War. He was born here in 1848, the youngest of seven sons of Phillip F. W. Peck and Mary Kent Peck. Arriving here in 1831 aboard the schooner "Telegraph" with a small store of goods, Phillip F. W. Peck became one of Chicago's earliest merchants. At that time Chicago was not yet incorporated as a city, and the population was only about two hundred and fifty. Fort Dearborn still protected the frontier village.

Commodore Peck's birth occurred in the family home at La Salle Street and Jackson Boulevard, where now stands the Continental Illinois National Bank and Trust Company of Chicago.

When he grew to manhood, Commodore Peck was admitted to the Chicago bar, but he devoted little time to the practice of law, preferring to engage in civic affairs and the building-up of his native city. He was one of the founders of the Art Institute, an officer both of the Illinois Humane Society and the exclusive Calumet Club, and one of the backers of the liberal Reverend David Swing in the establishment of the Central Church of Chicago. He also promoted the city's first opera festival, staged here in 1885.

Ferdinand Peck continued to live in the Michigan Avenue house until his death at the age of seventy-six. For several years afterward the house was occupied by his son, Ferdinand, Jr., and then it was sold. Today it is occupied by Albert Sandring and his family. Still living is Commodore Peck's widow, Mrs. Tilla Spalding Peck, now ninety-three years old. She resides with her son, Ferdinand, Jr., at 2238 Lincoln Park West.

The House of a Thousand Curios

~~~~~~

ANYONE making a study of Chicago's interesting old houses would undoubtedly conclude, after visiting its interior, that one of the most unusual is the three-story, gray-stone mansion at 2816 South Michigan Avenue. For this house, successively the abode of two notable and socially prominent families, is today a private museum containing antiques, objects of art, curios, and rare furnishings from more than a score of other famous old Chicago houses.

Here may be found a "gold" rug from the home of the late Mrs. Edith Rockefeller McCormick, stained glass from the Watson Armour home, a set of brass andirons from the P. D. Armour residence, mahogany paneling from the John V. Farwell mansion, a highly carved birchwood bookcase from the Victor F. Lawson house, a gold-plated gas chandelier from the Kate Buckingham house, and an actual dining-room—complete with glassware, china, paneling, furniture, and all—from the residence of Mrs. T. B. Blackstone.

This is only a hint of what the house contains. Although there are more than a thousand items here, not only from Chicago houses but from dwellings elsewhere in this country and abroad, the entire collection is arranged harmoniously in the twenty-two sumptuous rooms of the Michigan Avenue mansion. The treasure is displayed in rooms called by the present owner the Music Room, the Gold Room, the Textile Room, the Curio Room, the Egyptian Room, the Crystal Room, and the Oriental Room.

The man who owns this private collection and who lives in this house of a thousand curios is Otto C. Lightner, a native of Kansas who came to Chicago as a young man and now has become known as "the hobby king of America." According to *Who's Who in Chicago*, Otto Lightner has been publisher of *Hobbies Magazine* for the last eighteen years. Hobbyists and collectors in all parts of the country know him as the impresario of the Hobby Show held each year in Chicago.

Not so well known has been his activity in other fields. He is the author of two books, *Thoughts of the Year*, a volume of verse, and *History of Business Depressions*, a work on economics. And for a time before the World War he was active in politics, serving as one of the leaders of the Progressive, or Bull Moose, party led by Theodore Roosevelt. Not active in politics since that date, he has devoted his full time to *Hobbies Magazine*.

"My aim is to establish a national hobbies museum here, with the old residence as the central unit," said Mr. Lightner. "Work is already under way on an adjoining building, which will be the second unit. This will connect with a third unit, the old Kohl mansion, where lived the man who conducted Kohl and Middleton's Dime Museum in Chicago during the 1890's.

Among other items in the Lightner home are Mrs. Kohl's collection of autographed photographs of theatrical stars of the 1890's, a completely furnished Egyptian room from the estate of Samuel E. Gross, real estate man and founder of Gross Park; statuary from the home of Ed V. Price; stained glass windows from the old Board of Trade Building; an expensive onyx fireplace from the James Patten home; a quilt

CHARLES W. BREGA MANSION
2816 South Michigan Avenue

made by Mrs. Lincoln; and paneled doors from the George M. Pullman mansion.

Mr. Lightner's collection of articles, curios, and souvenirs from the World's Columbian Exposition of 1893 is regarded as one of the largest in the country. He also has large collections of Parian, bisque, and majolica pieces, as well as old-style barber bottles, quilts, parasols, lithographs, porcelains, musical instruments, Chinese and Japanese curios, rare books, old maps, and Bohemian glass. One of his most cherished exhibits is a fine quilt made by his mother, Maria Lightner, in the old Lightner home in Kansas.

In 1933 Mr. Lightner acquired the house from Franklin P. Smith, wire and iron manufacturer and socially prominent Chicagoan, who had lived in it with his family in the years before the World War. Son of a pioneer Chicagoan, Franklin Smith had founded his manufacturing concern in the 1880's, and since that time he has been a leader in business, social, and cultural circles. He is one of the early settlers of Lake Forest and still resides there.

During the time the Smiths lived in the South Michigan Avenue residence, Mrs. Smith, who was Daisy Durand, daughter of a pioneer Chicago wholesale grocer, won wide admiration as a hostess and cultural leader. She died in 1934 in her Lake Forest home. Her son, Durand Smith, is an Oxford graduate, a devotee of music, and an official of his father's firm. Durand and his brother, Hoyt, live with their father. Their sister is Mrs. John T. Pirie, Jr.

The man who built this residence and who made it widely known in the 1890's as a gathering-place of the social élite was Charles W. Brega, capitalist and member of the Chicago Board of Trade half a century ago. The house, designed by S. S. Beman, notable architect of the period, was erected in the late 1880's, when South Michigan Avenue was an elegant street of wealth and fashion.

Charles Brega had come to Chicago in 1863 from his birthplace at Hamilton, Ontario. After serving as director of the North Waukegan Harbor and Dock Company, he became a member of the Board of Trade and an associate member of the Chicago Real Estate Board. As a successful and wealthy man he was active in many clubs of his time, including the Calumet, Chicago, Caxton, and Ontwentsia.

Among notables who were entertained by Mr. and Mrs. Brega in their home were the Robert Todd Lincolns, the Potter Palmers, and the Harlow N. Higgenbothams. Charles Brega died in 1906. His widow afterward moved to London, where she resided with her daughter, Louise, wife of a British army officer, Lieutenant Colonel Ralph H. James. Mrs. Brega died in London in 1919.

Now returned to her native city, where she and her husband live at 220 East Walton Place, Mrs. James often visits her old family home in South Michigan Avenue, taking warm interest in the antique collections on display there. Her son, Charles James, is a well-known designer.

A Transformed Residence

~~~~~~

NOT all the old mansions that composed the city's one-time Millionaires' Row on South Michigan Avenue, below Twenty-sixth Street, have been abandoned to cobwebs and dust or else changed into cheap rooming-houses. Once owned by the exclusive rich, some of them, as charitable institutions, are now devoted to aiding the poor.

Of this latter group, one of the most interesting, both for its history and for its present-day status, is the three-story, gray-stone residence at 2959 South Michigan Avenue. It is located across the street from the John W. ("Bet-a-Million") Gates mansion, which now is a Catholic Youth Organization hotel for needy young men.

Although not so large and costly as the Gates's abode, this residence was at one time associated with the names of notable and wealthy people. Here, as a child, lived the man who married the only daughter of Andrew Carnegie, famed as the "Ironmaster," and here, too, resided for many years the daughter-in-law of Chicago's own "Ironmaster," Richard T. Crane, founder of the Crane Company.

Not only this, but the house was originally the property of one of the city's outstanding railroad men of the 1890's, Roswell Miller, long a president and chairman of the board of the Chicago, Milwaukee and St. Paul Railroad, now the Chicago, Milwaukee, St. Paul and Pacific Railroad. He is believed to have built the house some years before the World's Columbian Exposition of 1893.

Today, all three floors of this well-preserved residence are occupied by offices and consulting rooms of the south central branch of the United Charities of Chicago. Even the coach house at the rear has been put to good use, for it now houses various projects for men and women conducted by the W.P.A. in conjunction with the United Charities.

It was Roswell Miller's son, Roswell, Jr., who, in 1919, became the husband of Margaret Carnegie, then an heiress to one of the largest fortunes in America. She was the only child of the Carnegies. At the time of the marriage the younger Miller, as well as his parents, had been away from Chicago for many years.

The Millers sold their Michigan Avenue residence to Richard T. Crane in 1900. Crane then presented it to his daughter-in-law, Mrs. Jessie D. Crane, and here she reared her four children and continued to occupy the house until 1914. In that year she moved to her Lake Geneva estate. She died there in 1932. Her daughter, Mrs. A. K. Maxwell, now lives at the Lake Geneva place. Mrs. Maxwell's brothers are Herbert P. Crane, Charles R. Crane, and Bal R. Crane.

In the years when Mrs. Crane lived in the Michigan Avenue house, her renowned father-in-law was a frequent visitor and enjoyed the company of his four grandchildren. It was only a short walk from his great mansion at 2541 South Michigan Avenue to the house of his daughter-in-law. The "Ironmaster's" mansion has since been torn down.

His granddaughter, Mrs. Maxwell, assisted him in the preparation of his unique autobiography, only one copy of which exists. It is hand illuminated in the manner of medieval books

ROSWELL MILLER HOME
2959 South Michigan Avenue

and is said to have cost more than $25,000 to prepare. Work on it was interrupted by the death of Mr. Crane in 1912, but it was later completed.

After Mrs. Crane moved to her Lake Geneva estate, the Michigan Avenue house was unoccupied, and then, in 1918, title to it was transferred to the United Charities with the stipulation that it be used as a charity center.

The house has been serving for that use, with very little remodeling, since that time and has aided thousands of underprivileged families in that section of the city.

Almost every day poorly dressed mothers, both white and Negro, can be seen walking up the stone steps of the old stone mansion in quest of aid or advice. These people come from ancient tumble-down shacks and stuffy tenements of decadent South Side neighborhoods.

In the large living-room on the first floor, a room lighted by an arched window, are the offices of the charity organization's legal aid bureau. The bureau staff, under the supervision of Mrs. Josephine Meyers, gives free legal advice to those who apply for it. The second floor is occupied by the offices of the family service bureau, directed by Mrs. Lillian Somers.

On the third floor, in addition to clerical offices, is located a large conference and study room used by students of the University of Chicago's Graduate School of Social Service Administration. This room, it was explained, was formerly a ballroom. On the walls of this room, as on the walls of all other rooms in the house, hang attractive and colorful oil paintings by artists of the W.P.A. art project.

In a small two-story brick coach house at the rear other activities are in progress. Here, under the auspices of the W.P.A., men and women can be seen reupholstering furniture, repairing toys, and doing small carpentry jobs. On the floor above, a dozen or so mothers may be observed sewing dresses while their young children romp and play in a small nursery at one corner.

PART IV

The Near North Side

Introduction

What Prairie Avenue was to the South Side of Chicago, Pine Street was to the North Side. On both sides of Pine Street—now North Michigan Avenue—in the years after the Chicago Fire stood many fine homes where lived a large group of old and socially prominent families. Among these were the Pooles, Leiters, Ryersons, McCormicks, Trees, Carpenters, Blairs, Medills, and Rumseys. They occupied residences on Pine and other streets adjoining the old Water Tower. These were the days when the Bourniques, father and son, taught the polka, gallop, waltz, schottische, and other dance steps of the time to the youngsters of the mansions. These were the days of gas lamps, hour-glass figures, family albums, top hats, and gold-headed canes. In the years following, fads and fashions changed, the automobile came, the city grew ever larger and larger, and the sedate and decorous social life of the Near North Side began to decline. One by one the wealthy families moved away, and in time Pine Street disappeared and became North Michigan Avenue—a broad thoroughfare of exclusive shops, stores, and tearooms. Still standing, however, are a few of the old residences of the Near North Side's fashionable past.

The Joseph T. Ryerson House

~~~~~~

NOT many old mansions north of the river have aroused more curiosity over a longer period of time than the venerable dwelling at 615 North Wabash Avenue. This is probably due to its proximity to Medinah Temple, where large gatherings are held regularly, and where the people who attend them cannot help noticing the imposing two-story residence standing in dignified, if time-battered, splendor across the street.

This curiosity is well merited, for here lived two of Chicago's first families in the days when this section was the bon ton neighborhood of Chicago, and millionaires' residences stood on all sides. The mansion was built by Joseph T. Ryerson, pioneer steel king, and here the Ryersons lived during the post-fire era of the 1870's. Afterward it became the home of A. A. Carpenter, pioneer lumber king.

When Joseph Ryerson built this house in 1873 at a cost of between $40,000 and $50,000, he was a wealthy and successful industrialist, one of the leading citizens of his day, and founder of a family that was to loom large in the later history of the city. The firm he established here in 1842, now known as Joseph T. Ryerson and Son, Incorporated, is today the largest independent steel service company in America.

Before this mansion was built the steel king and his family lived in an earlier residence on the same site, built in 1860 and destroyed in the fire of 1871. The destruction of this earlier home is described in a fire narrative reprinted in Andreas' *History of Chicago*. The author, George M. Higginson,

JOSEPH T. RYERSON RESIDENCE
615 North Wabash Avenue

says that Joseph Ryerson "was obliged to take a hurried departure in his carriage, saving little or nothing from the house."

When the new house was completed, Ryerson and his wife, Ellen Griffin Larned Ryerson, and their four children moved into it, held many brilliant functions here in the 1870's, entertained visiting celebrities, and mingled with their neighbors, who included the Joseph Medills, Lambert Trees, Edward T. Blairs, and Cyrus Hall McCormicks. The Ryersons were also active in affairs of St. James Episcopal Church, which stood just north of them.

One of Ryerson's sons, Edward Larned Ryerson, was twenty years old when his family moved into the new house. Two years later he entered business in his father's firm, became a partner in 1879, and served as president of the company from 1888 until 1911, after which he became chairman of the board. He died in 1928 at the age of seventy-four, leaving an estate estimated at $4,600,000, of which $300,000 was bequeathed to civic, educational, and religious institutions in Chicago.

While still living with his father in the Cass Street home—Cass Street has since been changed to North Wabash Avenue—young E. L. Ryerson became acquainted with a Connecticut girl, Mary Pringle Mitchell, whom he later married. She was the daughter of Donald G. Mitchell, who, under the pen name of "Ik Marvel," wrote *Reveries of a Bachelor*, *My Farm at Edgewood*, and other books.

It was but natural that a son of this union should "take to books." But few expected that young Joseph T. Ryerson, when he grew to manhood, would show an interest in a particular class of books. Today, Joseph T. Ryerson occupies a unique position here as the possessor of one of the largest collections of old and rare books on Chicago, as well as other printed matter in this field, to be found in America.

Not only does his collection consist of books, leaflets, old magazines, and theater programs, but it includes etchings, paintings, wood blocks, and photographs of unusual Chicago scenes.

When Mr. Ryerson was three years old, his grandfather

sold the big Cass Street mansion to A. A. Carpenter, one of
the founders of the Kirby-Carpenter Company, a lumber
firm established here in 1872. The Carpenters lived in the
house during the eighties and nineties and here reared a son,
A. A. Carpenter, Jr., and a daughter, Amie. The handsome
carriages of many society and civic leaders in Chicago during
the nineties were often seen before the stone portals of the
Carpenter ménage, say old-time social historians.

For all during this time Augustus Alvord Carpenter was
active in social, civic, and business affairs of the city. He was
then called the Nestor of the Chicago lumber trade. The year
before moving into the Ryerson house he served as president
of the Lumberman's Exchange, an institution he helped to
found.

After the Carpenters had vacated the Cass Street house, it
was for a time occupied by the late Joseph H. Biggs, caterer
to Chicago society people since 1882. Today, the house is
leased to Miss Elizabeth MacDonald, who has converted its
numerous rooms, with their Italian marble fireplaces, tall
mirrors, leaded windows, and trim of fine inlaid woods, into
studio apartments without destroying the old-time grandeur.
Several well-known commercial artists occupy some of these
apartments.

What this mansion was like in its heyday is revealed in a
large bound volume of photographs taken at the time the
Ryersons lived in it. One of Joseph T. Ryerson's most prized
items, this book, with its many detailed views, should prove
a valuable sourcebook for future social historians, showing as
it does the furnishings and interior of a typical great house
of the seventies.

Recently, Mr. Ryerson demonstrated his devotion to Chicago in a commendable and constructive way by initiating

the publication of the late Thomas E. Tallmadge's *Architecture in Old Chicago*, a work that was practically completed when Mr. Tallmadge was killed in a train wreck. In sponsoring this valuable book, Mr. Ryerson, a close friend of the deceased architect, was joined by three other sponsors and Tallmadge friends, John A. Holabird, Charles West, and Ralph Fletcher Seymour. The volume was published by the University of Chicago Press.

Period House

~~~~~~

ONE of the most attractive "period houses" in Chicago today, an old mansion that to an unusual degree retains, both inside and out, all the decorative charm of the age of Queen Victoria, is the red-brick residence at 1149 North La Salle Street. Redolent of Chicago life in the years after the fire of 1871, the house is still the abode of an elderly society woman whose family goes back almost to the beginning of Chicago.

For more than half a century this house has been presided over by Miss Mary Pomeroy Green, descendant of an old New England family and daughter of O. B. Green, pioneer harbor builder and religious and cultural leader of Chicago. She also is a niece of Andrew H. Green, known as the "Father of Greater New York." Today, Miss Green still reigns over this house and now holds the distinction of being one of the last of the aristocratic "old guard" that flourished on La Salle Street—then called "avenue"—in the 1870's and 1880's.

One of Miss Green's most prized possessions is a stout old copy-book in which her father, using skilful English, described events in the Green household. The first page, dated November 6, 1873, contains this entry: "This day we take our first meal in our restored home on La Salle Avenue." Lower on the page we read that "Hugh is four years old today."

The date on which the residence was completed being established by this entry, the house survives today as one of the first to be built on that street following the great conflagration of 1871. Before the fire the Greens lived in a brick

O. B. GREEN MANSION
1149 North La Salle Street

house on the same site—a house that had originally belonged to Hugh McLennan, one-time partner of O. B. Green. This dwelling was destroyed in the fire.

When the house was completed in 1873, Oliver Bourne Green was one of the city's leading citizens. As a dredging and general harbor contractor he organized the Green Dredging Company and supervised many improvements in the Chicago River and along the lake front. He first began this type of work in 1858, three years after his arrival in Chicago. In addition to his business activity, he took part in civic and philanthropic work.

"Mr. Green," says a newspaper account the day after his death, "was interested in educational and philanthropic work in Chicago and elsewhere and was a liberal contributor to such causes. He was a member of the New England Congregational Church, and as chairman of its board of trustees for many years showed his interest in its welfare."

From *The Book of Chicagoans* we learn that O. B. Green was born January 1, 1826, at Green Hill, his ancestral home at Worcester, Massachusetts. This estate is now a park in the Massachusetts city. One of Green's ancestors was General Timothy Ruggles, officer of the Colonial Army. After being educated in his native city, O. B. Green became a civil engineer and as such engaged in the first surveys for the New York Central Railroad from New York to Albany.

Attracted to Chicago, which was then rapidly expanding with the introduction of railroads and lake shipping, Oliver Green arrived here in 1855. That same year he married Emily Louise Pomeroy, a Canadian-born girl. The couple afterward acquired the original La Salle Street house, and here were born three children—Mary, Olivia, and Andrew Hugh. The last named was the youngster who was four years old when the Greens occupied their new mansion for the first time.

In the years that followed Mrs. Green was just as active as her husband in civic and welfare projects. She was, says an old newspaper account, "an elderly woman with a kindly, motherly character, who has always taken the deepest interest in works of charity, especially that connected with the home for young women which was erected by the association [Y.W.C.A.]."

The master of the La Salle Street house died in it in 1906 at the age of eighty. His widow survived him for a few years, and then, with her passing, it was taken over by the daughter, Miss Green, and her brother. Subsequently, Andrew Green acquired a plantation in the West Indian island of Dominica, and there he lived until his death a few years ago.

What makes this residence unusual today is that the original interior has been preserved by Miss Green. But there is no overcrowding of bric-a-brac such as characterized many Victorian interiors. Here the visitor finds everything chastely arranged. Many of the articles of furniture are family heirlooms dating from early New England days and saved from the Chicago Fire. One who appreciates antiques would find this dwelling a treasure-house.

The main rooms on the first floor, with their tall windows, inside shutters, parquet floors, and fine woodwork, are enhanced by fireplaces of various kinds of marble, and over these are suspended great mirrors. From the ceilings hang the original brass chandeliers, now wired for electricity. In the dining-room stands a large buffet containing family china and other heirlooms.

This house was the scene, a few years ago, of a fashionable gathering. This was when Miss Green's grandniece, Katherine Dole Baird, was a debutante and Miss Green gave a tea for her. The old mansion, on that occasion, was filled with the social élite of the city, and all marveled at the way Miss Green had maintained her dwelling in a world of rapid change.

The Cyrus H. McCormick Mansion

UNLIKE so many of the great town houses of the Gilded Age which still stand in Chicago, the sixty-two-year-old Cyrus Hall McCormick mansion at 675 Rush Street continues to be occupied by a member of the family that made it great.

Here lives, when he is in town, Harold F. McCormick, son of the reaper king and himself as famous today as was his father in the 1870's. In fact, three generations of the internationally renowned McCormick clan have lived here, as it was the abode, for a time, of the children of Harold F. McCormick and the late Edith Rockefeller McCormick after they were divorced in 1921.

In view of this, the three-story mansion on the Near North Side may be easily designated as one of the most famous houses in Chicago today. But it is rarely recognized as such by hurrying citizens of the present generation because few of them see it in their daily comings and goings. Owing to physical changes in the city, the house is now off the beaten path, located on a quiet street.

Although the exterior of this commanding house shows signs of its comparatively great age, the soot and smoke and

dust of Chicago having darkened its brownstone façade and
walls, the interior, with its luxurious furnishings, is just as

CYRUS HALL McCORMICK MANSION
675 Rush Street

well preserved, bright, and elegantly appointed as when the
inventor of the reaper first moved into it in 1879.

It was not until Cyrus Hall McCormick was seventy
years old that he decided to erect a great town house that
would be the equal of any built by other Chicago "giants" of

the 1870's. He secured the services of a noted architectual firm, Cudell and Blumenthal, to design such an abode, and when it was completed the McCormicks moved into it. Here they reigned for many years as one of the city's first families.

"Far more famous than Aldine Square, in fact only second to Potter Palmer's castle on the Drive, was and is the Cyrus McCormick house," wrote Thomas E. Tallmadge in his book, *Architecture in Old Chicago*. "This house was begun in 1875 and completed in 1879. The interior was designed and installed by L. Marcott and Company of New York. This huge brown stone mansion proclaims to even a greater extent than Aldine Square its French ancestry. Here, however, the inspiration has been the new additions to the Louvre and the Paris Opera, rather than the *Néo-Grec*. The Louvre is announced by the high mansard roof with its elaborate cresting, its mansard cupola, its bull's-eye windows and its rusticated stone work done exactly after the fashion of, say, the Pavilion Richelieu, while the banded columns, the garlands, the richness of ornament, certainly stem from Charles Garnier's famous Nouvelle Opéra, the architectural wonder of the world in the reign of Napoleon III."

Cyrus Hall McCormick might well have felt some pride in contemplating the contrast between his luxurious mansion and the humble dwelling in Virginia where he was reared and of that July day in 1831 when, as a young man, he had cut a strip of grain with his newly invented reaper, an invention that was afterward to bring him world-wide fame as "the liberator of the farmer."

He could have thought, too, of his struggle to establish the first reaper factory in Chicago in 1847; of how his wife, whom he married in 1858, had helped and encouraged him; of the great fire of 1871 when his factory near the mouth of the river was destroyed, and of how, soon afterward, he established his plant at Twenty-sixth Street and Western Avenue, which became the International Harvester Company.

But the reaper king was destined to enjoy his new mansion only a comparatively brief period. Five years after it was built he died in the Rush Street house. From then on it was presided over by his widow, the former Nettie Fowler of Clayton, New York, and here she reared her children, including young Harold F. McCormick.

It seems certain, from all accounts, that Mrs. Cyrus Hall McCormick did almost as much to make this house one of the most famous in the city as did her late husband. For she was a notable personality, possessed of a keen mind, rare charm, and quick wit, and her donations and gifts to missions, schools, and medical centers were world-wide in scope.

Here she consistently carried out the one big objective of her life—to assist in the spread of Christianity and Christian education and to introduce the latest advances in medical science to countries of the Far East. It was from this house, too, that she sent out more funds to the Presbyterian church than any other person in America.

A large part of this went to the old McCormick Theological Seminary (now Presbyterian Theological Seminary) on the North Side, an institution originally endowed by her husband in 1859.

An unusual event in the Rush Street residence occurred in 1915 when students and faculty of the McCormick seminary held a surprise party for Mrs. McCormick. She was eighty years old that day. Cablegrams and telegrams of congratulations came to her from famous persons all over the world.

Mrs. McCormick died in 1923 at the age of eighty-eight, leaving an estate estimated at ten million dollars. After her death the mansion was taken over by her son, Harold F.

McCormick, and he has maintained it in first-rate condition ever since.

The interior is a veritable palace, resplendent with fine old tapestried chairs, heavy silken draperies, richly carved mantels, crystal and gold chandeliers, rare rugs, old masterpieces and family portraits, walnut dressers, paneled walls, inlaid ceilings with mahogany beams, and rare and historic art objects.

An adjunct of this great mansion, the coach house on the north, has been converted into an interesting institution. It now houses the library of the McCormick Historical Association, composed of 1,500 printed and 1,500,000 manuscript items, all dealing with the activities and interests of the McCormick family.

Mayor Rumsey's Residence

~~~~~~

INCLUDED in the Near North Side itinerary of the W.P.A. tours to Chicago points of interest is a three-story residence of faded red brick at the northeast corner of Huron Street and Wabash Avenue. In a section of many such ancient houses this edifice is conspicuous because its architecture is obviously of an older era than most of the homes around it.

The man who built this house, lived in it for many years, reared his family here, and made it something of a social center in the 1870's was Julian S. Rumsey, now best known in local history as the Civil War mayor of Chicago. His career, however, goes back much farther than that.

It was in 1835 that Rumsey, then a very young man, came to Chicago. His uncle, George W. Dole, was founder of Newberry and Dole, the city's first storage, forwarding, and commission house. In 1847 Julian Rumsey and his brother, George F., became members of the firm of Newberry and Dole upon the retirement of Oliver Newberry, a Detroit shipowner. The Rumsey's evidently were successful in this business, for by 1854 they had taken over the firm completely, and the new name was Rumsey Brothers and Company.

Julian and George Rumsey were central figures in a colorful incident involving a brass cannon from Fort Dearborn. Prized as a historic relic, the cannon became a bone of contention between Whigs and Democrats during the exciting presidential campaign of 1840. In the midst of the struggle

JULIAN S. RUMSEY RESIDENCE
40 East Huron Street

for its possession, the cannon disappeared. The Rumsey brothers, during the night, had hidden it in a bin of wheat in the Newberry and Dole warehouse.

After his marriage in 1848 to Martha Ann Turner, daughter of John B. Turner, who afterward became president of the Chicago and North Western Railway, Julian Rumsey built a two-story frame house on the site of the present mansion. This location disturbed Mr. Turner. He said the house was too far "out in the woods" and that Indians might be a source of trouble.

In her book, *Recollections of a Pioneer's Daughter*, Eliza Voluntine Rumsey writes of this first Rumsey house:

"Father was mayor of the city in 1861 and many celebrities were at our house. Mr. Lincoln came, after his first nomination for President, and during that call wrote for Brother George the few lines, with his signature, that Nathaniel Wheeler now has. Mr. Lincoln also went upstairs to see the doll house."

Eleven children were born to the Rumseys in this frame house. The fire of 1871 destroyed the home, and in 1874 Rumsey built the present mansion on the same site at a cost of $40,000.

The following item appeared in a newspaper of the day: "St. James Episcopal Industrial Society gave a pleasant affair this week in the handsome ballroom of the Julian Rumsey home, Cass and Huron streets. The worthy cause, the popularity of the Rumsey family and perhaps the desire to see this lovely new home brought a crowd of the élite."

Society leaders present at that gathering were Mr. and Mrs. Mahlon Ogden, N. K. Fairbank, L. Z. Leiter, John N. Jewett, and the Joseph T. Ryersons, "besides many other prominent people." Although Julian Rumsey died in 1886, the house was occupied by members of the Rumsey family until 1922, when it was sold to Cyrus McCormick.

Eleven years ago the residence was taken over by Miss Annie Sara Bock, who had previously conducted a small restaurant, the Southern Tea Shop, in an old dwelling at 745 Rush Street. Under the same name the venerable Rumsey residence today attracts people who not only appreciate the appetizing southern dishes offered here but who also enjoy its atmosphere of old-time elegance. For Miss Bock, whose hobby is the collecting of antiques, has outfitted her tea shop in almost the same manner as it was furnished when the Rumseys lived here.

In the first-floor rooms of this house, handsome rooms of ample proportions and notable for their trim of burled walnut, high decorative ceilings, ornamental chandeliers, tall, narrow windows with inside folding shutters, fireplaces of marble and tile, and great gilded mirrors, the visitor finds furniture and objects of art dating from the era in which the residence was built. All these furnishings are tastefully arranged and well spaced, so that the visitor here does not have a feeling of stuffiness. This also is true of the reception hall, from which a richly carved grand staircase leads to the second floor. On this floor a number of Miss Bock's friends— artists, writers, and professional people—live in private quarters.

One of these is Miss Herma Clark, whose "When Chicago Was Young" column in the Sunday edition of the *Chicago Tribune* is widely read and enjoyed. The writer of such a column, which deals with the personalities as well as fads and fancies of the late Victorian era in Chicago, could not live in a more appropriate dwelling. A book of hers, *The Elegant Eighties*, was recently published.

The R. Hall McCormick Mansion

AMONG the numerous "brownstones" on the Near North Side that flourished before the turn of the century, few were better known than the stately, if comparatively plain, mansion at the northwest corner of Rush and Erie streets. Its fame rested not only on the prominence of the man who lived here but also on what it housed—one of the largest and most expensive private collections of paintings in this part of the country. Until recently, this once exclusive residence was open to the public as a tea room.

It was in 1875, just four years after the great fire, that this three-and-a-half-story abode was completed for R. Hall McCormick, member of the world-famous McCormick clan of Chicago. Into it he brought his wife and children, as well as the nucleus of what was to become his art collection, and here he lived until his death in 1917 at the age of seventy. During the forty-two years he dwelt here, R. Hall McCormick reigned as an outstanding Chicago industrialist, philanthropist, and art collector.

An interesting side light on this residence is that it is one of a group of such mansions all of which were once occupied

by McCormicks and all of which stood within a radius of two
blocks of this homesite. Across the street from it still stands
the most costly and commanding of these homes, that of
R. Hall McCormick's uncle, Cyrus Hall McCormick. Incidentally, it was in the same general neighborhood, before it
became residential, that the first McCormick reaper factory
was opened in 1848.

A frequent guest in the R. Hall McCormick home during
its heyday was the owner's father, Leander J. McCormick,
who was associated with his brother, Cyrus, in the manufacture of the McCormick reaper. During the year in which the
first McCormick factory was opened, R. Hall McCormick
was brought here by his parents. He was then a year old.
He grew up in the neighborhood where later he was to erect
his town house at what is now 660 Rush Street.

To this house, in the 1880's and 1890's, there came as
guests many of the prominent folk of the city and of the
nation. The mistress of this house, who was the former Sarah
Lord Day, daughter of a well-known New York attorney, was
a noted hostess of her time, and her dinners and other social
functions were outstanding events in society of the years
before and after the World's Columbian Exposition of 1893.

Much of the appeal of the Rush Street house, of course, was
due to the display of rare paintings and costly objects of art
that were on view in the many rooms of the dwelling. The
Book of Chicagoans, published in 1905, says this of R. Hall
McCormick: "Always interested in art; has made a special
study of the British school; has examples of most of the leading artists of that school in his collection; has published an
elaborate illustrated catalogue of the collection, which is in
the principal art galleries of the United States and Europe."

On the walls of the McCormick residence, during its great
days, hung such famous English canvases as "Portrait of Mrs.

MacNeil," by Raeburn (which in later years brought $30,000 at a New York auction), and "Portrait of the Marchioness of Ely," by Sir Thomas Lawrence (which, at the same auction,

R. HALL McCORMICK MANSION
660 Rush Street

brought $18,000). The McCormick collection also included masterpieces by Gainsborough, Reynolds, Cole, Beechey, and Wilson.

Among the antiques and objects of art that enhanced the drawing-room, dining-room, library, and other rooms of this house were collections of Bavarian and Venetian glass,

Wedgwood china, rare tapestries, teakwood tables from China, Persian rugs, and historic pieces of furniture.

During the years when R. Hall McCormick was adding to his collection and serving as superintendent of manufacturing for the McCormick Harvesting Machine Company, he and his wife reared five children. These children are Robert Hall McCormick, Henrietta (now Mrs. Nelson Williams), Miss Elizabeth D., Phoebe (now the widow of Walter Ayer, manufacturer and member of an old Chicago family), and Miss Mildred D.

After the death of R. Hall McCormick in 1917, the house was occupied for a time by his widow and then finally was closed. Subsequently it was acquired by the Surgical Publishing Company, publishers of the official journal of the American College of Surgeons, which occupies headquarters next door in Erie Street.

For several years this company leased the old mansion to Mr. and Mrs. L. C. Levering, who conducted a tearoom in it called "Kentucky Serves a Meal." They specialized in southern dishes. Although their main interest was cookery, the Leverings were also collectors of antique furniture and objects of art. As a result, the old McCormick residence, when they occupied it, was slightly—it could never be fully—restored to its former atmosphere of charm and grace. It was not difficult for the Leverings to do this, as the interior, with its attractive fireplaces, great mirrors, rose-colored damask walls, and marble pillars, was largely intact.

Queen Anne Architecture

BOTH of these mansions have commanding situations and are among the richest residences in the city." Thus are described, in a guidebook to Chicago published during the World's Fair of 1893, the impressive dwellings of the brothers John V. and Charles B. Farwell, two of Chicago's wealthiest and best-known citizens of the 1890's. The houses stood side by side on East Pearson Street.

Today only one of the residences is still standing. This is the Charles Farwell home at 120 East Pearson Street. And it still occupies a "commanding situation." Standing there in lonely grandeur, its red-brick façade dark and time stained, this great mansion opposite the old Chicago Avenue Water Tower long has aroused the curiosity of passers-by in near-by Michigan Avenue. It has been vacant for many years.

When this imposing house was in its prime there was no Michigan Avenue. What later became the city's most important boulevard was then a quiet, tree-lined, residential street called Pine Street that led through an area of millionaires' homes clustering around the Gothic Water Tower. Among Charles Farwell's closest neighbors, other than his brother, were E. S. Isham, member of Lincoln's law firm; Levi Z. Leiter, former partner of Marshall Field; and Sartell Prentice, noted lawyer.

In his posthumously published book, *Architecture in Old Chicago*, the late Thomas E. Tallmadge discusses the Farwell mansion at some length. Among other things, he says: "Of

CHARLES FARWELL RESIDENCE
120 East Pearson Street

the countless examples of Queen Anne [style of architecture in Chicago in the 1880's] there is none better than the Charles B. Farwell [home] on Pearson Street, just west of the Drive. That of his brother, John V. Farwell, was next door on the corner. These two houses were 'projected' in 1882 and each cost over $100,000."

Tallmadge continues: "The architects of the Charles Farwell house were Treat and Foltz. This house has all the characteristics of real Queen Anne—Classic detail used in an unorthodox but not in a debased way. Note the entrance columns, the high roof and elaborate chimneys and particularly the very steep pediments, especially characteristic, as is also the all over red color scheme, brick and sandstone in this case."

A glimpse of the interior is given us by Mr. Tallmadge. "The interior of the Charles B. Farwell house," he writes, "as illustrated in the *Inland Architect*, was typical of the mansions of the eighties. The great entrance hall aspired to the ideal of a baronial manor house with panelled wainscot (of golden oak), an enormous fireplace niche (with a microscopic grate opening), a beamed ceiling, walls and ceilings covered with stenciled canvas, and here and there crossed scimitars, bronze statues, brass plaques, antlers, inlaid tables, Jacobean furniture and two early American Windsor chairs looking very self-conscious and out of place."

The author adds: "You may walk in it today, fifty-five years later, and have the thrill of comparing it with the photograph. It is just the same, minus the furniture and the lamps and the peace and plenty of the romantic eighties."

At the time Charles Farwell—in his later years he was Senator Farwell—lived in the house on Pearson Street, he was widely respected as a pioneer of Chicago, one of its most successful businessmen and a leader in public life. So, too, was his brother John, founder of the early wholesale dry goods house of John V. Farwell and Company.

After being established in his new house, Charles Farwell was chosen United States senator for Illinois to fill a vacancy in that office cause by the death of General John A. Logan. Senator Farwell served four years in the upper house, ending his term in 1891. Before being sent to the Senate he had represented his section of Chicago for several terms in the lower house, having first been elected congressman in 1870. His opponent that year was "Long John" Wentworth, former mayor of Chicago.

But Senator Farwell had been in politics even earlier than this. Back in 1853, one year after his marriage here to Mary Eveline Smith of South Williamstown, Massachusetts, he was elected clerk of Cook County. He served in this office until 1861. A few years later he joined his brother, John, in the latter's dry goods establishment and retained this connection until late in life.

Previous to Charles' entry into the firm, it was known as Farwell, Field and Company, one of the partners being Marshall Field. The "company" was Levi Z. Leiter and S. N. Kellogg. This establishment grew out of a still earlier firm known as Cooley, Wadsworth and Company, in which John V. Farwell had been a partner and Marshall Field a clerk.

Senator Farwell first came to Chicago in 1844 at the age of twenty-one. The story is told that he arrived here from downstate Illinois on a wagonload of wheat with only ten dollars in his pocket and no prospect of a job. He soon obtained employment, however, as an assistant in the office of the county clerk. He also worked evenings in a mercantile store.

With such a showing of industry he was able to obtain extra cash, and with this he purchased his first land in Chicago. The *Dictionary of American Biography* says of him: "Successful real-estate speculation laid the foundation of his fortune." It adds that he "had probably been financially interested in the mercantile transactions of his brother" for some time before becoming a member of the firm.

In the magnificent house on Pearson Street, with its mansard roof and Queen Anne façade dominating the little adjoining park, Senator Farwell held sway and entertained many celebrities of the late Victorian era in America. Among his close friends were Archbishop Feehan and Generals U. S. Grant and Philip Sheridan. Here, too, when not entertaining, he pored over the rare sixteenth-century volumes that composed a large part of his extensive library.

Senator Farwell died in 1903 at the age of eighty. In the years after the first World War the Farwell mansion was vacant, but in 1931 it came to life as a French restaurant called "Chez Louis." In this capacity it attracted many of the city's leading epicures. Diners reveled in the old-time grandeur of the mansion, admiring its richly carved grand staircase, beamed oak ceilings, leaded windows, marble fireplaces, and glittering chandeliers. But the restaurant lasted only a year or two. Since then the mansion has been closed.

"Nickerson's Marble Palace"

‹‹

IN MAKING a study of noteworthy old Chicago mansions, one often comes upon surprises. Such a surprise is in store for one entering for the first time the three-story stone residence at the northeast corner of Wabash Avenue and Erie Street. Outwardly plain, its soot-darkened façade marked by very little decoration, this mansion reveals, in its interior, such richness, profusion, and magnificence of ornamental detail and trim as to cause amazement.

So highly regarded was this house, with its many elegant rooms, that in 1919 more than a hundred leading citizens formed a group to purchase the house. This was done, and they presented it to the American College of Surgeons, an association of surgeons in the United States and Canada. It has been used as an administrative building by the association ever since. The names of the donors are inscribed on a bronze tablet outside the main doorway.

The house is nationally known in the medical world. The establishment of the surgeons' headquarters here had much to do with making Chicago the world-famous medical center it is today. A neoclassical memorial building to the great Chicago surgeon, Dr. John B. Murphy, was erected next door to the old mansion some years ago.

The marble entrance hall, onyx pillars, alabaster balusters, tiled fireplaces, parquet floors, mantels of rare inlaid woods, beamed ceilings, brass, copper, and glass chandeliers, leather-paneled walls, and richly carved woodwork of this Erie Street mansion are little less than awesome in their grandeur. Obvi-

SAMUEL M. NICKERSON MANSION
40 East Erie Street

ously, the builder must have been a person of great wealth and high position in Chicago life.

And so he was. This big stone residence was erected by a prominent Chicago banker of the 1880's, Samuel M. Nickerson. He was one of the founders of the First National Bank, oldest of the national banks in Chicago, organized in 1863. Later he was elected its president and was serving in this capacity when, in 1883, he built his sumptuous abode on the Near North Side.

"Mr. Nickerson," says a volume of biographical sketches published in 1900, "has manifested great interest in art and music and was a promoter of and liberal contributor to those May festivals that were among the earliest developments of musical culture in Chicago.

"He has acted as a member of the Lincoln Park Board of Commissioners, and was very active in the transformation of what, during his term of office, was little more than a stretch of waste sand into an artistic pleasure place. Mr. Nickerson has traveled extensively in Europe and once had circumnavigated the globe."

Born in Massachusetts of Puritan stock, Samuel Nickerson came to Chicago in 1858 with but a few dollars in his pocket. He soon became successful in the distilling business and, after acquiring a considerable fortune, entered the banking field. He was also a founder and first president of the old Chicago City Street Railway Company.

Another institution he helped to establish, and which he served as first president, was the Union Stock Yards National Bank. All of these activities were engaged in before he built the Erie Street residence. When the time came for the erection of this house, Samuel Nickerson was one of the wealthiest men in Chicago.

The story is told that he built his mansion regardless of cost. It is now known that the house represents an investment of $450,000. After being completed, it became a show place of the 1880's and was widely known as "Nickerson's Marble Palace." A leading Chicago architect of that day, Edward Burling, designed it. Much of the woodwork was hand carved by artisans and craftsmen working under the direction of A. Fiedler, famous wood designer.

Although many varieties of rare and costly woods decorate the interior, the house is even more distinguished for its marble work. The main hall has a marble floor, onyx panels on the walls, and a lofty ceiling of marble panels. The stair rails are of alabaster open work, and on each side of the grand stairway stand two onyx columns of stately proportions.

Mr. and Mrs. Nickerson, with their son Roland, lived and entertained in this great house until 1900, when they sold it and moved to New York. The purchaser was Lucius G. Fisher, paper-bag manufacturer and long-time resident of Chicago. He moved into it with his family, and here two of his daughters were married. They are Mrs. Homer Dixon and Mrs. William W. Dixon, both of Chicago.

No alterations were made after the Fishers acquired the Nickerson mansion, but a new decorative element appeared. Here and there, on the first and second floors, were hung heads of buffalo, deer, and other animals gathered together as a hobby by Lucius Fisher, who was also a collector of old-time weapons. Many of the animal heads are still on display in the house.

In charge of the Erie Street dwelling today and serving as administrative heads of the surgeons' association are Drs. Bowman C. Crowell and Malcolm T. MacEachern. Under them a large clerical staff work in the various rooms of the palace-like mansion—rooms that have been converted into offices without destroying or altering the original ornamentation.

The L. Hamilton McCormick Residence

~~~~~~

IN THE vicinity of Rush and Erie streets, clustering around and dominated by the old Cyrus Hall McCormick mansion, stands a group of venerable residences erected by various members of the renowned McCormick family. So numerous are these stately Victorian dwellings that the neighborhood is often referred to as "McCormickville." And as an interesting demonstration of the changes wrought by time, one of these once-exclusive town houses is today open to the public in the form of a restaurant.

This is the four-story abode of Italian Renaissance architecture at the northeast corner of Rush and Ontario streets. It was built almost half a century ago by L. Hamilton McCormick, inventor, writer, art collector, and nephew of the Reaper King. His father was Leander J. McCormick, brother and business associate of Cyrus Hall McCormick in the manufacturing of farm implements. Incidentally, it was in this same general neighborhood that the first McCormick reaper plant was set up in 1848.

A few years after his mansion was built, L. Hamilton McCormick and his English-born wife—she was Constance Plummer of Canterbury, England—moved to England and lived there for many years. During their absence from Chicago the Ontario Street residence was occupied successively by several leading Chicago families, including the Levi Z.

L. HAMILTON McCORMICK MANSION
631 Rush Street

Leiters, W. P. Rends, Chatfield-Taylors, and the William A. Gages. The owners of the house returned to Chicago shortly after the outbreak of the first World War and once more took up residence in their big, stately dwelling, which cost $125,000 to build. It was designed by the Chicago architectural firm of Cowles and Ohrenstein.

During the year of the World's Columbian Exposition, when the Hamilton McCormicks still lived in it, this house was the scene of many brilliant functions. Here came the society leaders of the 1890's and here were held those elegant dinners that made Mrs. McCormick widely known as one of the city's great hostesses. It was at this time, too, that L. Hamilton McCormick began collecting objects of art and making his first studies in the field of character-reading.

While abroad, Hamilton McCormick and his wife acquired a large quantity of pictures, bronzes, enamels, statuary, armor, and old furniture. They brought these valuables to Chicago, upon their return in 1917, and installed them in their Ontario Street house. These collections added to the fame of this mansion.

It was in this house that L. Hamilton McCormick completed his studies in what he called "characterology." A volume bearing this title was published by him in 1920. He had written several other works in the same field. As a matter of fact, he had spent most of his mature years in studying the reading of character through physical appearance. He had also perfected several inventions.

His three sons were reared in the Ontario Street house. They are Alister, Leander J., and Edward Hamilton McCormick. The family continued to occupy the house during the World War years, and here many war benefits and other charitable affairs were staged; but after the war Mr. and Mrs. McCormick spent most of their time in California. The master of the house died in Florida in 1934 at the age of seventy-four. After his death Mrs. McCormick moved to a hotel and leased the great house in Ontario Street to outside interests.

She no longer wanted to live in the old mansion. The downtown district had crept northward, and her house was practically engulfed by hotels and business institutions. The neighborhood had changed. About three or four years ago a well-known Chicago restaurateur of Danish birth, Fredrik A. Chramer, rented the venerable McCormick mansion, remodeled the interior at a cost of $63,000, and set up an elegant restaurant specializing in Scandinavian dishes and a lavish "smörgasbörd."

He has been conducting it as such since that time. The many rooms of the great house, with their inviting fireplaces, tall gilt mirrors, splendid woodwork, and wide doorways, have been redecorated by Mr. Chramer so that they now represent the best in what is known as Swedish modern. Woven into the detail of royal blue, gold, and pink are numerous coats-of-arms bearing three crowns, which symbolize the three Scandinavian countries.

In most of the dining-rooms of The Kingsholm are cabinets containing collections of Copenhagen china gathered together by Mr. Chramer over a long period of years. He has outfitted each room with fine old pieces of furniture which do not conflict with the Swedish modern atmosphere. One of these rooms is known as the Lauritz Melchior Room, named after the noted Danish opera singer who has dined here frequently. Other rooms are called the Viking Lounge and the Swedish Room.

In addition to collecting china, Mr. Chramer has several other interests, including classical music and motion-picture and still photography. The walls of his restaurant are lined with photographs of famous persons who have dined here. Among these are Dr. Frederick Stock, Jean Hersholt, William Knudsen, and Lily Pons, as well as descendants of the several McCormicks and other old-time Chicago families.

Where once was the ballroom on the fourth floor Mr. Chramer has installed his particular pride—a home-movie theater. Here he invites his friends and favored diners to see colored movies he has taken himself, as well as travel, sports, educational, and war films. Here also his guests may listen to his large collection of classical music records. A national movie magazine pronounced this the most perfect home-movie house in the Middle West.

It is plain to see that Mr. Chramer carries on the tradition of gracious and elegant living established when this house was built almost fifty years ago. The story is told that shortly before her death three years ago Mrs. L. Hamilton McCormick dined in the restaurant occupying her house and, observing the luxurious manner in which it was redecorated and furnished, said to the host: "My, if I had known it could be redecorated in such grand style I would have hesitated about renting it to you."

PART V

On the Gold Coast

Introduction

When the Near North Side began to decline as a bon ton neighborhood, the Gold Coast along Lake Shore Drive began to rise. Here was a wide, quiet thoroughfare, shaded by rows of trees, that paralleled the shore of the lake for almost half a mile before reaching Lincoln Park. It was an ideal residential street, fronting on a blue inland sea. One after another came new mansions on either side of the Potter Palmer "castle" until Lake Shore Drive was solidly built up with fine houses. Upon reaching that stage, it presented an unusual and interesting parade of what is called the Eclectic Period in American architecture. Here were Gothic turrets, Moorish doorways, French Renaissance mansards, Romanesque arches, Georgian balustrades, Italian balconies, and Spanish patios. Today some of these residences are disappearing and are being replaced by fourteen-story apartment hotels. Meanwhile, the half-mile stretch of beach across "the Drive" from the mansions is crowded, on hot summer days, with thousands of men, women, and children from the middle-class and poorer districts of the city.

The Castle on the Drive

I F ANY house in Chicago is entitled to be called "great," none would fit that designation better than the Potter Palmer castle on Lake Shore Drive. Although now vacant, its blinds down, its doors locked, only a caretaker occupying limited space in it, the Palmer castle was in its day one of the most eminent houses in America.

"By far the most famous, probably the largest, and by all odds the most imposing house in our city," writes Tallmadge in his *Architecture in Old Chicago*, "is the Potter Palmer mansion, a mansion to end all mansions, which at this writing it seems to have done. . . . . As architectural fashions have flowed and ebbed it has been admired and derided, along with its more venerable neighbor, the Water Tower, but no citizen in Chicago or lover of her traditions or her beauty could see the towers of this castle overthrown without real sorrow."

This magnificent residence was designed by two prominent architects—Henry Ives Cobb and Charles Sumner Frost. Tallmadge tells us that it was built in 1882. "It came," he continues, "very early in the Romanesque–Queen Anne regime. As a matter of fact it has nothing to do with either. It's an American architect's best thought of what a baronial castle should be. Early photographs and illustrations in the periodicals of the time show a building not nearly as pleasing as the castle we see today. The lighter limestone trim made a startling and agitating pattern. Now the kindly patina of smoke and weather have toned it down to a uniform hue."

Not only was it famous because of its glamorous chatelaine but also because of the man who built it. For Potter Palmer is remembered today as the "Father of State Street," as the founder of an early mercantile firm which later became Marshall Field and Company, and as the builder of one of the city's oldest and most renowned hotels. He is truly a titan of early Chicago.

As for the style of architecture in which the Potter Palmer castle was built, we are told by Tallmadge that it is English Gothic. This style is characterized by square windows instead of the arched windows usually associated with Gothic. As Tallmadge indicated, the house today has a mellow, medieval appearance which was not evident during its great days of half a century ago. This is made all the more effective by the English ivy which covers most of its exterior.

When Potter Palmer built this house at a cost of one million dollars, it immediately became a show place of the city. During the World's Columbian Exposition of 1893 it was one of the two leading sights of the city outside the fair grounds, the other attraction being the Masonic Temple, then the highest building in the world.

It was in these World's Fair years that the stone castle by the lake was at the peak of its glory. Here Mrs. Palmer, stately, regal, handsome, wearing her diamond tiara and famous rope of pearls, ruled as social queen of America's second largest city and presided over brilliant functions and noble dinners. As president of the Board of Lady Managers of the World's Fair, Mrs. Palmer was the dominant figure of all social events at which visiting celebrities of America and Europe were then entertained.

Among distinguished guests entertained in the "castle on the Drive" were Presidents Grant and McKinley, the Infanta Eulalia of Spain, the Duke and Duchess of Veragua (the duke was said to have been a descendant of Columbus), various Russian princes and princesses, and many other leading figures of the late Victorian era.

POTTER PALMER MANSION
1350 Lake Shore Drive

In the years after the World's Fair the great house continued to be the social center of Chicago. Its most notable functions were the New Year's Eve balls.

During this time Mrs. Palmer also maintained houses in Paris and London. She was as well known in European social circles as in American.

Mrs. Palmer continued to live in the castle after the death

of her husband in 1902. She carried on his business enterprises. She became noted as an art collector, and on the vel-
vet-hung walls of the castle's art gallery were many European
and American masterpieces. Here, also, was a notable portrait of Mrs. Palmer by Anders Zorn. Fifty of these paintings
are now part of the Potter Palmer Collection in the Art Institute.

Mrs. Palmer died in 1918, leaving a fortune estimated at
sixteen million dollars. From the date of her death until the
spring of 1921 the fabulous castle was unoccupied. In that
year, after some remodeling and redecorating of the interior,
Potter, Jr., and his family moved into it.

But in 1928 Potter Palmer, Jr., sold the great mansion to
Vincent Bendix, wealthy head of the Bendix Aviation Corpo-
ration, for a reported consideration of three million dollars.
Then, in 1933, Mr. Bendix conveyed title to the mansion back
to Potter Palmer, Jr., and once more the castle came into the
Palmer family.

Before this occurred, however, the mansion was thrown
open for a two-day charity benefit, and then for the first time
the ordinary folk of Chicago saw its fabulous interior. They
crowded under the colonnade of the porte-cochere and into
the big rotunda of the reception hall. They gazed in wonder
at the mosaic marble floor, paneled oak walls, and the great
fireplace in the corner with its handsome clock set into the
mantle.

They looked up in awe at the elaborate brass chandeliers,
touched the carved doors of the library, felt the wine-red velvet which draped the walls of the ballroom, and saw the per-
fection of the parquet floors. And they walked up the great
carved staircase to the second floor and saw another maze of
richly ornamented, high-ceilinged rooms. Visitors with artistic inclinations looked in wonder at the famous murals by
Gabriel Ferrier and other noted artists.

A House of Celebrities

WHEN the Gold Coast on Lake Shore Drive began to take form in the early 1880's, one of the first houses to be erected there was the William Borden mansion. Still standing at the northwest corner of Lake Shore Drive and Bellevue Place, it is of less interest today, however, as a Gold Coast landmark than as the one-time home of a Chicago family which produced many talented and noted persons.

William Borden, then a lawyer and successful mining engineer, and Potter Palmer laid out the Palmer and Borden subdivision on the shore of the lake, north of the downtown district, and thus became the "fathers" of Lake Shore Drive. Borden built his residence in 1884, Potter Palmer erected his "castle" in 1882, and a few years afterward was built the mansion later owned by the late Mrs. Edith Rockefeller McCormick. William Borden's father, John Borden, had come to Chicago in 1835.

William Borden became wealthy as the result of a mining venture at Leadville, Colorado, in association with Marshall Field and Levi Z. Leiter. He was financially able to build a house of imposing design, and the architect he chose to plan it was Richard M. Hunt, best-known American architect of the 1870's. Hunt had designed the Vanderbilt, Astor, Schwab, and other famous mansions in New York.

As with the New York residences he had created, Hunt planned the Borden home in the French Renaissance style, which was then fashionable. The house is of gray stone, four stories high, and its slate roof is marked by numerous turrets and dormers. It is said to be a smaller version of the château-like Charles Schwab mansion on Riverside Drive in New York City.

In this gray-stone mansion was born Mary Borden Spears, famous today as an Anglo-American novelist and as the wife of Brigadier General Edward L. Spears, a British military leader and member of Parliament. It was in this house that Mary Borden's talent for writing was nurtured, and it was here she wrote some of her books, which now number almost a dozen. Since her marriage in 1918 she has made her home in London.

Here, too, was born and reared Mary Borden's brother, William Whiting Borden. In 1912 young William startled Chicago by renouncing a promising business career and social position and becoming a foreign missionary. But he did not live to carry out his ambition of bringing Christianity to heathen peoples. He died in Cairo, Egypt, a year after he set forth on his missionary work.

Although better known to Chicagoans than his late brother or any of his sisters, John Borden was not born in the Lake Shore Drive mansion. He came into this world in New York City, but when only a year old was brought to Chicago by his parents and reared in the family home. When his father, William, died in 1906, John Borden became master of the mansion, and here he lived until he and his first wife were divorced in 1924.

While living here John Borden achieved fame as an Arctic

explorer. His numerous expeditions to the Bering Sea and north of the Arctic Circle are known to most Chicagoans, as are the names of the vessels he owned and commanded—the schooner "Adventuress," the three-masted sailing vessel

WILLIAM BORDEN RESIDENCE
1020 Lake Shore Drive

"The Great Bear" (in which he and his crew were wrecked), the steam yacht "Kanawha" (commissioned as a submarine chaser during the World War), and the schooner "Northern Light."

A younger sister of John Borden who showed exceptional talent was Joyce, now the wife of Zlatko Balokovic, Yugoslav violinist. Before her marriage Joyce Borden spent some months on the stage, making her debut in New York in the English opera, *The Immortal Hour*. After acquiring the schooner "Northern Light" from her brother, she and her husband sailed it around the world in 1932. Mrs. Balokovic is now noted as a collector of Balinese art.

John Borden's second wife, Courtney Letts Borden, showed unusual ability as a writer in her book, *Adventures in a Man's World*, which described life at Glenwild, the five-thousand-acre Borden plantation in Mississippi. The book was for a time a best seller. She and Mr. Borden were divorced in 1933.

Today, the great gray-stone house on "the Drive" is occupied by John Borden's first wife—who was Ellen Waller, daughter of a pioneer Chicago businessman—and her husband, John Alden Carpenter, Chicago composer. The house is now the property of John Borden's two daughters by his first marriage. These two are now Mrs. Adlai Stevenson and Mrs. Robert Pirie, both prominent in Chicago society.

The Mansion of a
Social Queen

~~~~~~

NOT so long ago one of the most glamorous houses in Chicago, where reigned a social queen whose status, wealth, and spectacular life equaled, if not exceeded, that of Mrs. Potter Palmer, the three-story, gray-stone mansion at 1000 Lake Shore Drive is gradually being forgotten by a citizenry that once knew it so well. Empty, its windows shuttered, its famous iron gate locked, the house is taking its place alongside the Potter Palmer castle and the Marshall Field mansion as a relic of Chicago's past.

If they are forgetting this mansion, citizens still know that it was the late Mrs. Edith Rockefeller McCormick's residence. For the name of this woman, daughter of the once richest man in the world and herself known in her day as the richest woman in Chicago, is still fresh in the minds of Chicagoans. She died only nine years ago.

As her name has been associated with this residence for more than forty years, many people believe that she and her husband, Harold F. McCormick, had it built soon after they were married in 1895. But this is not the case. It was back in the early 1880's, after Mr. and Mrs. Potter Palmer had built their castle on Lake Shore Drive, that Nathaniel S. Jones, a millionaire, erected the stone mansion that afterward became the McCormick abode. It was designed by S. S. Beman.

Born in Ohio in 1841, Nathaniel Jones came to Chicago in 1875, entered the grain and provision business, prospered, became a member of the Board of Trade, and founded the com-

MRS. EDITH ROCKEFELLER McCORMICK MANSION
1000 Lake Shore Drive

mission house of Jones, Kennett and Hopkins. Describing him as "one of the wealthiest and most successful business-men in Chicago," a journal of 1889 goes on to say that he has "a palatial home on the Lake Shore Drive."

In this house, continues the same article, Jones "has liberally indulged his cultural tastes, his house being adorned with many costly paintings and rare works of art, while his library overflows with literary gems, ancient and modern."

On what a grander, and much more costly, scale did Mrs.

McCormick, not many years later, outfit this house with artistic furnishings and rare antiques!

But before she and her husband moved into it, the mansion for a time was the abode of another wealthy Chicagoan, General Joseph T. Torrence, father of the system of belt-line railroads around Chicago which facilitate the transfer of east- and west-bound freight. General Torrence, who earned his military title in the Illinois National Guard, first came to Chicago as an engineer in charge of furnaces for the Chicago Iron Works.

It was several years after their marriage in New York—a marriage that united two of the largest fortunes in the United States at that time—that Harold McCormick and his wife came to Chicago. There is a persistent story that the bride's father, John D. Rockefeller, bought the mansion at 1000 Lake Shore Drive and presented it to the couple as a wedding gift, but this was denied by Mrs. McCormick.

In the years following—years marked by long absences from Chicago of its one-time social queen, Mrs. Potter Palmer—the chatelaine of the stone mansion at 1000 Lake Shore Drive was on her way toward the throne of the absentee queen. When Mrs. Palmer died, Mrs. McCormick ascended the throne and ruled Chicago society until her death in 1932.

In this great house, with its turrets, its arched entrance and wide stone steps, and with its front protected by a highly ornamental grillwork iron gate, Mrs. McCormick held court in the years before the first World War. Here she reared her three children, Muriel, Mathilde, and Fowler. And here, too, as the city's foremost art patron, she installed those rare and costly paintings and art objects that made her name famous throughout the world as a collector.

It was in the Empire Room of this house that Mrs. Mc-

Cormick held sway at brilliant functions and entertained royalty in later years—Queen Marie of Rumania in 1926 and Prince William of Sweden in 1927. It was in this room that great personages walked on the most famous of her rugs, the Emperor's Carpet, for which she is said to have paid $125,000. It was made in Persia six hundred years ago and was once the property of Peter the Great of Russia.

Under the roof of this house were treasures Mrs. McCormick had gathered in all parts of the world—gilded chairs that once belonged to Napoleon, a gold dinner service which Napoleon gave to the princess Pauline Borghese, a precious rug internationally known for its beauty, a private library of first editions and literary rarities, a collection of old lace said to rival that of the Vatican, and matchless jewels.

The McCormicks lived in this house until 1913, when, following a nervous breakdown, Mrs. McCormick went to Switzerland to study psychology under the famous Dr. Jung. She remained in Switzerland eight years. Then she returned to Chicago, accompanied by the young Swiss architect, Edwin Krenn, and not long afterward she divorced McCormick, who later married Ganna Walska, Polish opera star.

Upon her return to Chicago, Mrs. McCormick became interested in real estate promotion. This marked the beginning of the most spectacular phase of her career. Her real estate operations, with the aid of her protégé, Edwin Krenn, and his friend, Edward A. Dato, skyrocketed to dizzy heights, then collapsed in 1929.

In 1930, for reasons of economy, she moved out of the great house on "the Drive" and occupied a suite in the Drake Hotel, across the street. Then this mansion, as well as her Lake Forest villa, both of which she bought from her husband at the time of their divorce and for which she paid a total of $2,500,000, were mortgaged for $770,000.

Mrs. Edith Rockefeller McCormick, once the richest woman in Chicago, was crushed. She never regained her health. She died not long afterward at the age of fifty-nine. The old gray-stone mansion was reopened once more for her funeral, and here, in the Empire Room where she had carved out her earthly career, Mrs. McCormick's body lay in state surrounded by Claude Pernet roses, the yellow blooms that were her favorite flowers.

The Home of Chicago's "First Citizen"

〰〰〰〰〰〰〰〰〰〰〰〰〰〰〰〰〰〰〰〰〰〰〰〰〰〰

O N ASTOR STREET, that quiet, tree-shaded street where many of the city's prominent families live today, there stands a stately, ivy-covered residence of unusual interest to Chicagoans of all classes. For here, in this simple but dignified Georgian house, dwells a white-haired, lively woman of eighty-two who is now widely acclaimed as the "First Citizen of Chicago."

It was in this house, which she and her husband built half a century ago, that Mrs. Joseph T. Bowen began a career that made her the most influential woman in Chicago for decades and brought her national prominence. That career is not ended. She is still as active as ever in the fight she has long waged for the betterment of the poor and underprivileged in Chicago.

In an article in the *Reader's Digest*, a Chicago writer, Milton S. Mayer, said this of the dynamic little chatelaine of the Astor Street house: "For fifty years Mrs. Bowen has been the social conscience of Chicago, and the one completely magic name in that rough, tough, cynical city."

Mayer continued: "For two generations she has led, or founded, or pushed every move for civic betterment. Ad-

141

mittedly she is Chicago's first citizen—not only because once upon a time the Republicans wanted her to run for mayor, or because once upon a time she received a bomb in the mail. For fifty years she has bullied decent laws out of politicians. Alone in the beginning, she now has solidly behind her all the men and women of Chicago who want to make their city and their world a better place to live in."

Not only is this Near North Side residence of interest because of Mrs. Bowen's wide influence in Chicago life but also because its mistress is a living link with the very beginnings of Chicago. Her mother was born within the palisades of the original Fort Dearborn. Her grandfather, Edward H. Hadduck, a government agent, had settled at the fort in 1835. And she herself was born just before the Civil War in a red-brick house at Wabash Avenue and Monroe Street.

She was the only child of John and Helen Hadduck de Koven and received the name of Louise. John de Koven had come to Chicago in 1856. His name is perpetuated today in De Koven Street. As a girl, Louise de Koven played one winter with "Tad" Lincoln, whose widowed mother was then living temporarily in the old Clifton House on Wabash Avenue.

When Louise de Koven became Mrs. Joseph T. Bowen in 1886, she and her husband began planning a home on the Near North Side suitable to their station but in no way ostentatious. They obtained the services of Frank Whitehouse, a leading architect of that day, and their dwelling was soon under construction. It was completed in 1891. Today its address is 1430 Astor Street.

"There were then only three or four houses on our street, a street that had just been redeemed from the beach," explained the white-haired dowager as she sat in the library of her residence. "The site of our house was an old graveyard from which most of the bodies had been removed. In digging the foundations of our house, however, workmen found numerous bones. At first we had great difficulty in getting servants because they feared our house was haunted. Nobody, it seemed, wanted to work for us.

MRS. JOSEPH T. BOWEN MANSION
1430 Astor Street

"We insisted on very plain architecture, similar to the Colonial style. As this was in contrast to the more pretentious French style then 'the rage,' our friends at first thought our house too plain.

"They would josh me and refer to our house as 'the jail.' But we didn't mind. The house suited our tastes, and we had plenty of room in it."

Describing the chestnut-shaded yard adjoining her house on the south and which connects it with the residence of her daughter, Mrs. William McCormick Blair, Mrs. Bowen said: "There were no trees in the yard at first. In the winter we turned it into an ice-skating rink. We also had a large snow slide. Often there were as many as a hundred children in the yard."

In this spacious house, with its forty tastefully decorated rooms, were reared the Bowen children—John de Koven Bowen, who died in 1917; Joseph T. Bowen, Jr., of Lake Forest; Mrs. Louise de Koven Phelps of Chicago; and Helen Bowen, now Mrs. William McCormick Blair. The master of this house, Joseph T. Bowen, died here in 1911. As a memorial to him Mrs. Bowen founded the Joseph T. Bowen Country Club for poor children from the West Side of Chicago.

An occasion of interest in this house was the day Theodore Roosevelt was entertained here. In her book, *Growing Up with a City*, Mrs. Bowen tells of it: "Later on, I had the pleasure of giving him a dinner at my house. About forty people sat down, and Mr. Roosevelt made a most excellent speech in which he said that if he had been elected he would have put a woman in his cabinet."

Among other well-known personages who came often to the Bowen house in Astor Street were John Dewey, philosopher and educator; Dr. Florence Allen, now a federal judge; the late Julius Rosenwald; Federal Judge Julian W. Mack; Anna Howard Shaw, early woman suffrage leader; and the late Jane Addams. It was in this house that Miss Addams died in 1935.

For more than forty years Mrs. Bowen was a co-worker of Miss Addams in the maintenance of Hull-House. During most of that time Mrs. Bowen was treasurer of the social settlement. She is now president of the institution.

Miss Addams, many years before her death, wrote about Mrs. Bowen in the *American Magazine:* "Whether Mrs.

Bowen receives in her charming house with her two daughters or presents the cause of school nurses before a committee of the Chicago common council; whether she applauds her sons as they win championships in tennis and golf or addresses a large audience upon the wrongs of neglected childhood and the prerogative of all youth to wholesome recreation, she always carries with her a reassuring sense of competence and power. She combines with cultivation and sympathetic understanding the acumen and hardihood of the pioneer men and women who built early Chicago."

Georgian Style

⌇⌇⌇

ELLEVUE PLACE has always been a favorite residential district, and immediately west of the Borden Château—such is the incongruity of our American individualism—stands the most perfect piece of Georgian architecture in Chicago, the personal design of Charles McKim for his great friend, the late Bryan Lathrop." These words are from that informative little volume *Chicago Welcomes You*, written by the late Alfred Granger, noted architect and admirer of the Chicago scene. The book was published by Adolph Kroch, the bookseller, during the 1933 Century of Progress Exposition. The "most perfect piece of Georgian architecture in Chicago" which Granger refers to is still standing in Bellevue Place, a spacious, dignified mansion now almost half a century old.

Today it is the home of one of the city's oldest and most exclusive women's clubs, the Fortnightly Club. To this organization belong many successful women artists, writers, and musicians as well as wealthy patrons and devotees of the arts. Granger wrote: "The members of this club appreciate the architectural value of their home, and all the necessary alterations to convert it from a residence to a club house were carried out by a former pupil of Charles McKim in the spirit of the original design."

Even if this house, one of three Gold Coast residences at Bellevue Place and Lake Shore Drive—the others being the Edith Rockefeller McCormick and William Borden homes— were not the one-time abode of a noted Chicagoan, it would still be of unusual interest as a sample of work by one of America's great architects.

In a lecture on American architecture given in Vienna a few years before his death, Granger said: "I have dwelt at some length upon Richardson and McKim because no other men have so deeply influenced the practice of architecture in America, and until the completion of the World's Fair in Chicago in 1893 their influence was unchallenged."

The architectural firm founded by Charles F. McKim, which included two other distinguished architects, William R. Mead and Stanford White, "had the largest and richest clientele in America, and the number of their buildings is legion," Granger said in his Vienna lecture. McKim and his associates restored the White House in Washington, designed the Morgan Library in New York and the Boston Public Library, and created "many sumptuous banks and private residences." McKim's influence was evident in many directions at the Columbian Exposition in Chicago in 1893, as Granger points out in his *Charles Follen McKim: A Study of His Life Work*, published in 1913. McKim not only designed the huge Agricultural Building and the "exquisite" New York State Building, but played an important part in laying out the Court of Honor, central point of the fair grounds.

It was in 1892, just before the opening of the fair, that McKim's three-story Georgian style house in Bellevue Place was completed and occupied by Bryan Lathrop, a notable personage in the Chicago of the 1890's and for many years afterward. Lathrop died in the Bellevue Place mansion in 1916 at the age of seventy-two.

During the years he occupied this residence, which was graciously presided over by his wife, the former Helen Lynde Aldis, whom he married in 1875, Bryan Lathrop accomplished the tasks that made him one of the city's greatest cultural benefactors. A Virginian by birth, he was educated in France

BRYAN LATHROP RESIDENCE
120 East Bellevue Place

and Germany by private tutors, and this gave him an intellectual and artistic background that increased as he grew in years.

He came to Chicago shortly after the Civil War, entered into management of Graceland Cemetery, and developed a real estate business that was the foundation of his fortune. Although active in business, he was interested also in art, music, and literature. He became an early trustee of the Art

Institute and three years after it was organized became a trustee of Chicago Orchestral Association.

To Lathrop, more than to any other man, is due the credit for erecting Orchestra Hall. He also aided the Newberry Library as a trustee. After being appointed to the Lincoln Park board in 1901, he brought about an extension of the park northward.

After his death, the Chicago Orchestral Association, which maintains the Chicago Symphony Orchestra, was found to be the beneficiary of a $700,000 bequest from the late civic and cultural leader.

Although the Lathrop residence in Bellevue Place often attracted attention as a gathering-place of distinguished persons, among whom were Mr. Lathrop's brother-in-law and sister, Ambassador and Mrs. Thomas Nelson Page, it attained greater renown for its collection of original Whistler etchings, said to be the largest in this country. The collection is now a permanent exhibit in the Art Institute.

When the Lathrop house was taken over by the Fortnightly Club in 1923 on the occasion of the club's fiftieth anniversary, few changes were made in the interior of the edifice. The rooms still retain their simple, dignified atmosphere, with here and there the decorative touches of the Four Georges era. And in keeping with the tasteful atmosphere of these rooms are the pieces of genuine Biedermeier furniture with which they are outfitted.

If Bryan Lathrop, with his familiar white beard and quiet, cultivated manner, were to visit his house today, he would undoubtedly be highly gratified at the way it has been preserved and its twenty-three rooms maintained with the same decorative charm as when he lived there. He would doubtless be pleased, too, with the use to which his residence is now being devoted—a gathering-place of people noted for their achievements in the arts.

The Home of Lincoln's Son

ALTHOUGH few, if any, landmarks in Chicago associated with Abraham Lincoln remain today, there still exists the residence in which Robert Todd Lincoln, son of the martyred president, lived with his family for almost two decades. It stands at the northwest corner of Scott Street and Lake Shore Drive.

This three-story brownstone mansion, plain but dignified and now partly covered with ivy, was erected by Robert Lincoln upon his return to Chicago in 1893 after having served for four years as United States minister to Great Britain. The architect Robert Lincoln selected to design the house was his friend, S. S. Beman, who had planned the model industrial town of Pullman. At that time Lake Shore Drive was beginning to supplant Prairie Avenue as the city's Gold Coast.

Before being sent to London, Lincoln had been a resident of Chicago and one of the city's notable lawyers. He had come to this city with his widowed mother soon after the assassination of President Lincoln. After being established as a lawyer here, he became counselor of the Pullman Company, supervisor of the township of South Chicago, and a trustee of the Illinois Central Railroad.

Then national honors came to him despite the fact that he

was averse to public life, preferring instead quietly to practice law. He was appointed secretary of war by President James A. Garfield, served in this high position competently, returned to Chicago, and then was called to public life once more when President Benjamin Harrison named him minister to England.

But when he and his family came back to Chicago in the year of the World's Columbian Exposition, Robert Lincoln was determined never again to accept an official appointment. He disliked public appearances. He did not want to create the impression he was capitalizing on his father's great name. It was this attitude that caused him to build a substantial home here which would be his permanent abode and in which he could live a quiet, simple existence and entertain a few close friends.

Not only was Robert Lincoln a reticent man but he was a considerably saddened person when he built his Lake Shore Drive residence. The memory of his own father's assassination still vivid in his mind, he was an eyewitness to the assassination of President Garfield in 1881. Then, in 1901, he was within earshot when President McKinley was fatally fired upon at the Buffalo exposition.

After becoming established in his Lake Shore Drive home, Lincoln resumed his connections with the Pullman Company, and a few years later, upon the death of George M. Pullman, he was named president of the company. He served in this capacity until 1906, when he retired to become chairman of the board. All during the years he was president of the company, Lincoln took little interest in outside affairs and rarely appeared in public.

He was content to occupy his leisure time in his home and enjoy intervals of companionship with his friends. Presiding over this home was his wife, Mary, daughter of James Harlan, who had been an Iowa senator during the Civil War. It is not known whether this house ever contained the six trunks of letters and other personal papers of President Lincoln that Robert Lincoln afterward placed in the Library of Congress, with the stipulation that they were not to be opened until 1947.

ROBERT TODD LINCOLN MANSION
1234 Lake Shore Drive

The house did contain, however, many art objects and articles of historic interest to which Robert fell heir. Among these was a large oil painting of the martyred president. The owner of these possessions valued them highly and was fully aware of their historical significance. He was, incidentally, at one time president of the Chicago Historical Society.

It is said that during his leisure moments in this Gold Coast mansion Robert Lincoln at times enjoyed working out algebraic equations. He was also an amateur of astronomy. For out-of-door recreation he sought the pleasures of golf with intimate companions or a drive in his carriage. Those who knew him said he was an inveterate smoker and, within his own small circle of friends, a good conversationalist and story-teller.

He is described as being physically unlike his illustrious father. He was shorter in stature and quicker in movement. As was the fashion among men of the time, Robert Lincoln wore a mustache and full beard. Although possessed of a re-tiring nature, he was not cold or taciturn among his friends and showed as much warmth toward them as President Lincoln had shown to his intimates.

The Lincolns and their two daughters lived in this residence until 1911, when they sold it to Charles A. Monroe, public utilities official and son-in-law of the late Frank G. Logan, Chicago capitalist and art patron. The Lincolns moved to their summer home at Manchester, Vermont, where Robert Lincoln died in 1926 at the age of eighty-two. His widow died there in 1937 at the age of ninety.

The only descendents of President Lincoln living today are the two daughters of the Robert Lincolns, Mrs. Jesse Randolph and Mrs. Charles Isham, both of Washington, and their children—Charles Isham, Jr., of New York and Robert Lincoln Beckwith and Mary Lincoln Beckwith, children of Mrs. Randolph by her first marriage.

The Lake Shore Drive residence is today occupied by Mrs. Nancy Clark. It is in well-kept condition and little altered since the time of the Lincolns. The reception hall is paneled entirely in oak and the parlor in mahogany. There are attractive fireplaces as well as parquetry floors in all important rooms. Mrs. Clark says that Lincoln students often come to visit the house.

PART VI

West of the River

Introduction

Across the river, on the West Side, there were aristocratic streets in the old days—streets that contained elegant homes on a par with those of Prairie Avenue or Pine Street. One of these streets was Washington Boulevard; another was Jackson Boulevard. Running north and south, Ashland Boulevard was a main avenue of the area. On all of these thoroughfares stood magnificent residences in which lived captains of industry and kings of finance. One of the best known of these was the spacious dwelling, set back on wide lawns, of Mayor Carter H. Harrison. It was located at Ashland and Jackson boulevards. Since the 1890's, these once sumptuous homes have gradually been deserted by the families who built them, until today most of them stand either vacant or occupied by roomers. Those that survive on Ashland Boulevard have been taken over by labor unions. Around all of them there have been neighborhood changes which brought factories, warehouses, and workshops to darken the old houses with the soot and dust of industry.

Hull-House

～～～～～～～～～～～～～～～～～～～～～～～～～～～～～～

IN HER book, *Twenty Years at Hull-House*, which has become a minor American classic, the late Jane Addams wrote: "Another Sunday afternoon in the early spring [of 1889], on the way to a Bohemian mission in the carriage of one of its founders, we passed a fine old house standing well back from the street, surrounded on three sides by a broad piazza which was supported by wooden pillars of exceptionally pure Corinthian design and proportion.

"I was so attracted by the house that I set forth to visit it the very next day, but though I searched for it then and for several days after, I could not find it, and at length I most reluctantly gave up the search."

Accompanied by Miss Ellen Gates Starr, Jane Addams had been searching for a house in which to establish a social settlement for the benefit of Chicago's poor. Some few weeks later Miss Addams succeeded in finding the dwelling with the piazza and Corinthian pillars, and here she established Hull-House, which became a world-famous social settlement.

The "fine old house" discovered by Miss Addams is still standing on its original site and is now eighty-five years old. Its first floor forms the reception room of the great social settlement, which today occupies thirteen buildings on two

square city blocks. On the second floor is the office of Miss
Charlotte Carr, successor to Jane Addams in directing Hull-
House. Although the original façade has been somewhat ob-
scured by remodeling and the addition of a third story, the

CHARLES J. HULL HOME
800 South Halsted Street

interior of the house remains much the same as when first
taken over by Miss Addams.

When the fiftieth anniversary of the founding of Hull-
House was celebrated in 1940, this old portion became a kind
of shrine to which pilgrims came to pay their respects to a
great American woman. For it was in this part of Hull-
House, among old-fashioned marble fireplaces, high windows,
ceilings adorned with rosettes, and carved woodwork, that

Jane Addams lived and planned the humanitarian works which made her name known throughout America and Europe.

The history of this Halsted Street landmark goes back to the pioneer days of Chicago. It was built in 1856 by Charles J. Hull, an early real estate promoter who did much to develop the West Side. An oil painting showing an artist's conception of the house when Hull first built it hangs in one of its rooms today.

It depicts a two-story, red-brick residence, topped by a cupola and surrounded by wide verandas. The house is set in the midst of an estate, with the grounds shaded by several big trees and enhanced in places by pergolas. At the time the house was built this section of Chicago was considered "suburban." Now it is in the very center of one of the city's most populous slum areas.

Soon after Hull moved into this residence, his wife died and left him with two young children. Before passing away she asked her husband's cousin, Miss Helen Culver, who was then teaching in Chicago, to give up this work and come into the Hull household to care for the youngsters. This Miss Culver did, and here she reared the children until the Civil War.

When the war broke out, Miss Culver became a field nurse and, at the close of the conflict, returned to the Hull residence and once more took over the care of the Hull children. Here she nursed them during illnesses which finally caused their deaths.

In 1868 Hull closed his residence and moved to another part of the city. Vacant, deserted, the house survived the fire of 1871. The West Side grew up around it, immigrants came and settled on all sides, and the neighborhood was soon a crowded tenement section.

Subsequently, the old mansion was taken over by the Little Sisters of the Poor and used for a time as a home for the aged. Afterward it was occupied by a secondhand furniture store, and when Miss Addams saw it that Sunday in 1889 the first floor was being used as an office and storeroom for a factory that had been built at the rear of it.

After Miss Addams and Miss Starr obtained the house, they sublet the second floor and the large drawing-room on the first floor. They moved in and began their work of aiding the poor and underprivileged in the neighborhood. Later, Miss Culver, who had inherited Hull's real estate interests, gave to Miss Addams and Miss Starr a free leasehold of the entire dwelling. And thus Hull-House was founded.

In Brighton Park

I N BRIGHTON PARK, that old but still lively community among the factories and switchyards of the Southwest Side where Mayor Kelly and numerous other public figures were reared, there stands in lonely splendor a tall residence of ancient vintage that inevitably catches the eye of the passer-by. It was once an important dwelling, for here lived, during the 1890's, the "Father of Brighton Park." It was, too, the home at different periods of numerous other Chicago persons of note.

Although widely known in that section as the old McCaffery home, after John McCaffery, early settler of Brighton Park, this two-story, red-brick residence was not built by him. The man who erected it and lived in it with his large family for some years was John Dolese, founder of the street-paving firm of Dolese and Shepard, a firm that paved most of the important streets and boulevards of Chicago just after the great fire of 1871.

Today this house stands at 3558 South Artesian Avenue, where its old-style architecture is noticeable to Western Avenue streetcar passengers. But this is not its original location. It was moved to this site about 1920 by its present owner. It had originally stood on Western Avenue in the midst of landscaped grounds, and around it were fruit trees and grape arbors, the whole estate being surrounded by a picket fence. Next door to it was the Tom Kelly residence of similar architecture, and the two dwellings were the outstanding buildings of the old village.

So far as can be determined, John Dolese built the house sometime in the middle 1860's. He was a native Chicagoan, having been born in a little frame house at the southeast corner of what is now the intersection of Lake and La Salle streets. His father, Peter, came to Chicago from Alsace-Lorraine in 1833.

After entering the teaming business at the youthful age of twenty, John Dolese later branched out and in 1868 formed a partnership with Jason H. Shepard in the business of paving streets. While living in his Brighton Park residence, Dolese looked after the firm's yards and quarries at Hawthorne. He dwelt in this house until 1890, reared a family of nine children here, and then sold the house to John McCaffery, who by that time was known as the "Father of Brighton Park."

John McCaffery and six other men incorporated the village of Brighton Park in 1851 and named it after a near-by race track. McCaffery had come here a little earlier and set up the first village store at Western and Archer avenues. He later sold this store to John and Matthew Larney, and they enlarged it to include a saloon and coal office. It became the main gathering-place of the village.

After the village was incoporated, John McCaffery bought up land owned by most of the other incorporators and began a development project. He was one of the organizers of the Brighton Cotton Mill and in 1871 became its president. He named Tom Kelly superintendent of the mill. Kelly afterward became a paving contractor and one of the most influential political figures of Chicago in the 1890's. Meanwhile,

McCaffery's fortune rose, and he became one of the original stockholders of the old Illinois Trust and Savings Bank.

By the time he purchased the Dolese residence, McCaffery was a well-to-do man. Not only had he helped build

JOHN McCAFFERY HOME
3558 South Artesian Avenue

Brighton Park and establish a cotton mill there but he had also joined the firm of Dolese and Shepard and supervised the paving of Drexel, Oakwood, Garfield, and other South Side boulevards. In his Western Avenue house McCaffery and his wife reared a son, John C. McCaffery, who grew up to become a circus proprietor and who at one time was president of the Showmen's League of America.

The elder McCaffery died in this house in 1900. His son continued to live in the house and several years later brought in a bride, Annabelle Adams, daughter of Henry E. Adams, first undertaker of Brighton Park. After the death of young McCaffery's wife the house was rented by Edward R. Litsinger, who afterward became a leading political figure.

About twenty-five years ago the house, by then a venerable landmark of Brighton Park, was acquired by Emil Klank and his wife, who was the former Emma Hampson, daughter of a pioneer stone contractor of the neighborhood. Emil Klank was afterward to become well known as the manager of Frank Gotch, heavyweight wrestling champion. He also piloted Stanislas Zbyszko and Yusouf Mahmut. These three champs of the mat often visited the Klank home in Brighton Park.

Emil Klank and his wife had the house moved across the street to the Artesian Avenue address. Klank died in June, 1940, and his widow continues to live in the spacious old residence. Living with her is her brother, James Hampson, who has spent most of his life in Brighton Park as a builder. The two have kept the house and grounds in good condition.

Some alterations have been made. A stone portico over the front door has been removed, as has a fancy wrought-iron railing that guarded the "captain's walk" on the roof. Otherwise, the façade is intact. Here are the decorative stone caps over windows, overhanging cornices, and mansard roof of a typical mansion of the 1860's.

Just as interesting is the interior. The rooms are large, with fine marble fireplaces and great mirrors, parquet floors, sliding doors, transoms of leaded glass, and gaslight chandeliers. The main rooms are decorated with antlers and antiques collected by Frank Klank in his many travels. Old-style furniture adds to the Victorian atmosphere of the house. Among these furnishings are a venerable parlor organ and a highly carved buffet.

Where Lived a Lumber King

ALTHOUGH built by an earlier Chicagoan of considerable renown in his day, the three-story mansion at the southwest corner of Jackson Boulevard and Sangamon Street has long been known as the one-time home of Jacob Beidler, lumber king and leading citizen of the 1870's. It is so designated in the files of the West Side Historical Society and is so regarded by many elderly residents of the neighborhood, who recall when this red-brick residence, with landscaped grounds around it, was a show place of that part of the city.

Not many of the mansions surviving from an earlier day stand so close to the Loop as the Beidler home. Surrounded by factories, warehouses, and office buildings, it is an object of curiosity and has long held the attention of passing bus riders and motorists. A casual glance at this once stately abode indicates that it must have been built or occupied by a man of some importance in the Chicago of an earlier day.

Such a conjecture is warranted. For not only was Jacob Beidler a lumber magnate and outstanding citizen but he was a pioneer settler who came to Chicago when it was nothing more than a small lakeside community of wooden buildings. Jacob Beidler was also a political figure of his time and served as alderman of the old Ninth, now Twenty-seventh, Ward for two terms. He was, furthermore, an active West Side Presbyterian.

But of equal importance, although less well known today, was Horatio H. Gardner, the man who built the Sangamon Street mansion and afterward sold it to Beidler. He, too, was a lumber magnate. He was better known in his time, however, as the builder and operator of the Gardner House, a hotel at the southwest corner of Michigan Avenue and Jackson Boulevard. This hostelry was afterward called the Leland Hotel and later was renamed the Stratford Hotel.

Gardner was the son of a wealthy lumberman who had come to Chicago in 1852 and set up a lumber yard. So far as can be determined, Horatio Gardner built the pretentious residence on Sangamon Street some time in the late 1860's, or soon after the close of the Civil War. At that time he had been admitted into partnership in his father's lumber firm, the Gardner and Spry Company.

His father, Freeland B. Gardner, was one of Chicago's first lumbermen. The elder Gardner first came here in 1839 and a few years later established a lumber yard west of the river. He prospered, and his son afterward increased the family fortune. Horatio Gardner's hotel was the first to be erected in the burned-over district after the great fire of 1871.

According to an account of the Beidler home supplied to the West Side Historical Society by George Beidler, son of the lumber king, the Sangamon Street mansion cost $80,000 to build. This figure, big at that time, seems likely, as the dwelling is impressive in proportions and is of expensive construction throughout. Here the Gardners lived in style until just after the fire of 1871. In that year the house was acquired by Jacob Beidler.

The latter, who had come to Chicago as a carpenter in 1844, moved into the mansion with his wife and five children,

Augustus F., William H., Francis, David, and George. Just before the fire, Jacob Beidler and nine other lumbermen established the lumber district along the south branch of the

JACOB BEIDLER HOUSE
308 South Sangamon Street

Chicago River. An official in one of the Beidler subsidiaries was Benjamin F. Ferguson, whose subsequent fortune was donated to the building of statues and monuments in Chicago.

Several years after moving into the big residence on the West Side, Jacob Beidler was elected alderman.

"His career as an alderman, like that of his business life," says an old historical work, "was characterized by unswerving honor and devotion to the city's interests. The city has no more substantial, honorable, or worthy citizen than Jacob Beidler."

During this time he was also active in affairs of the Third Presbyterian Church at Ashland Avenue and Monroe Street.

While living in this house, Jacob Beidler helped organize the Presbyterian Hospital, provided funds for the establishing of the West Side branch of the Y.M.C.A., and endowed the chair of natural sciences at Lake Forest University. It is recorded that he gave liberally to various Presbyterian churches and to the Presbyterian Theological Seminary. He also entertained many lay leaders of that faith in his home, where Mrs. Beidler served as a gracious hostess.

In 1898 Jacob Beidler died, and his widow continued to occupy the house with her children. She died in 1900. After that, the mansion, without much alteration, was converted into the Frances E. Willard Temperance Home. A few years later, the tall cupola on the roof and the spacious veranda were removed. In 1910 the residence was acquired by a group of nuns and converted into a Catholic social center for the care of neighborhood children. It is still being used for this purpose.

Architecturally, the mansion is in the French style, a style marked by the mansard roof. The interior is typical of its era. There are many high-ceilinged rooms with marble fireplaces, massive doors, parquet floors, and richly carved balusters, as well as a large framed mirror of imported glass in what was formerly the drawing-room. The house is set back on part of the original Gardner grounds.

Not far from the old Beidler home is located the office of J. Beidler Camp, grandson of Jacob, real estate broker and leader in civic affairs of the West Side. On the wall of Camp's office hangs a large portrait of Jacob Beidler, the man who helped build the West Side and who presided over the old residential landmark on Sangamon Street.

A "Garden City" Survivor

~~~~~~

IT WAS built in the days when Chicago called itself the "Garden City." Like many other homes and residences at that time, it stood in the midst of landscaped grounds on a quiet street shaded by rows of elms, lindens, and cottonwoods. Today, it stands in the center of a deteriorated section of the city where factories and warehouses loom above men's boarding-houses and the grinding brakes of trucks and motor vans echo among brick walls.

That, in brief, is the story of the old, red-brick residence at the northwest corner of Adams Street and Racine Avenue. Topped by an ornamental cupola and surrounded by an equally ornamental cast-iron fence, this venerable West Side dwelling has been standing on the same spot ever since it was built some time in the early 1860's. Few residents of the neighborhood are left, however, who remember the name of the man who built it and lived in it during the stirring period of the Civil War.

If that man's name is obscure today, not so is the name of the man who lived in the house during the 1880's and 1890's, when this part of the West Side was a fashionable neighborhood. He was David R. Fraser, pioneer machinery manufacturer and prominent citizen in the World's Fair era. For years he was associated with Thomas Chalmers and his son, William J., in the machinery manufacturing business.

When David Fraser and his wife, Lydia, acquired the house at 134 South Racine Avenue—it was then 57 Centre Avenue —in 1881, they were a well-known and popular couple in West Side society. A year after they moved into it, their house

DAVID R. FRASER HOUSE
132 South Racine Avenue

was the scene of a fashionable wedding. This was the marriage of their son, Norman, to Miss Ariadne Preble, daughter of a pioneer Chicago family.

In Andreas' *History of Chicago* we learn that David Fraser was among a group of leading Chicago citizens, including the city's first mayor, William B. Ogden, who about 1850 organized the Chicago Locomotive Company. This company prospered, supplying lomomotives to the then infant railroad industry. It was an outgrowth of the Scoville Iron Works, established in 1842 by Hiram H. Scoville and his son-in-law, P. W. Gates.

At the time David Fraser reigned as master of the Racine Avenue house, he was one of the heads of the firm of Fraser and Chalmers, which was supplying mining machinery to the famous gold, silver, and lead mines of the West. His associate was William J. Chalmers, who was afterward an outstanding Chicago philanthropist, art patron, and civic leader. The firm they conducted is now known as the Allis-Chalmers Manufacturing Company.

In addition to many other prominent citizens of the time, the Frasers frequently entertained Mr. and Mrs. Chalmers in their home. Even at that period Mrs. Chalmers, daughter of Allan Pinkerton, head of President Lincoln's secret service agency during the Civil War, was known for her engaging personality. She was to become, like her husband, a philanthropist whose gifts were widespread and generous.

The Frasers continued to live in the big West Side residence during the 1890's. At this time, for a period of about four years, their son, Norman, and his wife and four children lived with them. About the turn of the century the elder Frasers sold their home and moved to a new dwelling on Washington Boulevard. David Fraser died in 1904. His son, Norman, was then president of the Chicago Portland Cement Company.

Thus ends the story of the old Racine Avenue house as it was known in the era between the Haymarket Riot and the Spanish-American War. Research discloses, however, that in the years immediately after it was built, or during the time Chicago still thought of itself as the "Garden City," this dwelling was as well known as when it was occupied by the Fraser family.

The man who built it and occupied it during the Civil War period was Frederick Letz, who, like David Fraser, was a pioneer iron and machinery manufacturer. He was also an early settler, having come here in 1836, before Chicago was incorporated as a city. In 1843 he established the Chicago Iron Works in a small shop on La Salle Street, between Randolph and Washington streets. The firm grew, and its name was changed to Letz and Company.

All during the time that Frederick Letz lived in his West Side residence he took a leading part in the building of Chicago by serving as a member of the city's board of public works. He and his wife, Kathrina, reared four daughters in the Racine Avenue house, and there they entertained their numerous friends. One of his intimates, Conrad Furst, a leading farm-implement manufacturer of the 1860's, is said to have been married in the Letz home.

The house today is surrounded by factories and warehouses. Its great age is plainly evident, but it is still sturdy and serviceable. It is now a men's rooming-house conducted by John Becker. The present owner, Ralph H. Burke, chief engineer for the city department of subways and traction, is a son of early West Side settlers. As a boy he often regarded with curiosity the old, red-brick house, behind its cast-iron fence.

The fence is still there, inclosing the original Letz grounds. In addition to the windowed cupola and ornamental cornices, the exterior is of interest for the decorative cast-iron lintels over the tall, narrow windows. All of this cast-iron work, obviously, is an indication of the profession pursued by the man who built this house more than eighty years ago.

Chicago's "Forgotten House"

NO HOUSE in Chicago stands on a locally more historic spot than the dilapidated, two-story stone and brick dwelling at 558 De Koven Street, just a mile or so southwest of the Loop. This may be said to be the city's No. 1 historic site. Here originated Chicago's greatest catastrophe—that devastating holocaust which marked a turning-point in the city's history.

Although every Chicago school child knows that the great fire of 1871 began here, few of them, to say nothing of their parents and Chicagoans in general, have the slightest knowledge of the house that stands on the spot today—the most memorable spot in the entire city. It is Chicago's "forgotten house." Everything has been written about the site and little, if anything, about the house.

This is natural enough. Still, the house should be of interest, even if it was only indirectly connected with what happened on its site. Its story has never been told. Local histories say nothing about it, and there is no information concerning it in old newspaper files.

When was it built? Who built it? Did its builder know he was erecting his home on the most historic site in Chicago? Who were the owners? Who lives in it now? Who is its present owner? These questions come into the visitor's mind as

ANTON KOLAR HOUSE
558 De Koven Street

he stands before the time-stained, weather-beaten stone front of this neglected house.

In the first place, the old and new historical markers imbedded in its façade might confuse the uninformed observer. They do not make clear that this is not the original O'Leary home from whose barn the great conflagration started. The O'Learys lived in a little frame cottage which was not destroyed in the fire but was torn down some years later and replaced by the present house.

We find that Patrick O'Leary and his wife, Catherine—she who is now immortalized in legend as the owner of the lantern-kicking cow—had sold their property on December 9, 1879—eight years after the fire—to one Anton Kolar and his wife. Under the old house-numbering system, the address of the property then was 137 De Koven Street.

A search of several city directories of the 1880's does not reveal an Anton Kolar at the De Koven Street address. In any case, he and his wife must have been well enough off, soon after they bought the O'Leary property, to erect a substantial two-story brick house with an English basement. The front was of smooth sandstone and was embellished at the top with a false mansard. Stone steps lead up to the tall entrance. In its day it would have been known as a "stone front."

This is the same house standing there today. There is little doubt but that it was built in 1880, which would make it sixty-one years old this year.

There is also no question but that the Kolars knew the world-fame of the spot they had chosen for their house, for only a year after it was built the Chicago Historical Society, through the efforts of its then secretary, Albert D. Hager, imbedded a marble tablet in the front of the house. It reads:

THE GREAT CHICAGO FIRE OF 1871
ORIGINATED HERE AND EXTENDED TO
LINCOLN PARK.
THE CHICAGO HISTORICAL SOCIETY, 1881.

During 1937, when Chicago observed the hundredth anniversary of its incorporation as a city, the Chicago Charter Jubilee Committee, in co-operation with the Chicago Historical Society, placed a new bronze marker on the house.

After living in the house for ten years, the Kolars sold it to one Michael Suchy. Then, on July 3, 1905, Mr. Suchy sold it to Christopher Pacelli and his wife, Angela. Mr. Pacelli was a distributor of the old *Chicago Journal* and was also an uncle of the present alderman of the Twentieth Ward, William V. Pacelli.

Here the Pacellis lived and reared their children. One of them is now Policeman Peter Pacelli of the Marquette Station. Sometime after the death of Mr. Pacelli, a resolution was introduced into the City Council by John Toman, then an alderman, proposing that the city buy the site, tear down the old Kolar house, and erect a memorial fire station on the spot.

Although the proposal was ridiculed in some quarters, one alderman suggesting that a huge statue of Mrs. O'Leary's cow be erected on the site and that it be used as an airplane beacon or mooring mast for airships, it nevertheless carried in the City Council, and the house and lot were purchased by the city from the Widow Pacelli on March 27, 1928. Then came the depression. The memorial fire station was never built.

As the city fathers have voted little or no funds for the repair and maintenance of the house, it is in a state of direst neglect. Occupying it as tenants today are Frank Constantino and his wife, Rose, with their children, Frank, Jr., and Sam, five-year-old twins, Joseph, ten, and Lucille, sixteen. On the floor below live Mr. and Mrs. Tony Miglore.

Turning back the pages of history, we find that the Kolar house stands on a lot originally owned by Cyrus Clarke and his wife Catherine, both of Buffalo, New York. Cyrus Clarke was related to Henry B. Clarke, who built the Widow Clarke's House in South Wabash Avenue. The records show that on March 24, 1864, the Clarkes sold the lot and a little cottage on it to Patrick O'Leary. That section of the city was then known as the West Division.

The O'Learys had five children. One of these later became the famous Jim O'Leary, a one-time gambling king of Chicago. Some idea of what the little O'Leary cottage was like can be gained from numerous similar cottages still standing to the west of the Kolar house, all of which are plain, gabled-roofed dwellings.

As an indication of the increase of realty values here since early days, the records show that Patrick O'Leary paid $500 to Cyrus Clarke for the cottage and lot in 1864. When Mrs. Angela Pacelli sold her house and lot to the city in 1928, she received $36,000.

Boyhood Home of "The Glorifier"

~~~~~~

I T IS a shabby old Victorian house in a shabby old section of the Near West Side. The red paint on the brick walls is peeling, the wooden steps leading to the second floor are rickety, and the metal cornice at the fourth-floor roof line is brown with rust. To a passer-by the house looks like just another of the old mansions clustering around the once fashionable Ashland Boulevard neighborhood.

But at one time this house, which stands at 1448 West Adams Street, was trim and elegant and known to many citizens, for it was then the home of a distinguished Chicagoan. And this Chicagoan had a son, reared in this house, who became internationally famous and whose name was a household word in America for three decades. The son's brilliant career was the subject, not so long ago, of a movie spectacle that thrilled millions.

That son was Flo Ziegfeld. While living in this house, he began the career that earned for him the title of "Glorifier of the American Girl." In this house, as a boy, he dreamed of becoming a great theatrical producer—a dream that all the world knows was realized.

When Florenz Ziegfeld was a young man living here, this

house was familiar to hundreds of Chicagoans. It was then the palatial home of Flo's father, Dr. Florenz Ziegfeld, for many years Chicago's beloved music master.

When he and his family moved into this house in 1882, Dr. Ziegfeld was at the height of his career as a music teacher —a career begun here in 1867 when he founded the Chicago Musical College. He had come from Germany many years earlier, had settled immediately in Chicago, and had served in the Civil War, rising to the rank of colonel. At the close of the war he married Rosalie de Hez, a French girl, who had settled in Chicago before he arrived.

The future creator of the "Follies" was thirteen years old when his family moved into the Adams Street house. It was then that young Flo got his first experience as a showman. He went to see Buffalo Bill's "Wild West" show at the old Academy of Music in Halsted Street. After staging a spectacular demonstration of marksmanship, Buffalo Bill challenged any member of the audience to duplicate his own performance. The thirteen-year-old Flo accepted the challenge, stepped up to the stage, and hit the bull's-eye. Buffalo Bill invited him to join the show, and young Ziegfeld accepted. He was gone three weeks, earning fifty dollars a week. His budding theatrical career was cut short, however, when his alarmed parents turned up and took him back to the Adams Street house.

Then came a ten-year period in which young Flo served as business manager of his father's music college. Life went along happily in the family home. During the World's Columbian Exposition of 1893, Florenz, Jr., made formal entry into the show business by procuring military bands from different countries in Europe for appearance at the fair—just as his father had done earlier for the Boston peace jubilee.

The young entrepreneur booked Sandow, the strong man

of Europe, and featured him in the Trocadero Theater on
Michigan Avenue, near Monroe Street. He spent five thou-

FLO ZIEGFELD HOME
1448 West Adams Street

sand dollars in exploiting Sandow, was successful in this venture, and managed the strong man for four years.

Young Ziegfeld was now started on his theatrical career.
He introduced Anna Held to America, married her, and from
then on soared to the heights of success and fortune.

Almost everybody knows his story. It was told in colorful and spectacular fashion not so long ago in a movie, *The Great Ziegfeld*, which recalled his glamorous "Follies" musical comedies and the stars of the stage he had discovered—Will Rogers, Anna Held, the Vernon Castles, Ed Wynn, Sophie Tucker, Bert Williams, Eddie Cantor, and dozens of others. Few people knew that the great producer, during his lifetime, never forgot the old house in West Adams Street.

He never forgot it because there lived the two persons to whom he was always devoted, his father and mother. He always visited them at the house whenever he was in Chicago. He was in this house, together with his brothers and sisters, when his parents celebrated their golden wedding anniversary in 1915. When his father died here in 1923 at the age of eighty-two, Flo was at the bedside. His show, *Kid Boots*, was then a Broadway success.

After the death of his father he was doubly zealous for the welfare of his mother. He wanted her to move away from the old house because the neighborhood had deteriorated, but she refused. She wanted to stay here with her memories of the great days of the 1880's and 1890's. So Flo came to the house each year for her birthday celebration, bringing gifts. Then his mother became ill and was in a coma for several months. At this time, in 1932, Flo himself was taken ill in California and died within a few days. Broadway said he died a poor man. Mother Ziegfeld, as she was affectionately called in the West Side neighborhood, died at the age of eighty-four in the Adams Street house without knowing that her son had preceded her in death.

The old house is now occupied by Guy Carlton Williams and his wife, Lillian, together with their daughter and son-in-law. The Williamses are serving as caretakers of the house for the Ziegfeld estate and are keeping it—at least the interior—in good condition. Mr. Williams, incidentally, is an author. His first published novel, *Streets of Death*, deals with the deterioration of the neighborhood in which the Ziegfeld house stands.

"It was a pathetic sight," recalled Mrs. Williams, "to see the public auction held in this house a few weeks after Mother Ziegfeld died. All of the articles and furnishings she loved so much, things like marble-topped tables, rugs, glassware and china, tapestried chairs, statuettes, books and the autographed pictures, were all placed under the hammer. It was among these things, as you know, that Flo Ziegfeld grew up to manhood."

Walnut Interior

T HE Madlener residence was a place to which invitations were never refused and whose doors were always open to friends with a certainty of glad and entertaining welcome." These words are from *Chicago and Its Makers*, a comprehensive reference work brought out some years ago by Felix Mendelsohn, Chicago publisher.

The mansion referred to was erected by Fridolin Madlener, pioneer resident, founder of an early liquor and distilling firm and a leading Chicagoan of the 1880's. The house still stands at 1239 West Washington Boulevard.

When first built, it compared favorably with any of the stately residences that lined both sides of Washington Street during late Victorian years. Today, almost lost among factories that have supplanted the mansions, it remains as one of the few survivors of the street's once aristocratic past. As such, it is held in sentimental esteem by many old-time West Siders and by members of the West Side Historical Society.

Information about the man who built this house, supplied by Mrs. Gertrude I. Jenkins, secretary-historian of the West Side Historical Society, reveals that Fridolin Madlener first came to Chicago from Baden, Germany, in 1858.

A young man of energy and foresight, he was soon in business for himself as a liquor wholesaler. He founded the firm of F. Madlener, which was later incoporated and became one of the best-known wholesale liquor houses in the Middle West. His company prospered, and in time he took his place in the city as a successful and wealthy citizen. In 1866 he was

FRIDOLIN MADLENER MANSION
1239 West Washington Street

married to Margaretha Blatz, daughter of Albert Blatz, leading brewer of Milwaukee.

When the Madlener mansion was built in 1883, the street on which it stood, as well as Ashland Avenue, were the fashionable thoroughfares of the West Side, where lived such personages as Carter Harrison and, a few years earlier, the widowed Mrs. Abraham Lincoln. Into his new home Mr.

Madlener brought his wife and two children, Albert F. and Angelina.

A notable social event in the house was the wedding in 1891 of Angelina Madlener to Edward A. Leight, lumber merchant of that day. It was while living here that Fridolin Madlener was most active among gymnastic and singing societies of the city.

It was not long, however, before the master of this Washington Street mansion began to observe signs of change in his neighborhood. In 1892 he and his family gave up their home and moved to the North Side.

The old Madlener residence had been in the hands of a succession of owners when it was bought in 1921 by Mr. and Mrs. Joseph Mandelbaum. The Mandelbaums have lived there ever since. Appreciating the value of their dwelling as a landmark, they are keeping it in good repair.

Except for the removal of the east veranda and minor alterations on the inside, this French-style mansion with mansard roof remains the same as when it was built more than half a century ago. The main porch is still there, as are the hand-wrought iron fence in front, the richly carved black-walnut entrance doors, and the big bay forming the west corner. The façade is of cream-colored brick.

The main rooms are of unusual interest. These are noteworthy for their fine walnut woodwork, thick sliding doors with burled walnut panels, decorative marble fireplaces, tall windows with inside folding shutters, and parquet floors. Most of the interior trim, from bedrooms upstairs to closets in the basement, is of black walnut.

One who is particularly interested in this house is Albert F. Madlener, Sr., seventy-two-year-old son of Fridolin Madlener, who was brought to this mansion as a youngster of fifteen. Succeeding his father as president of F. Madlener,

Incorporated, he directed the firm until 1911 and then entered the investment business.

A devotee of Chicago and its history and a member of the Chicago Historical Society, Mr. Madlener has hung numerous etchings of city scenes on the walls of his office in the First National Bank Building in Dearborn Street. And in his inner office hangs a large engraving of his father—a bearded man with a high forehead and a faint twinkle of humor in his eyes.

The B. F. Ferguson Home

IN MANY parts of Chicago stand monuments and statues commemorating "worthy men or women of America or important events of American history." These bronze and stone memorials were made possible by a million-dollar bequest—one of the largest such bequests in Chicago history—from a pioneer Chicago lumber magnate, art patron, and devotee of the city in which he made his large fortune.

The mansion in which this man lived still stands. Not only is it of interest because of the generous gift to Chicago by its one-time occupant but it is also worthy of attention as an example of residential architecture fashionable in the 1880's and 1890's. Its exterior and interior construction unchanged since the day it was built, this dwelling survives at 1503 West Jackson Boulevard in the midst of a changing neighborhood.

Here lived, during the years immediately preceding and following the World's Columbian Exposition of 1893, when this section of the West Side was fashionable, Benjamin Franklin Ferguson, millionaire lumber executive who had come practically penniless to Chicago in 1865 after being mustered out of the Union Army. Before joining the army, he had worked in his father's lumber yard at Columbia, Pennsylvania.

Upon his arrival here, according to data in the files of the West Side Historical Society, Benjamin F. Ferguson found employment in the lumber firm of Jesse Spalding, after whom a well-known institution of today, the Jesse Spalding School for Crippled Children, is named. It appears that Jesse Spalding started many young men in the lumber business who afterward became successful.

BENJAMIN F. FERGUSON HOME
1503 West Jackson Boulevard

But B. F. Ferguson did not remain along in the Spalding firm. He branched out for himself, and, by 1871, he and an associate, Philip L. Auten, had established a planing mill on Throop Street, near what is now Cermak Road. When this mill was destroyed by fire soon afterward, the firm of Ferguson and Auten was dissolved, and Ferguson joined a lumber company in which he was to remain for many years. This was the firm founded by Jacob Beidler, whose mansion still stands at the southwest corner of Jackson Boulevard and Sangamon Street.

Ferguson was elected treasurer of the Beidler firm, then known as the South Branch Lumber Company. It was at that time the leading lumber company of the city and maintained this position until 1893, when it ceased operations in Chicago but continued to conduct its mills at Tonawanda, New York, with B. F. Ferguson in charge.

"In addition to the eastern business," says an old historical work, "Mr. Ferguson is actively connected with the Santee River Cypress Lumber Company, being its president. It has mills on the Santee River at Ferguson, Berkeley County, South Carolina, where, with two band saws and a full complement of machinery for the manufacture of mouldings and fine house finish, the company will add the beautiful yellow cypress of the South to the stock of ornamental woods which have of late years taken the place of the varieties which for so many years were considered standard."

While still with the Beidler company, Ferguson, now wealthy, began to think of a home suitable to his position in Chicago life. It was at this time that he heard of the mansion in West Jackson Boulevard. Begun by John Curran, a leading West Side contractor, in 1884, the house was partially completed when it was purchased and finished by Ferguson the following year. Curran had intended living in it himself, but business reverses forced him to give it up.

The present owner of the house, Mrs. Arthur H. Brumback, has in her possession a letter written by B. F. Ferguson to his friend, Charles L. Hutchinson, in which he explains that he had acquired the house for $25,000 and had spent $2,800 in completing and decorating it. Ferguson adds that, after he and his wife moved out of the house, he presented it to the Chicago Orphan Asylum.

Here, in this fourteen-room dwelling with mansard roof, high ceilings, mahogany paneling, sliding doors, leaded windows, parquet floors, and onyx fireplaces, the Fergusons dwelt in the years when Jackson Boulevard was a street of fashion. Sometime in the late 1890's they gave up the residence and moved to Massachusetts.

The dwelling remained closed for a number of years, and then the Chicago Orphan Asylum sold it. The purchasers were Dr. and Mrs. Brumback. They acquired it in 1902 and have been living in it ever since. When the Brumbacks took it over, they brought with them their two children, Mrs. Brumback's father and two brothers, and her niece and the latter's husband and two children.

Since becoming chatelaine of this West Side mansion, Mrs. Brumback has been active in women's club affairs of the city. For seventeen years she was president of the Chicago Federation of Aged and Adult Charities, which holds a tag day each year in May. She was also former president of the West End Woman's Club.

While a member of the West End Woman's Club, Mrs. Brumback served on a committee seeking to obtain a statue for the West Side out of the income of the million-dollar B. F. Ferguson Monument Fund. The committee's request was turned down by the trustees of the Art Institute, administrators of the fund, on the ground that the money was needed to build an east wing to the Art Institute.

Twin Mansions

~~~~~~

IN 1833 there came to the little lakeside settlement of Chicago a young man named Orsemus Morrison. His arrival was unheralded, but he was destined to become a prominent Chicagoan, to have a modern forty-two-story hotel named after him, and to become the father-in-law of two notable men of the 1890's—men whose homes are now landmarks of the West Side. They occupied twin mansions at the southeast corner of Washington and Homan boulevards, overlooking Garfield Park.

These houses were once show places of the Garfield Park district. The corner one, at 3355 West Washington Boulevard, was the home of George W. Spofford, pioneer school principal and real estate man. The residence adjoining, at No. 3341, was the abode of his brother-in-law, Daniel W. Mills, warden of the Cook County Hospital and West Side alderman and congressman.

A frequent guest in the Spofford and Mills homes was Captain Edward W. Morrison, colorful and eccentric nephew of Orsemus Morrison and owner of the site on which the Morrison Hotel stands. Captain Edward, who had gone to sea in a whaler, had inherited the site upon the death of his father, James Morrison, in 1868. James was a brother of Orsemus and had purchased the Morrison Hotel site from the latter.

It was often recalled in the Spofford home how Orsemus Morrison, who had been overseer of construction on the famous Erie Canal before coming to Chicago, had purchased the hotel site, as well as several adjacent lots, for $250. For this amount, says an old Chicago history, Orsemus "received

MILLS-SPOFFORD HOMES
3341–3355 West Washington Boulevard

a title by patent, signed by Andrew Jackson, president of the United States."

The two houses, of the same architectural design, were built after Spofford and Mills had married the Morrison daughters. It was on Christmas Eve, in 1859, that George Spofford, who had been appointed principal of the Foster School on the West Side, became the husband of Hannah Morrison. About ten years later he resigned from his school position and entered the real estate business.

During this time there was a young man in the city named Daniel Mills who had come to Chicago at the close of the Civil War and engaged in the manufacture of candy. Afterward he went into the lake shipping trade, prospered, and then gave this up to become a realty operator. In 1871 he married Lucy Morrison, sister of Mrs. Spofford. He subsequently became a leader in Republican politics of the city and was elected to several public offices.

By this time the Spoffords and the Millses were ready to erect residences in keeping with their social position. They chose sites on Washington Boulevard—then a fashionable thoroughfare—which overlooked Garfield Park. Here they built their mansions next door to each other some time in the late 1880's. The houses, which stood on landscaped grounds inclosed by a tall iron fence, were designed in the Queen Anne style of architecture.

After the Spoffords and the Millses moved into their new domiciles many well-known citizens of the 1890's were entertained in the spacious drawing-rooms. George Spofford was living here at the time he received the city's homage for having been successful in swinging enough votes to win for Chicago the site of the World's Columbian Exposition, scheduled to be held in 1892–93.

Orsemus Morrison had died some twenty-five years before the two Washington Boulevard residences were built. George Spofford's family consisted of his wife, Hannah, and two children, Percy H. and Florence M. Spofford. In his later years the master of the house spent much time in his library pursuing studies in which he had become interested while a student at Phillips Exeter Academy.

He died on January 10, 1909, at the age of seventy-eight. His widow and her daughter, Florence, continued to live in the mansion. During the World War Florence Spofford served with the Red Cross motor corps in France and attained the rank of captain. In 1922 she and her mother gave up the residence and moved to another section of the city.

Some years before this, Congressman Mills had died, but his widow remained in the home until her death in 1919. A number of families have lived in the two residences since, but in recent years the houses have been vacant. The elaborate stone coach houses at the rear of the mansions are occupied by the families of caretakers.

Each house is three stories high and notable for the half-timbered English design of the exterior of the upper floors. The walls of the first floors are of roughhewn limestone blocks. A story is told in the neighborhood that these limestone walls, during hot weather, exude traces of crude petroleum. Whether this is true or not, there are no oil stains visible on the walls today.

An Ashland Boulevard Residence

O
F THE numerous mansions remaining from the great days of Ashland Boulevard, one of the most imposing and interesting is the former Case residence at 220 South Ashland Boulevard. Built of roughhewn granite blocks and designed in the grand manner of the 1890's, this mansion was well known at the time Carter Harrison, the younger, and other noted personages of the city dwelt on Ashland Boulevard and made it one of the society strongholds of Chicago.

As with many of the other dwellings on the street, the Case house is now and has been for the last nineteen years a labor-union headquarters. Today, this part of Ashland Boulevard is known as "Union Row," for here are located, in the stately residences where once lived captains of finance, industry, and commerce, the meeting places of many of Chicago's leading unions. This is logical, for today more working people live on the West Side than in any other section of the city.

When Ashland Boulevard—then called "avenue"—was a sedate, elm-shaded thoroughfare, where ladies in bustles and gentlemen in top hats could be seen riding past in highly polished victorias, the residence at No. 220 was the home, according to records of the West Side Historical Society, of Charles Hosmer Case, well-known fire insurance underwriter of the 1880's and 1890's, religious leader, and one-time West Side alderman.

Before moving into this big mansion Charles H. Case, in addition to his vocation as an insurance executive, had served one term as an alderman of the old Thirteenth Ward, which embraced the territory now bounded by Ashland Boulevard, Pulaski Road, Lake Street, and Roosevelt Road. He was elected to this office in 1874 during the regime of Mayor Harvey D. Colvin.

At the same time he and his wife, Laura, were active in affairs of the First Congregational Church at Washington and Ashland boulevards. He served as a deacon and trustee of the church and was the superintendent of its Sunday school and a member of the American Board of Commissioners for Foreign Missions, a Congregationalist organization. He and his wife, both natives of prohibitionist Vermont, were also leaders in the temperance movement of that day.

From Andreas' *History of Chicago* we learn that Mrs. Case served on a committee of leading Chicago women, including Miss Frances E. Willard, founder of the W.C.T.U., which carried a petition signed by 100,000 women to the state assembly urging passage of a law allowing women to vote on questions involving the liquor traffic. Such a law was introduced but failed to pass. During the same period, her husband was serving as president of the board of directors of the Washingtonian Home, an institution for the cure of inebriates.

Sometime after the World's Fair of 1893, the Cases moved into the residence on Ashland Avenue. By then Charles Case was a wealthy and influential citizen. He had been a manager, since after the Chicago Fire, of the Royal Insurance

Company of England, representing that company throughout all of the northwestern states. He had also served as president of the local board of underwriters.

CHARLES H. CASE HOME
220 South Ashland Boulevard

As chief representative of the English insurance firm in Chicago, Charles Case superintended the erection of the Royal Insurance Building on Jackson Boulevard near La Salle Street. It was a ten-story edifice costing more than a million dollars. From this building Charles Case directed the activities of his firm in Middle West America and attained eminence in the insurance field.

He was born at Coventry, Vermont, on September 8, 1829, the son of a minister. After being educated in the schools and academies of his native state, he married a Vermont girl, Laura Farnsworth, and came West with her in 1852. He served as superintendent of schools at Warsaw, Illinois, for five years, entered the insurance field, and arrived in Chicago in 1867 as an ambitious, if obscure, insurance agent.

As occupants of the spacious mansion in Ashland Avenue, the Cases played important roles in the civic, cultural, and religious life of Chicago. In addition to his temperance work, Charles Case had helped to organize a reform group called the Chicago Citizens League and had served as president of the Newsboys Home and the Chicago Relief Society. He was also a charter member of various literary societies and of the Union League Club and was a member of the board of trustees of Wheaton College.

A man of unusual energy, he also indulged in numerous hobbies while living in his great West Side residence. It is said that he was a student of electricity, performing many experiments in this field, and that he was also interested in psychology, bacteriology, and archeology. The records show that when he died in 1917 most of his fortune was willed to various organizations of the Congregational church and to Wheaton College.

Following his death, the Ashland Boulevard house was vacant for a time, after which it was occupied by the Chicago branch of the Socialist party. In 1922 it was acquired by the Milk Wagon Drivers Union, Local 753, an affiliate of the A.F. of L. with a membership of some fifty thousand. Since that date this union has maintained its headquarters here, and a bronze memorial tablet at the front entrance explains that the house is called the William A. Neer Memorial Building, in honor of the late labor leader.

The union is now headed by Henry Weber. On duty in the old residence as secretary-treasurer of the union is Thomas J. Haggerty. Although some alterations have been made in the interior, the main rooms still retain their old-time grandeur. Here may be seen mantels of carved mahogany, built-in cabinets and bookcases of cherry wood, stained-glass windows, and big sliding doors of paneled oak.

PART VII

In Old Lake View

Introduction

North of Chicago's downtown district, between the north branch of the river and the shore of the lake, lies that vast middle-class residential territory known as the North Side. Until 1889 this territory was outside Chicago in the old township of Lake View, whose southern boundary was Fullerton Avenue. In that year it was annexed to Chicago, and the city's northern boundary thus jumped many miles north to Howard Street. Following the annexation, farms and prairies were subdivided into lots, streets were laid out, houses built, and small shopping and business communities grew up at strategic intersections. One of these shopping communities emerged as the large Uptown Chicago of today. Originally settled by German, Luxembourger, and Swiss immigrants, who established truck farms specializing mostly in celery, Lake View grew to include all nationalities. Today it is an area of more than four hundred thousand population.

A West Ridge Farmhouse

I N ANDREAS' *History of Cook County* we learn that
Peter Muno was among a dozen or so farmers who, between 1844 and 1847, settled in the region now known
as West Ridge. As with the others, he built a farmhouse soon
after his arrival there and in it lived out his career. That
house is still standing on its original site, a small, two-story
frame dwelling looking quaint and old fashioned in contrast
to the modern brick bungalows and apartment buildings surrounding it.

The Muno farmhouse is set back on a wide lawn shaded by
old elms and cottonwoods at 7504 Ridge Avenue. It is still as
trim, comfortable, and sturdy, according to those who know
its history, as when Peter Muno built it almost a century
ago. Unchanged is the wide porch across the front and side,
where Peter Muno often sat in a rocking-chair smoking and
contemplating his own and his neighbors' truck farms, which
spread out in all directions from his dwelling on "The Ridge."

Among some of the farms and gardens he might have seen
were those of his kinsmen. For there were other Munos in
the region—John, Henry, and another Peter—who had come
here earlier or later and taken claims to government land out
in the country north of the little frontier city of Chicago.
Most of these Munos, including the subject of the present
sketch, came from the vicinity of Trier, Germany, in the
1840's.

By the time Peter Muno was established as a successful farmer he owned some eighty acres west of "the Ridge." He had come over from Germany in 1845 with his wife and ten-year-old son, Henry, and had arrived in Chicago the same year, going out immediately to the country to become a homesteader. A patient and hard-working man, he

PETER MUNO HOME
7504 Ridge Avenue

built the house and cleared his land and soon had most of it under cultivation. As the son grew older, he helped with the chores.

During the first years that Peter Muno occupied his farmhouse the region was known as Ridgeville. It was formally organized as a township in 1850 under the same name and included a large part of what is today Evanston and what was formerly Lake View. A few years later Evanston and Lake View were organized into townships. By this time the small settlement of Ridgeville began to be populated by Luxembourgers.

Muno became the father of three more children, all girls. He continued farming, helped to found St. Henry's Roman Catholic Church at Ridge and Devon avenues, saw the coming of the North Western Railroad, and was still among the living when his friend and neighbor to the east, Phillips Rogers, subdivided and laid out what was to become Rogers Park. Peter Muno died, however, before Ridgeville, along with Rogers Park and Lake View in general, was annexed to Chicago.

Had he been alive several years later his life would have been saddened by a tragedy that came to the family. His son, Henry, a married man with children who occupied a home of his own on Touhy Avenue, near Western Avenue, was waylaid and murdered by a robber.

He had been returning on foot from a visit to his mother-in-law, Mrs. John Zender, wife of another early settler of Ridgeville. The murderer was never found, but he is believed to have been a hired hand of the neighborhood who thought that Henry Muno was carrying twenty-five dollars in his pockets. His widow, Anna Maria, was left with seven sons and one daughter to care for.

When this occurred, Mrs. Peter Muno, mother of the slain man, was living alone in the little farmhouse on "The Ridge." But she was by no means deserted by her three daughters, all of whom were married then and living in homes in the vicinity. They came to visit her almost daily. One of them—Mrs. John Weber—occupied a house just north of the old Muno homestead. There, too, went her widowed daughter-in-law and her grandchildren.

After the death of Mrs. Muno in 1895 the farmhouse was vacant for a number of years. Then it was acquired by Joseph Winkin, who moved into it with his bride. The Winkin family has occupied it since. They have kept it in shipshape condition, and the landscaped grounds around it are as attractive as any along Ridge Avenue. Just south of the ninety-six-year-old farmhouse stands the modern brick edifice of St. Scholastica's Academy, a leading Roman Catholic institution.

Reigning today as patriarch of the Muno clan on the North Side is Peter Muno, seventy-one-year-old grandson of the early settler of Ridgeville and son of the slain Henry Muno. He lives with his family in a modern apartment building on Arthur Avenue, not far from the farmhouse where his grandfather and grandmother lived. For many years he was the proprietor of greenhouses on the North Side and afterward head of a livery concern.

Standing under its great elms, the white-painted farmhouse on Ridge Avenue is today an object of veneration among members of the large Muno clan living in all parts of the Far North Side. It is similarly revered by students of the early history of Lake View, for not only does it date from the very beginning of that section but, under its roof, in the early days were entertained many of Lake View's first settlers— the Rogerses, Touhys, Zenders, Marshalls, Kyles, Schers, Phillips, and Schneiders.

The Turner Homestead

WHEN the carillon in the spire of Chicago's famous "skyscraper church" at Washington and Clark streets sounds out the hours resonantly over the crowded, noisy canyons of the downtown district, few, if any, of the hurrying Loop office workers who hear it know that this carillon was the gift of a devout, elderly man living in a little old farmhouse on the North Side—one of the few early farmhouses still standing within the metropolitan limits.

Among old Chicago houses which have survived rapid changes and a devastating fire, that small white farmhouse ranks high in interest and historical associations. The story of this dwelling goes back to 1859, the year its original portion was built. In that year, when the nation was plunging toward the Civil War, horsecars first appeared here, wooden blocks were first used in Clark Street, the city held its first art exhibition, Abraham Lincoln was being groomed for the presidency, and John C. Haines was mayor.

That same year, too, the proprietor of a flourishing livery stable just across the river on the Near North Side, one John Turner, leased part of his eighty-acre tract outside the city to a tenant farmer. The tenant farmer immediately went to work and built a house. Soon the leased land was under cultivation, and one more farm was added to the many in the township of Lake View. Today, the farmhouse built by the Turner tenant is still standing—at 1854 Addison Street.

You can see it as you walk a block west from the Addison Street Elevated Station. It is a small, gable-roofed, white

JOHN TURNER HOUSE
1854 Addison Street

dwelling with porches around it and old-fashioned shutters on its windows. The house stands at the rear of spacious grounds that in summer are refreshingly green with lawns, bushes, and trees. Around it on all sides stand the tall apartment houses and two-story brick dwellings of modern Chicago.

Several generations of citizens in Northcenter, as the community in which the house stands is now called, have admired the quaint Turner homestead ever since they were children. Not only did they like the trim lawns, snowball bushes, tulip beds, and shady elms in front, but they held—and still hold—in high esteem the man who lives in the house, William Turner, son of the original landowner.

When old John Turner, the livery man, rented the land and saw his tenant build a comfortable house on it, he did not realize that within twelve years he would be forced to move his family, including his son, William, out to the farmhouse and occupy it himself. It was the only place he could go. The great fire of 1871 had destroyed his livery stable and home near the downtown district.

So, after taking care of the tenant farmer and his family, John Turner set up his household in the little farmhouse and here, with his wife, Sarah, and his children, remained for the rest of his life. In the years following he raised sheep, pastured cattle and horses for other people in Lake View, and rented what remained of his tract to hard-working, thrifty German truck farmers.

If John Turner had moved "out in the country" and become a farmer, he did not lost sight of his civic and religious duties. While still a resident of Chicago before the fire, he had been active in community and church affairs and had been one of the charter members of the then exclusive Calumet Club.

He had also been one of the founders of the Old Settlers Society, established at a meeting of early citizens in the Tremont House just before the great fire. He evidently carried this spirit of civic zeal with him when he moved to the farm, for Andreas, in his *History of Cook County*, says that John Turner was one of the founders and leading supporters of the

First Methodist Church of Ravenswood, then a new residential community northeast of the Turner farm.

Before the fire had wiped out Mr. Turner's livery stable, he was making a successful business of it. He had come from England as a young man and landed in New York. He did not stay in Manhattan long, however. Chicago beckoned, and he arrived here in 1836—one year before Chicago was incorporated as a city.

Having prospered in Chicago, he bought the eighty-acre tract in Lake View from William B. Ogden, the city's first mayor and a large landowner. The Turner farm subsequently developed interesting, if indirect, connections with American literature and the early rise of movies in this country. It was on streets that passed through what once was the Turner farm that Charles T. Yerkes, Chicago traction magnate of the 1890's, laid streetcar tracks. And Yerkes, informed readers will remember, is the prototype of Frank Cowperwood, central character of two of Theodore Dreiser's novels, *The Titan* and *The Financier*.

Before Yerkes laid his tracks, however, there came Samuel Eberly Gross, who, besides being a real estate operator and subdivider, was an amateur novelist who had published several books. Gross bought half of the Turner tract, subdivided it, and opened Gross Park. This subdivision later became a community of frugal German-American families.

Then, as recently as 1919, life itself as it was lived among the German-Americans of Gross Park and near-by sections became the subject of a novel. This was *The Flail*, by the late Newton Fuessle, who had been born and reared in the community.

What was once part of the Turner farm became, in 1907, the site of the Selig Polyscope Company, first movie studio in Chicago. It stood at Byron Street and Western Avenue.

Here were made "The Adventures of Kathleen" and other thrillers of the early movie days.

The present occupant of the farmhouse, William E. Turner, is in his eighty-second year. In 1935 he presented the carillon to Chicago Temple as a memorial to his father and mother, John and Sarah Turner, and his sister and brother, Mary P. and John V. Turner.

Early Ravenswood Home

~~~~~~

MARTIN VAN ALLEN, now generally regarded as the "Father of Ravenswood," one of the first suburbs of the old township of Lake View, built a two-story frame dwelling in 1868, the year Ravenswood was established, and lived in it afterward with his wife and three children. Today there are no Van Allens left in Ravenswood, but their house still stands, an object of interest to students of the early history of the North Side.

Not only was Martin Van Allen the founder of Ravenswood but he was an early settler of Chicago, having come here in 1854 to take his place as one of the builders of the infant city. The full story of this man, and of his Ravenswood home, has been compiled by Miss Helen Zatterberg, secretary-historian of the Ravenswood–Lake View Historical Society. Photographs and letters of the Van Allen family are on display in the society's rooms in the Hild Branch of the Chicago Public Library in Lincoln Avenue.

"Before Van Allen built his home in Ravenswood," explained Miss Zatterberg, "he had been a civil engineer in Chicago and in this capacity helped to build the Illinois Central Railroad. His birthplace was New York State, where he studied engineering. He went back there in 1857, married Martha Bowen, and returned with her to Chicago."

We learn that Van Allen, after serving as head of a patriotic organization called the "Spartan Brotherhood," formed to prevent the carrying-out of a plot to free the Confederate

MARTIN VAN ALLEN HOUSE
4506 North Winchester Avenue

prisoners at Camp Douglas, became interested in real estate and by the end of the Civil War had combined engineering with real estate activity. He was a staunch supporter of President Lincoln in the political campaign of 1864.

In the year 1868 Van Allen and nineteen other businessmen

formed the Ravenswood Land Company for the purpose of developing a residential suburb north of the city. The company acquired 194 acres in the old township of Lake View, adjacent to the tracks of the Chicago and North Western Railroad, laid out lots and street, and chose Van Allen as secretary.

At this time there were only two houses on the tract purchased by the land company—the stately, southern-style residence of Conrad Sulzer, first settler of Lake View, and the home of a Mr. Wood, who maintained a large nursery around his house. The first dwelling to be built after the new subdivision was opened was the Van Allen home.

The street on which it was erected was then called Palmer Street, but this name has since been changed to Winchester Avenue. The address of the house today is 4506 North Winchester Avenue. When the Van Allens lived here in those early days, the house was on a landscaped estate in a grove of evergreens, and around it were lilac bushes and rose gardens. Flowers and shrubs were Mrs. Van Allen's hobby. A white picket fence surrounded the grounds.

In the parlor of the Van Allen home were held religious meetings which led to the founding of the Methodist Church of Ravenswood. The leader of these meetings was Malcolm McDowell. Among those who attended were his daughter, Mary McDowell, afterward to become famous as a social worker, and his son, Malcolm McDowell, Jr., former staff member of the *Chicago Daily News* and now a contributor. Another who attended was Charles M. Bowen, father of Mrs. Van Allen and first postmaster of Ravenswood.

A year after moving into his house "west of the tracks," Van Allen became an active leader in affairs of the township of Lake View. He was elected a school trustee in 1869 and the following year was elected town assessor and a member of the town board. Subsequently, he became town collector and, while holding this office, aided in building the first schoolhouse in Lake View.

What the suburb of Ravenswood looked like when the Van Allen abode was in its prime is indicated in a passage from A. T. Andreas' *History of Cook County*, which reads: "Ravenswood certainly presents as 'rich' an appearance as any of the younger suburbs on the North Western road, its avenues and streets being wide and well graded and lined with costly and tastefully constructed residences."

Another book, *Chicago and Its Suburbs*, written by Everett Chamberlain in 1874, has this to say: "Among the leading residents of Ravenswood are the following: Mr. Van Allen, dealer in real estate, owns a handsome residence and 900 feet of nicely laid out grounds, considered worth $26,000. The ornamentation of Mr. Van Allen's grounds is very artistic and effective."

In 1890, soon after Van Allen's son, Dr. Frank Van Allen, left Ravenswood to become a medical missionary in India, the house was remodeled and a brick basement was added. Left untouched was Mrs. Van Allen's special pride, a large conservatory on the south side where she tended her plants during the winter months. This has since disappeared, but the house in general still retains its fanciful, old-style architectural trim.

After the death of Martin Van Allen in 1903, the house was sold to a family named Phelps. One of the Van Allen daughters, Martha Louise, became Mrs. Winegard and now lives in Elmhurst. The other daughter, Jennie, writer and song composer, lives in Los Angeles. The son, Dr. Frank, died in 1923 after founding one of the largest hospitals in South India.

Today, the Van Allen home, still as trim and neat as in the days when it was a gathering-place of the élite of old Ravenswood, is occupied by Mrs. Ida Bloemer and her family, and on summer evenings the quaint, gable-roofed porch is often the scene of informal neighborhood get-togethers similar to the ones presided over by Mr. and Mrs. Van Allen more than half a century ago.

The House on "The Ridge"

〰〰〰〰〰〰〰〰〰〰〰〰〰〰〰〰〰〰〰〰〰〰〰〰〰〰〰〰〰

I T IS rare in Chicago for a citizen who has gone beyond the usual three-score years and ten to be living in a house on practically the same spot where he was born. In view of this, the man* who occupies the old stucco-covered house at 6440 Ridge Avenue is worthy of especial attention. He is now eighty-seven years old, and the little farmhouse in which he was born stood only a few yards distant from his present home.

This man is Dominick Schreiber. Now retired and living quietly in his two-story house on "The Ridge," Mr. Schreiber engaged in truck farming and the florist business on the Far North Side for more than half a century. During that time he was widely known among residents of Rogers Park and other communities in that section of the city.

But Mr. Schreiber has another distinction. He is the son of an early Chicago settler after whom Schreiber Avenue in Rogers Park is named. This pioneer was Nicholas Schreiber, who came to the United States in 1848 with his wife, Katherine. That same year the couple arrived in Chicago. Deciding to become a farmer instead of a city dweller, Nicholas Schreiber went out into the country north of Chicago and purchased forty acres of land in what was then called Ridgeville.

* Deceased since this book went to press.

He went to work clearing his land and soon had it all under cultivation. Four years later, however, he became ill and died. A few months after his death, on June 18, 1853, there were born to Mrs. Schreiber twin boys. They were named

DOMINICK SCHREIBER HOUSE
6440 Ridge Avenue

Dominick and Michael. Mrs. Schreiber reared them in the little farmhouse while an older son, John, took care of the farm.

As youngsters, the twins helped their older brother cultivate the land and do the chores around the Schreiber farmhouse. They studied in old St. Henry's parish school near by and, upon reaching maturity, took over control of the original Schreiber farm. Afterward, Dominick entered the floral business, and the blooms from his greenhouses on "The Ridge" were admired by residents of that area for many years.

In 1877, when he was twenty-four years old, Dominick Schreiber married Miss Anna Hartman, daughter of an early settler of the neighborhood. That same year he erected a two-story frame house on Ridge Avenue—the house in which he is living today. Here were born his seven children. For a time he could look through the window of his home and see the adjacent farmhouse where he was born.

When Dominick Schreiber built his Ridge Avenue house, that section was still a sparsely settled farming community outside the city limits. It was not until 1889 that Lake View, as the area was called, was annexed to Chicago. The neighborhood began to change then, and soon the farms were subdivided, streets laid out, and homes built.

Mr. Schreiber continued as a truck farmer and florist. At this time he was an active leader in affairs of St. Henry's Church. He donated three acres of the original Schreiber farm to the church for a cemetery. He was also a generous supporter of many other church projects.

In these years he was a widower, for his wife had died in 1899. After retiring some years ago, his business was carried on by a son, Joseph A. Schreiber, who also dwells on Ridge Avenue.

The house in which Dominick Schreiber lives contains fourteen rooms. It stands on a rise of ground under several aged poplar trees planted by his father. Some remodeling has been done since the house was built. The original siding has been covered with stucco, and many improvements have been made in the interior. The old-fashioned arched window frames, however, have been preserved.

Here Dominick Schreiber spends his days, and often he looks out of the window of his old home in wonderment at the way the city, with its bungalows and apartment houses, has crept up and surrounded his dwelling-place. And here, too, he is often visited by some of his seven children, ten grandchildren, and nine great-grandchildren.

A Swedish-American's Home

~~~~~~

ARRIVING on the front porch of the ancient frame house at the southwest corner of Wilton Avenue and School Street, in old Lake View, the observant visitor immediately notices that the frosted glass door in front of him contains an elaborate design, the main part of which is an unusual coat-of-arms surrounded by symbolic representations. Below is a date—1883. This date is the year in which the dwelling was built, as the visitor learns afterward.

Close study of that coat-of-arms gives some hint of the character and career of the man who once lived here. Half of the shield is a reproduction of the royal coat-of-arms of Sweden and the other half is a reproduction of the American flag. Above the shield are designs of a Greek lamp, symbolizing knowledge, and of a Greek lyre, symbolizing music and poetry. Here, also, is a crossed quill pen and sword, representing the art of literature and the art of war.

The house entered through this door was the abode of Dr. John A. Enander, famous Swedish-American leader of the 1890's, editor, poet, historian, orator, and educator. A monument to his memory, erected by nation-wide subscription among Swedish-Americans, stands today in Oakhill Cemetery.

It has been said that with the exception of John Ericsson, who designed the Civil War ship "Monitor," Dr. Enander was the best-known Swedish-born citizen who ever lived in America. "His name," wrote the head of Bethany College to President McKinley, "is a household word among Swedish-Americans from one end of America to the other."

JOHN A. ENANDER HOME
3256 Wilton Avenue

While living in this picturesque frame house, with its gables, tower, and ornamental scrollwork trim, Dr. Enander achieved success in his chosen field—that of making loyal Americans out of those of his countrymen who had settled in the United States. It was for this, as well as his services to Swedish literature, that King Oscar of Sweden honored him with a decoration in 1910, which was presented to him at a banquet of the Swedish Business Men's Club in Chicago.

Dr. Enander was living in the Wilton Avenue house—the street was then called Oak Place—when he was appointed United States Minister to Denmark by President Harrison in 1889. Owing to severe illness, however, he was forced to resign this post. He had been a personal friend not only of President Harrison but of Presidents McKinley and Theodore Roosevelt and of hundreds of other well-known persons of his day.

In the years after taking up his residence in the Wilton Avenue house, then, as now, in the midst of the North Side colony of Swedish-Americans, Dr. Enander served as a speaker for the Republican National Committee, addressing Swedish-Americans in all parts of the country during presidential campaigns from 1888 to 1904. During this time, too, he was editor of the Swedish-language newspaper *Hemlandet*, as well as a leader in Swedish clubs and societies.

In the library of his Lake View home, Dr. Enander wrote an autobiographical sketch, telling of his youth in Sweden, where he was born of poor parents, and of his first days in America. He was born in the province of Westgothia, Sweden, on May 22, 1842. After working his way through Wenersborg College, in his native province, he came to America in 1869 and entered Augustana College at Rock Island, Illinois.

A short time later he became editor of *Hemlandet* and retained this position for the rest of his life, except for a three-year period when he served as professor of Swedish language and literature at Augustana College. This college awarded him the degree of Doctor of Laws in 1893. Before this time, he had served as a member of the Illinois State Board of Education.

When Dr. Enander built his house in 1883, Lake View was a town outside the boundaries of Chicago. Soon afterward other Swedish-Americans erected homes around the Enander abode, and thus was begun a Swedish-American colony in Lake View that today numbers several thousand. While living in this house, Dr. Enander wrote his best-known work, *The History of the United States*. It was published in two volumes and has been translated into several languages.

He wrote a total of seven books, including several volumes of poetry. In 1905 he was elected first president of the newly organized Swedish-American Historical Society. He continued with his writing until his death in the Wilton Avenue house in 1910 at the age of sixty-eight. His widow, Malinda Lawson Enander, remained in the dwelling until 1918. The couple had reared a son and two daughters there, and there, also, in the early years of the century, they had entertained many distinguished Chicagoans and visitors to the city.

Today the house is occupied, and has been since 1918, by officers of Corps No. 7 of the Swedish branch of the Salvation Army. Twelve of these live here under the direction of Captain S. W. Franzen. The house has been kept in good condition by the Salvation Army, and there has been little remodeling of the exterior or interior. Two stories high with an English basement, the dwelling is noticeable for its old-style architecture.

The rooms are simple and dignified. Dr. Enander's onetime library, where he studied, wrote, or conversed with friends, is on the second floor.

Among prized articles in the possession of the Salvation Army officers occupying the house is a volume called *Selected Writings of John A. Enander*. It was published in 1892 and contains the best of Dr. Enander's speeches, lectures, essays, and poems.

Edgewater's First Brick House

ALTHOUGH known in the neighborhood as "the first brick house built north of Lawrence Avenue," the two-story residence at 5896 Ridge Avenue is of greater interest to students of the city's past as the abode of a Chicago family that first settled in this region more than one hundred years ago. Four generations of this family have frequently gathered under its roof, and many early settlers have sat in its parlor and recalled pioneer days of the neighborhood.

The house, however, does not date from the pioneer days. It was built in 1881 by Peter P. Kransz, son of a successful farmer and tavern-keeper of old Lake View who first settled here in 1846. Peter Kransz, with his family, has occupied the house ever since it was built. He is now eighty-two years old and is still active in an insurance business, with offices in North Clark Street. Just as active is his wife, Katherine, who still presides over the Ridge Avenue landmark and entertains, at intervals, her children, grandchildren, and old-time neighbors.

When this house was built, the region around it was largely vacant prairie, sand waste, and swampland. In the immediate vicinity, however, lay the Kransz farm, owned by Peter's father, and, at what is now Clark Street and Ridge Avenue, stood the original Kransz home and inn, known in the old days as the Seven-Mile House. Today this region, called Edgewater, is a neighborhood of homes and apartment buildings. Standing on part of the old Kransz farm is Senn High School, one of the largest in the city.

Although not a survivor of the very early days, the Kransz home may be considered a landmark of the North Side, for it was erected when that part of the city was outside the municipal boundaries in the township of Lake View. Eight years later, however, Lake View was annexed to Chicago, and soon the city crept up around the brick dwelling on Ridge Avenue.

Still standing when this domicile was built was the Seven-Mile House, erected by Nicholas Kransz, Peter's father, in 1848. This edifice, in fact, remained standing until five years ago, when it was razed to make way for an open-air market. Before being torn down, its history was obtained by the Ravenswood–Lake View Historical Society under the direction of Miss Helen Zatterberg, secretary-historian, and considerable material on it is now in the files of the society's rooms on North Lincoln Avenue.

From this source we learn that Nicholas Kransz, a native of Buschrodt, Luxembourg, came to America in 1845, worked for a year as a laborer in Chicago, and then bought one hundred and twenty acres of land on the old Green Bay Road (now North Clark Street) north of Chicago in what later became Lake View Township. A few other Luxembourgers were living in the vicinity at that time.

Nicholas Kransz cleared his land, cultivated it, and built the frame homestead that was to become the Seven-Mile House. A one-time visitor to the Seven-Mile House, according to Peter Kransz, was Abraham Lincoln.

"Lincoln was brought to my father's place to attend a

Republican caucus of the farmers in the vicinity," says the white-haired insurance executive. "That was when Lincoln was a candidate for president. My father was a Republican and an admirer of Lincoln."

PETER P. KRANSZ HOUSE
5896 Ridge Avenue

A volume of biographical sketches published in 1897 says of the elder Kransz: "Mr. Kransz, immediately upon settling in Lake View, took an active part in local public affairs. His townsmen soon recognized his fitness for office, and he was elected to all the offices of the township excepting that of supervisor. He possessed good executive ability, was usually accurate in his judgment, and candor and absolute fairness characterized every move of his life."

The Kransz biographical sketch continues: "Mr. Kransz was generous and charitable. On December 1, 1886, he endowed a school in his native village (in Luxembourg) with $1,500 for the education of poor children. This fund was so invested that the income from it supports and pays tuition for one pupil each year."

After becoming a successful farmer, Nicholas Kransz entered the insurance business. Following the marriage of his son, Peter, to Katherine Becker, daughter of another early settler, Nicholas urged the newlyweds to build a brick house instead of a frame one. Peter followed his father's suggestion, and in 1881, several months after the marriage, the brick edifice was completed at a cost of seven thousand dollars. It soon became a show place of that section.

Installed in his spacious brick house, with its numerous rooms and large porch, Peter Kransz lived as a member of one of the first families of Lake View, often entertained some of the old-time Luxembourgers of the neighborhood, and carved out his career as a successful insurance man. For years he was consul in Chicago for Luxembourg and in 1924 was presented with the decoration of the Order of the Oak Leaves by the Grand Duchess Charlotte.

In the years of his retirement and before his death in 1896, Nicholas Kransz was often a visitor in his son's brick home across the street from the old Seven-Mile House. Here he would sit with other early settlers of "The Ridge" and talk about the days when Indians could still be seen on Green Bay Road and Lake View was the celery-growing center of the Middle West. Here he would often meet his other sons, Henry P. and Nicholas H., both successful businessmen, and his daughters, Mary and Anna.

Here, too, he played with his grandchildren, Alois and Elsie, son and daughter of Mr. and Mrs. Peter Kransz. Alois is now associated with his father in the insurance business. Still shading the ancient brick edifice are some of the hard maples and elms that the elder Kransz helped his son plant.

The ten-room house has been little altered since it was built. The rooms are high, large, and decorated with fine woodwork and parquet floors. Seated on the large front porch of a summer evening, Mr. and Mrs. Kransz often recall the years when their neighborhood was farm and prairie land and horsecars went up and down North Clark Street.

The Frederick Sulzer Home

〜〜〜〜〜〜〜〜〜〜〜〜〜〜〜〜〜〜〜〜〜〜〜〜〜〜〜〜〜〜

WHEN, in 1939, the old township of Lake View celebrated the fiftieth anniversary of its annexation to Chicago, an object of particular interest was the large, gable-roofed brick residence at 4223 North Greenview Avenue. Although it had been built a year or two before the annexation, which in itself makes it notable, the house is of greater significance today as a link with the very beginnings of Lake View.

For here lived the son of Conrad Sulzer, first settler of Lake View. Coming to this region as long ago as 1837, the same year the little frontier town of Chicago was incorporated as a city, the Swiss-born Conrad Sulzer brought with him his wife and their one-year-old son. That son was Frederick Sulzer. He was reared in the Sulzer residence, then located on an estate out in the country some miles north of the city, and before his death in 1891 he was widely esteemed as one of Lake View's outstanding citizens.

In the year 1871, some months before the city to the south had been devastated by a great fire, Frederick Sulzer married Anna M. C. Buether, daughter of a Chicagoan. Then, in the period between 1886 and 1888, he erected the big, comfortable residence which stands today on Greenview Avenue. It occupies a site on the original one hundred acres of land which his father had purchased when he first settled in the region. At the time of his marriage, Frederick was conducting a large nursery and floral business, and his greenhouses occupied a portion of the elder Sulzer's land.

It was natural for Frederick to be an admirer of flowers, for both his father and mother were nature lovers as well as persons of education and good taste. The family residence originally stood at the southeast corner of old Green Bay Road (now North Clark Street) and Sulzer Road (now Montrose Avenue). This site is now part of Graceland Cemetery and here may be found, still growing, some of the ornamental shrubs and trees of the original Sulzer place.

Soon after Graceland Cemetery was established, Conrad Sulzer moved his residence across Green Bay Road to the southwest corner of the intersection. This home site is the one best remembered by early settlers of Lake View. It was considered one of the most attractive homes in that region and was often admired by farmers going by in buggies and wagons.

The house was set back some distance from the road on landscaped grounds. A picket fence, partially hidden by arbor vitae hedges and rows of trim cedars, surrounded the grounds. The driveway from the main gate led through formal gardens where grew roses, poppies, heliotrope, iris, lilies, and other varieties of flowers. Here, too, were lilac, honeysuckle, and syringa hedges. Footpaths were bordered with alyssum, clove pinks, pansies, and mignonette. A fountain added to the appeal of the place.

The house itself is described as a southern type of dwelling, two stories high, with a large wing on each side. Three front entrances opened on a latticed, vine-covered porch of ample proportions. At the south end of the house stood the conservatory, which was the particular pride of Mrs. Sulzer.

South of the house stood a cherry orchard whose white blossoms, in early spring, were greatly admired. Some protection from the prevailing west winds was afforded the Sulzer home by a windbreak of large willow trees. Later this windbreak was enhanced by groves of evergreens, flowering

FREDERICK SULZER HOME
4223 North Greenview Avenue

shrubs, and cherry, pear, and apple trees of the Sulzer Brothers' Nursery. The Sulzer place was maintained until 1888, when the house was moved.

In these surroundings Frederick Sulzer grew up. The young boy saw more and more settlement in the region, observed the Lake View House being built in 1853, saw the region formed into a township in 1857, watched the coming of Rosehill and Graceland cemeteries and the United States Marine Hospital, and witnessed the establishment in 1869 of a new residential subdivision called Ravenswood (which included forty of his father's original one hundred acres).

When Frederick reached his maturity, he began to take an active interest in affairs of the newly formed township of Lake View. His father, incidentally, had been elected first assessor of the township.

In time Frederick became a well-known citizen of Lake View. He was elected town clerk in 1867, commissioner of highways in 1868, and town supervisor in 1875. For sixteen years he had served as a member of the township school board and helped to establish many schools, including Lake View High School, which are still in existence on the North Side. Meanwhile, in the city to the south, he was widely known as a florist and later as a real estate man.

When Frederick Sulzer's fine brick residence on Greenview Avenue was completed, it was one of the largest and most commanding homes in that section of Lake View. Here he and his wife reared a family of four daughters and one son. After the death of the elder Sulzer in 1873, Frederick's mother came to live with him in the new house on Greenview Avenue, and in time the Sulzer abode became a rendezvous, at intervals, of many old settlers of Lake View.

Although in an isolated position when first built, the Sulzer house was surrounded by other dwellings at the time Lake View was annexed to Chicago in 1889. The house remains the same today as when first built. Its two stories are surmounted by a high-gabled roof which provides a spacious attic. The northwest corner is marked by a very wide porch. The rooms are tall, comfortable, and well lighted by numerous windows. A sense of space and roominess is gained by large doorways, which are framed in Georgia pine. The large reception hall is finished in oak.

Living in the house today are Frederick's widow, Mrs. Anna Sulzer, and three of her daughters, Angeline, Grace, and Mrs. Julia S. Griffith. The last named is an artist, and many of her oils are on display in the house. Mrs. Sulzer's only son, Albert F. H., lives in Rochester, New York, where he is an official of the Eastman Kodak Company. Another daughter, Harriet, died in 1939.

A Hermitage Avenue House

A RELIC of the days when old Lake View ceased to exist as a separate town and became the North Side of Chicago, the many-gabled, half-timbered mansion of red brick and shingle at the northeast corner of Hermitage and Berteau avenues is of interest not only as a typical example of Queen Anne architecture but as the home, at different periods, of several notable Chicagoans.

Although most people in Ravenswood, where the residence is located, know the identity of its second owner, few are familiar with the man who built it fifty-one years ago. Information on him has been uncovered by Miss Helen Zatterberg, secretary-historian of the Ravenswood–Lake View Historical Society.

This costly mansion, which was considered rather impressive for the Ravenswood of half a century ago, was erected by James S. McDonald, a leading Chicago manufacturer of the 1870's and 1880's. His plant, where stationery, record-books, and office supplies were made, was then located at the southeast corner of Irving Park Boulevard and East Ravenswood Avenue, opposite the Cuyler Station of the Chicago and North Western Railroad. This building is now occupied by Curt Teich and Company, Incorporated, makers of post cards and stationery.

A photograph of James McDonald in *Chicago: The Book of Its Board of Trade and Other Public Bodies*, written by George W. Engelhart and published in 1900, reveals him as a white-haired man with a mustache, regular features, and keen, intelligent eyes. The book also contains an engraving of his factory and a photograph of his residence. This last shows several scrawny young trees standing in front of the house and vacant land on all sides of it.

When James McDonald erected his big mansion here, this part of Ravenswood, then in its boom period as an attractive residential district, was still largely unsettled. But he knew it would soon be built up. Only a year earlier the town of Lake View had been annexed to Chicago by popular vote. This resulted in an influx of many home-seekers, and one by one they began building houses on new streets and on such older thoroughfares as Hermitage Avenue, then called Commercial Avenue.

Installed in his new house, McDonald became one of the best-known residents of Ravenswood, a suburb that was founded by successful businessmen. His dwelling was widely admired, as were his carriage and sleek black horses that waited for him each morning under the porte-cochere on the north side of the house. Many businessmen and their wives were entertained at functions in the dignified, oak-paneled rooms of the McDonald house.

In 1903, thirteen years after it was built, this Hermitage Avenue house came into the possession of the Reverend George F. Hall, a leading minister of the Disciples of Christ. He moved into it with his family and in the years following conceived here the sermons which brought him wide attention and a large following. For a long time he occupied the pulpit of the Bush Temple Church at Chicago Avenue and Clark Street.

It was while living here that the Reverend Hall laid plans for the founding of a colony of his followers in Florida. He saw his dream realized, and this colony is now Hall City, a community in Glades County, Florida, west of Lake Okee-

JAMES S. McDONALD HOUSE
4211 North Hermitage Avenue

chobee. In addition to preaching and looking after the affairs of his colony, Hall found time to write numerous religious books and pamphlets.

One of his sons, who was seven years old when the family moved into the Hermitage Avenue house, showed exceptional musical ability as he grew older. Later the young man began composing songs for his father's congregation. That son is

Wendell Hall, well known today as a radio singer and composer and called "the redheaded music-maker." One of his most popular songs is "It Ain't Gonna Rain No More."

After the death of the Reverend Mr. Hall in 1925, the big North Side residence was bought by the Evangelical Free Church of America, a denomination that came into being among Swedish-American settlements of the Middle West during pioneer days. In 1926 the church opened a Bible institute and seminary in the house, and the mansion has been a religious headquarters since that time. Students come here from all parts of the country and study in the many rooms of the old house.

A regular lecturer at the seminary is Dr. E. A. Halleen of Minneapolis, president of the Evangelical Free Church of America. Others who teach are the Reverend Axel L. Wedell, president of the seminary, and Dr. Gustav Edwards, dean of the school. In charge of the entire house as matron is Miss Hilda Carlson, who has been with the institution since it was established here. Some of the rooms in the house have been remodeled into offices, a library, a chapel, and classrooms.

The residence stands back on wide, grassy grounds, and both house and grounds are shaded by great tall elms and maples—the same trees that looked so young and scrawny in the 1900 photograph of the McDonald house. The house is three stories high, and the third story, roofed by many gables and a pointed tower, is covered with a siding of shingle.

Interesting activities at the seminary include frequent gatherings of the school's "Fireside Friends," an informal group that meets in front of the big fireplace of the large entrance hall. The mantel of this fireplace, hand carved of oak and designed in the Gothic style, is a fine piece of woodcraft.

PART VIII

Early Hyde Park

Introduction

In 1853 a young Chicago lawyer named Paul Cornell bought three hundred acres of land on the shore of the lake some six miles south of Chicago. That was the beginning of Hyde Park. In 1861 the township of Hyde Park was formed. By 1867 its boundaries were Thirty-ninth Street on the north, State Street on the west, One Hundred and Thirty-eighth Street on the south, and the lake on the east. This large township included the hamlets and settlements of Oakland, Kenwood, Grand Crossing, Brookline, South Chicago, Hegewisch, Riverdale, Pullman, Roseland, and Kensington. The main part of the township, however, was in the community of Hyde Park, where Paul Cornell had built a hotel and a station on the Illinois Central Railroad. In the same year that Lake View was annexed to Chicago (1889), Hyde Park, then a village, was also annexed. Two years later the University of Chicago was founded in the one-time village of Hyde Park, and here also the World's Columbian Exposition of 1893 was held. A walk through old Hyde Park today takes one among modern apartment houses, hotels, business districts, and rows of new homes; but often the curious observer comes upon ancient dwellings surviving from Hyde Park's village days.

Hyde Park's Oldest House

F EW old dwellings on the South Side have aroused more curiosity among passers-by than the big odd- ly shaped double house with gable roof standing on Hyde Park Boulevard across from East End Park. More than ordinary interest was shown in this ancient abode during the celebration in 1939 of the fiftieth anniversary of Hyde Park's annexation to Chicago.

Research discloses that this appears to be the oldest house in Hyde Park, there being no evidence to the contrary so far. It also has another distinction, for it was in the parlor of the original section of this house that St. Paul's Episcopal Church, now at Fiftieth Street and Dorchester Avenue, was founded eighty years ago. This was the first church of that denomination established on the South Side of Chicago.

While digging into the past history of Hyde Park in prep- aration for the community's jubilee celebration, Alderman Paul Douglas of the Fifth Ward, who served as chairman of the jubilee committee, found that the original portion of the big twin house at 5152–5200 Hyde Park Boulevard was built in 1857 by Dr. Jacob Bockee, who had arrived in this section that year from Poughkeepsie, New York.

When Dr. Bockee built his two-story, gable-roofed frame house at what is now Cornell Avenue and Fiftieth Street, there was no legally incorporated Hyde Park. This section was then a sand waste in the old town of Lake. Only five years earlier Paul Cornell, a young lawyer, had purchased three hundred acres here with the intention of building up a suburb. He called it Hyde Park.

As Dr. Bockee, in addition to being a physician, was a licensed lay reader of the Episcopal church, he conducted services in the parlor of his little home, and in 1859 he held a meeting there which led to the founding of St. Pauls' Church. His wife, Catherine, organized a Sunday school. During the Civil War Dr. Bockee served as a surgeon in the Union forces.

Among the small group of settlers who attended the first town meeting of the newly incorporated town of Hyde Park, an assemblage which was held in the Illinois Central Station at Fifty-third Street in 1861, was Abraham Bockee, son of the physician. He was named clerk of the meeting. When Dr. Bockee returned from the Civil War, he had his frame house moved opposite the small park which Paul Cornell had donated to the new town and which today is East End Park.

Meanwhile, there was a man in Chicago who was prospering in the lumber business. His name was James Morgan. He was related to the Thomas Morgan who owned most of the land which became Morgan Park. In 1873 he and his wife, Rebecca, and their daughter, Clara, came to Hyde Park for a visit, liked the quiet, shady suburb to the south of Chicago, and not long afterward acquired the Bockee house, which then overlooked the lake. Dr. Bockee went back to his boyhood home in New York.

James Morgan enlarged the house. He also became interested in affairs of the town and was elected a member of the village board of trustees. Later he became president of the South Park Commission—a group organized by Paul Cornell. This was the parent-body of Chicago's present world-famous park system.

As Mrs. Morgan was a Maryland belle and therefore not used to the idea of cooking being done in the house, her husband built an addition in the rear to accommodate a kitchen. He also built a roomy southern-style porch on the south side of the house to get the full effect of the sunlight. Then, when

JACOB BOCKEE HOUSE
5152 Hyde Park Boulevard

his daughter became the wife of Dr. H. H. Frothingham, he built the north section, put a new roof over all, and thus it became a twin house.

Here the Frothinghams lived for many years, and Dr. Frothingham became one of the best-known physicians in Hyde Park. But in 1906 the house was sold to George Owens Clinch, and he and his wife and their daughter moved into it.

Mrs. Clinch was the former Frances Van Schaick, a native-born Chicagoan. Mr. Clinch, before his death in 1930, was vice-president of the Crerar-Clinch Coal Company, a firm founded by his brother, F. Floyd Clinch.

If Dr. Bockee were to visit his house today, he would hardly recognize it. For, in addition to the remodeling and enlargements done by James Morgan, a further enlargement was made when the Clinches built an addition to the north section which now contains their dining-room. But the original Bockee house still composes the south section of the twin house, and here you can see the Bockee bay window and fine walnut stairway.

Today this oldest of Hyde Park houses is as neat and well kept up as any of the modern apartment hotels near it. As the chatelaine of this ancient ménage, Mrs. Clinch has decorated it with rare pieces of mid-Victorian furniture and other household articles, many of these having been brought from her husband's home in Georgia.

Not only is this place notable for its interior furnishings and its great age but it is also a house known to most of the older members of Chicago society. The Clinches have been socially prominent for many years and have entertained here many of the personages of old Prairie Avenue and of Lake Shore Drive. Mrs. Clinch, now seventy-five years old, is still active in society.

An interesting side light on this landmark is that all of its successive owners, like its builder, were of the Episcopal faith and worshiped in the church that was founded in its parlor. Before his death, Mr. Owens was a vestryman of St. Paul's. One of his brothers was the Reverend N. Bayard Clinch, an Episcopalian World War chaplain. His daughter, Eleanor, is the wife of the Reverend Charles P. Melcher, of the same faith. And today Mrs. Clinch continues to worship in St. Paul's Church.

A Composer's Cottage

~~~~~~

A N UNUSUAL discovery was made in connection with the celebration in 1939 of the fiftieth anniversary of Hyde Park's annexation to Chicago. In the rear of 5317 Dorchester Avenue was found the humble little cottage in which lived Henry C. Work, composer of "Marching through Georgia," "Kingdom Coming," "Wake Nicodemus," and other popular Civil War and plantation songs and of the famous temperance song, "Father, Dear Father, Come Home with Me Now."

Those who found the cottage feel reasonably sure that these songs, once sung throughout the nation and in the Union Army camps, were composed in the tiny dwelling on the South Side. All of them were written between 1860 and 1867, the period in which Work and his family occupied the cottage.

As viewed today, the cottage hardly looks big enough to house a piano. Plain, with a high-peaked gable roof, weather-beaten clapboarded sides, and a small porch, it looks more like a shed than a cottage.

It was in 1859, not long after Paul Cornell opened up a new subdivision south of Chicago called "Hyde Park," that Henry C. Work purchased a lot from Cornell for $175. It had a twenty-five-foot frontage. The cottage is believed to have been built about 1860.

At that time Work was employed as a journeyman printer and composed songs during his leisure moments. Born at Middletown, Connecticut, on October 1, 1832, he was brought to Illinois by his father, an ardent abolitionist who operated a "station" of the Underground Railroad at Quincy.

HENRY C. WORK HOME
5317 Dorchester Avenue

After learning the printer's trade, Henry Work came to Chicago, obtained a job here, got married, and bought the lot in Hyde Park.

Henry Work and his wife, Sarah, were among the organizers of the First Presbyterian Church of Hyde Park, established in 1860 by Paul Cornell and a few other residents of the new suburb. After Hyde Park was incorporated as a township, Work was elected township clerk in 1864 and served in this office until 1866.

It was during these years that he wrote "Marching through Georgia," with its familiar opening lines: "Bring the good old bugle, boys, we'll sing another song." While living here, too, he wrote that popular plantation ditty, "Kingdom Coming," with its rousing chorus.

Of the same period was "Wake Nicodemus," another plantation song. It has been revived today at parties of the younger set in Hyde Park, and until lately none of these people knew that its composer had once lived in their neighborhood.

In 1864 he wrote "Father, Dear Father, Come Home with Me Now," that song interlude of *Ten Nights in a Barroom*.

The story is told that it was George F. Root, head of a Chicago music firm, who urged Work to write war songs.

In any case, Work became a successful song-writer, and soon after the close of the Civil War he made a tour of Europe. In later years he composed "Grandfather's Clock," which sold more than 800,000 copies and brought him $4,000 in royalties. He is said to have written almost a hundred songs. He wrote, also, a once popular seriocomic poem, "The Upshot Family."

His financial circumstances being somewhat improved, Work sold the cottage and land in 1867 to Guy C. Sampson, afterward a justice of the peace in Hyde Park Township.

Work died on June 8, 1884, at Hartford, Connecticut, where he had gone to visit his mother. He was buried there in Spring Grove Cemetery beside his wife, who had died a year earlier. The couple had three children, two of whom died while the family was still living in Chicago.

Sampson, with his family, lived in a new two-story house and used the cottage in the rear for a dining-room. A few years after Sampson's death in 1878, the house was sold to another family. Henry C. Work was forgotten, and no one ever thought of the little cottage. It remained in obscurity until the Hyde Park anniversary celebration.

Becoming interested in this celebration, Mrs. Dora M. Scott, resident of Hyde Park and a granddaughter of Guy C. Sampson, remembered the Henry C. Work cottage at the rear of her grandfather's home. She went to see if it was still standing. She found it intact, if a bit the worse for wear.

Mrs. Scott reported her discovery to Mrs. Alice Manning Dickey, chairman of the Hyde Park jubilee historical committee and niece of Paul Cornell, the "Father of Hyde Park."

The result was that when the premier of the Stephen Foster American folk ballet, "Thunder in the Hills," was staged at the University of Chicago as part of the Hyde Park celebration, a feature of the program was the singing of Henry C. Work's songs.

Home of a
"Painter of Presidents"

～～～～～～～～～～～～～～～～～～～～～～～～～～～～～

AMONG old houses remaining from the village days of Hyde Park none is better known than the venerable dwelling at 5714 Dorchester Avenue. Here lived several notable Chicagoans, and one of them, a woman, became a famous American portrait and miniature painter several years after leaving this house and moving with her husband to Washington. In her day she was known as the "painter of presidents." Many of her oils are still on display in some of the public buildings of the nation's capital.

This woman artist was Cornelia Adele Fassett, who presided over the Dorchester Avenue house in the early 1860's. She was the wife of Samuel Montague Fassett, one of Chicago's pioneer photographers in the era before and during the Civil War. The couple were married in New York State in 1851 and came to Chicago in 1854. Here Samuel Fassett set up a photographer's studio at Lake and Clark streets.

In Andreas' *History of Cook County* we learn that the Fassetts were among the first settlers of South Park, a small residential community in the village of Hyde Park.

The site of that community today is occupied chiefly by the homes of professors at the near-by University of Chicago.

When the Fassetts lived here, however, there were few dwell-ings in the vicinity, Hyde Park was still a quiet village out-side Chicago, and the site of the University of Chicago was a muddy prairie.

It is believed that the house occupied by the Fassetts was built in 1860 by another early settler of South Park named Charles H. Botsford. Some, however, say the house was erected by an Englishman named Hughes. The Fassetts ac-quired it in 1863. In his "suburban" home, which he called "Bonnie Venture," Fassett entertained some of the other pioneer settlers of South Park, including James P. Root, manager of Abraham Lincoln's campaign in Illinois and later founder with Robert Todd Lincoln of the Chicago Bar As-sociation.

"Mrs. Fassett assisted her husband in conducting the pho-tographic studio and was considered a very fine painter of portraits," says Mrs. Claiborne A. Wilson, of Chicago, daugh-ter of James P. Root. "She was beautiful herself and was the subject of a study by the famous portrait painter of that time, G. P. A. Healy." The Healy portrait mentioned is now in the possession of a Fassett granddaughter living at Upper Monclair, New Jersey.

The *Dictionary of American Biography* says of Mrs. Fas-sett: "For twenty years she pursued her art career in Chi-cago, near the end of which time she was elected a member of the Chicago Academy of Design. In 1875 she moved to Washington, D.C., where she was elected to membership in the Washington Art Club and where her studio entertain-ments became a notable feature of the social life of the city.

"Her works include numerous portraits in miniature and many in oils. Among the studies painted from life were those of Presidents Grant, Hayes and Garfield; Vice-President Henry Wilson, said to be one of the most successful for which he ever sat; Charles Foster, then governor of Ohio (now in the State House at Columbus); Dr. Rankin, president of Howard University, and many other prominent persons of Chicago and Washington."

SAMUEL M. FASSETT HOME
5714 Dorchester Avenue

Authorities agree that Mrs. Fassett's best picture is a large oil painting called "The Florida Case before the Electoral Commission." Painted from life-sittings, it is a representation of the famous Hayes-Tilden controversy of 1877, and on it are the portraits of some 260 men and women, all "well-known figures in the political, social, and journalistic life of Washington at that period." The canvas was purchased by Congress and now hangs in the eastern gallery of the Senate wing of the Capitol.

While the Fassetts were living in the South Park dwelling two sons were born to them, Raphael and Montague. They reared a total of eight children. The next to the youngest, Clara, was the wife of the late W. W. Delano. She now resides with her married daughter in Berkeley, California.

After the Fassetts left the Dorchester Avenue house it was acquired by Claudius B. Nelson, who had come to Chicago in 1842 from Erie, Pennsylvania. Soon after his arrival here he became active in the First Presbyterian Church. At the time he purchased the Fassett house he was a partner in the hardware firm of William Blair and Company, oldest hardware house in Chicago. Later, he became one of the founders of Lake Forest College and a director of the Presbyterian Theological Seminary of the Northwest. He died in his South Park home in 1885 at the age of sixty-five.

"When I first knew the house occupied by the Nelsons, which was about 1876, it was surrounded by a garden," says Mrs. C. P. van Inwegen of Oregon, Illinois. "The garden extended a block to the west. I remember the grape arbor, strawberry patch, and flower bed. I used to admire them so much. There were stables at the west end of the grounds."

In these attractive surroundings the Nelsons lived and reared their son, Walter C., who in his mature years became a well-known Hyde Park building contractor. A later marriage of the elder Nelson brought him a daughter, Minnie Rutherford Nelson, and she became the wife of the Reverend John C. Parsons. A few years later the Parsons lived in the old Fassett house, and here they reared their children.

In a letter to the author, the Reverend Mr. Parsons writes: "Old Hyde Parkers will recall that originally the veranda of the Fassett house extended across its entire front, that there was a small conservatory connected with it for keeping plants in winter, and that the cupola was adorned with a heavy timber railing. In the center of the cupola rose a tall flagstaff. On national holidays and state occasions a flag fluttered from the staff."

In 1920 the house was sold to Professor Bertram G. Nelson of the English department at the University of Chicago. He was not related to the earlier Nelson. The dwelling is now owned by a son of Professor Nelson, Dr. Bertram G. Nelson, Jr. Living in it today is another professor of the University of Chicago, W. Lloyd Warner, who teaches in the sociology department. He is the author of several books, including *Black Civilization*. Occupying it with him are his wife and three young children, William, Caroline, and Ann.

The exterior of the house is marked by an old-style portico over the main entrance and by numerous tall, arched windows. A squat cupola surmounts the low-pitched roof. The rooms are large, and some are adorned by tiled fireplaces with wooden mantels. The Warners have furnished the house with eighteenth-century chairs, tables, and chests from Mrs. Warner's ancestral New England home. An interesting feature of the dwelling is that it is built of brick with wood veneer.

Swords and Books

~~~~~~

B Y A curious turn of events, two extremes of human activity—warfare and scholarship—come together on a friendly basis in the history of the old dwelling at 5704 Dorchester Avenue, for years a landmark of Hyde Park. Not only have notable wielders of the sword dwelt here or been frequent guests but the structure has also housed many burners of the midnight oil who have contributed much to education and culture in the city, state, and nation.

Although erected a few years after the Civil War, this house has more associations with that conflict than perhaps any other dwelling on the South Side. For the men of this house—that is, the men who lived in it during its earlier period—played important roles in the War of the Rebellion, and here, in the years following, gathered others who performed their share in the making of American military history.

The man who built this house, William H. Hoyt, an early Chicago settler who became a leading realtor here in the 1870's, headed a supply expedition sent out by the Chicago Board of Trade during the Civil War. He took five hundred blankets to the Seventy-second Regiment at Memphis and an equal number to the One Hundred and Thirteenth Regiment at Vicksburg.

His son, Judson Q. Hoyt, was among the Chicago residents who signed the call for a patriotic mass-meeting on the outbreak of the war in 1860. A year later the son was elected alderman of the then Second Ward.

It was in 1874 that William Hoyt went out to the suburban village of Hyde Park, purchased a parcel of land in a new

WILLIAM H. HOYT HOUSE
5704 Dorchester Avenue

subdivision of the village known as South Park, and erected the two-story brick house now standing at 5704 Dorchester Avenue. This all happened when South Park was far removed from the city. In the same year Hoyt built a two-story frame caravansary at Fifty-first Street and Cottage Grove Avenue and called it the South Park Hotel.

In the house on Dorchester Avenue—then called Madison Avenue—lived William Hoyt and his family, and here they entertained some of the early settlers of Hyde Park. It was from one of these early settlers, Hassan Hopkins, that Hoyt purchased the land on which he built his residence.

Then, in 1888, when Hyde Park was still a suburban village outside Chicago, the Hoyt home was jointly purchased by Mrs. Clarence Gordon Sholes and her sister, Mrs. William P. Campbell. Their husbands were out of town on business trips at the time, and the Dorchester Avenue house was to be a "surprise package" for them upon their return.

With the entry of these two families into the house the Civil War tradition was continued. For Clarence Gordon Sholes occupies a place in history as General Sherman's personal telegrapher on the famous march to the sea, and his brother-in-law, William P. Campbell, is on record as one of the first three clerks of the Railway Mail Service, founded at the outbreak of the Civil War.

As the new house out in South Park was large, there came to live here the father and mother of the joint owners, Major and Mrs. Tenedor Ten Eyck. While a young officer in the army, Major Ten Eyck went through the Fetterman Massacre at Fort Phil Kearny in Wyoming. He earlier had served in the Civil War.

A frequent guest in the Sholes-Campbell abode some years later was Brigadier General William Wallace Robinson, brother-in-law of the two sisters who owned the house. Also a veteran of the War of the Rebellion, General Robinson later served in the campaign against the Indians following the massacre of Custer and his men on the Little Big Horn in 1876.

When the World's Columbian Exposition was held in 1893, this house became noteworthy for the number of distinguished military men entertained there. Mrs. Ten Eyck was a member of the Board of Lady Managers of the fair, appointed by the chairman, Mrs. Potter Palmer. Another visitor who came often at this time was Mrs. Sholes's father-in-law, Christopher Latham Sholes, inventor of the type-writer.

At some of the gatherings of Civil War military men in this abode there would be a great outburst of singing when Mrs. Sholes, seated at the piano, played "Marching through Georgia"—a song composed by Henry C. Work, who in the 1860's lived in a small cottage several blocks north of the Sholes house. It was in this house, in 1899, that Mr. and Mrs. Sholes's daughter, Pauline, was married to Dr. George Francis James, then secretary of the Chicago Educational Commission.

Dr. James later became dean of the college of education at the University of Minnesota and afterward founded the Citizens Military Training Camps Association. He and his wife often returned to the Sholes house on Dorchester Avenue, and here, too, came his brother, Dr. Edmund James, for sixteen years president of the University of Illinois. Another frequent visitor was Bertha Ten Eyck James, poetess, daughter of Dr. and Mrs. George F. James and now wife of Daniel Catton Rich, director of fine arts at the Art Institute.

For the last fifteen years the house has been operated as a tearoom by Mrs. Ann Douglas, and her clientele consists largely of professors and their wives from the University of Chicago near by. Called "The Gargoyle," the tearoom is also a favorite rendezvous of old-time residents of Hyde Park, among whom were Mr. and Mrs. Horace Spencer Fiske.

Although some modernistic details and colors have been added, the interior of the house remains largely intact. Here may be seen the fine marble fireplaces, ornamented ceilings, and mahogany trim of the days when this house, shaded by elms and surrounded by flowering bushes, was a show place of old Hyde Park.

The Faulkner House

~~~~~~

IN THE years just after the Chicago Fire of 1871, many well-to-do business and professional men of the city, wanting to avoid the dangers of any repetition of the great conflagration, built comfortable homes in what were then residential suburbs outside the city limits. Since that time, many of these suburban communities have been annexed to Chicago, and much of their old-time atmosphere of leisure and quiet has disappeared. Still surviving, however, from these early suburbs are several score of the residences that once were the homes of prominent Chicagoans.

One of the most interesting of these, because it was the abode, successively, of half-a-dozen such Chicagoans and because of the activity being carried on in it today, is the venerable red-brick dwelling at 4746 Dorchester Avenue. Now known as the Faulkner House, having been occupied for the last thirty years by the Faulkner School for Girls, this building exists as a residential landmark of the early days of Kenwood, one of the most exclusive suburbs of the 1870's.

It was in 1874 that Alexander Bishop, pioneer Chicago furrier and hatter who had achieved wealth and position through the firm he founded, built the residence which today houses scores of girl students. A native of Ireland, Bishop had come to America while a young man and found employment at Albany, New York, in the fur plant of George C. Treadwell and Company, first in the world to dress and dye Alaskan seal.

He soon turned his eyes westward in search of larger opportunities. He arrived in Chicago in 1860 and the same year founded the firm of A. Bishop and Company, which is still in existence. After his first store, located at Lake and Dearborn streets, was burned in the fire, he set up business on State Street and there remained many years. The firm is now on Wabash Avenue.

At the time Bishop built his house in Kenwood he was a successful man. In his new dwelling during the 1870's he and his wife entertained the Kennicotts, Judds, and other early settlers of the fashionable suburb. And here, too, they reared a son, Walter, now an elderly man residing at Athens, Georgia.

But the Bishops did not remain long in their Kenwood house. The records show that in 1884 the house was sold to John C. Neemes, founder of the confectionery firm of John C. Neemes and Company. The Neemeses, with their two daughters, lived in the Dorchester Avenue—then called Madison Avenue—dwelling during the late 1880's, and in 1890 it changed hands again, becoming the property of Miss Kate B. Martin.

Here Miss Martin established a day and boarding school called Ascham Hall after the English writer, humanist, and classical scholar, Roger Ascham. By this time Kenwood, along with Hyde Park and other suburbs south of the city, had been annexed to Chicago, and new houses began to appear on all sides. Kenwood was growing in population, and in these years Ascham Hall was the leading private school of that section.

Then, in 1909, Miss Martin retired from public life and

sold her school, good will and all, to Miss Elizabeth Faulkner, daughter of an early settler of Oakland, suburb just north of Kenwood. Before this, Miss Faulkner had been a teacher in the old Kenwood Institute, an affiliate of the University of Chicago. Upon taking over Ascham Hall, Miss Faulkner

ALEXANDER BISHOP HOME
4746 Dorchester Avenue

started a new school and changed the name to Faulkner School for Girls.

Since the school occupied only the two lower floors of the Kenwood dwelling, Miss Faulkner and her family, including her mother and father, set up living-quarters on the third floor. Her father, Samuel Faulkner, had come to Chicago in 1851, where he entered the wholesale grocery business and formed the firm of Wells and Faulkner. Afterward, for many years he was western representative of Procter and Gamble, soap manufacturers.

"In his years of business activity," according to *Chicago and Its Makers*, a volume published some years ago, "Mr. Faulkner was closely associated with men such as Marshall Field, Levi Z. Leiter, the Gould brothers, the Spragues, the Farwells, the Durands, the Rumseys, and Marvin Hughitt."

Aiding Elizabeth Faulkner in conducting the school is her sister, Miss Georgene Faulkner, well known throughout the country today as "the Story Lady." Her many appearances on school platforms, in churches and auditoriums, and over the radio, have made her one of the most popular tellers of children's stories to appear in recent years. Another Faulkner daughter, also well known, is Mrs. Marx E. Oberndorfer, who, with her husband, has lectured widely on musical subjects.

Since taking over the old Bishop residence, Elizabeth Faulkner has made only a few changes in the interior. The exterior remains intact and is of interest for its spacious wooden porch, tall windows, great bay, and ornamental cornice.

The main rooms of the interior are furnished with old-style walnut chairs, marble-topped tables, chandeliers, and other furnishings of a typical dwelling of the late Victorian era. Still here are the attractive white marble fireplaces, topped by great mirrors, that were the pride of the Bishop family more than a half-century ago.

Senator Trumbull's House

I THINK Lyman Trumbull was one of the great men of Illinois. I hope that Illinois will thus suitably recognize the merits of one of her most distinguished sons." So wrote the late William Howard Taft in a letter to a Chicagoan, expressing approval of a plan to erect a statue of Lyman Trumbull in Chicago. Today the name of this celebrated Illinoisan is remembered in Trumbull Park.

But a far better memorial to Trumbull than a statue or a park already exists in Chicago. This is the house in which he lived for more than three decades, or during the height of his brilliant public career. It is located at 4008 Lake Park Avenue—an old section of the city noted for its numerous pre-fire homes.

In tribute to the historical importance of the Trumbull House, the Chicago Charter Jubilee Committee placed a bronze marker on its front which reads in part:

LYMAN TRUMBULL.
FRIEND OF LINCOLN,
SENATOR FROM ILLINOIS;
SUPPORTED LINCOLN;
SECURED PASSAGE OF THE
14TH AMENDMENT.
WAS ONE OF THE REPUBLICANS
WHO VOTED AGAINST
IMPEACHMENT OF
ANDREW JOHNSON.

This was the house in which Senator Trumbull lived and in which he died. By a curious turn of events, the house stands today within a few blocks of a section of the city where thousands of Negroes live—an American racial group that

LYMAN TRUMBULL HOME
4008 Lake Park Avenue

owes its citizenship to a constitutional amendment introduced by Senator Trumbull.

Although there is a persistent legend that Trumbull's friend, Abraham Lincoln, once visited this dwelling as a guest of the senator and his wife, historians specializing on Lincoln's movements in Chicago have not been able to verify this. An old Negro servant of the Trumbulls claimed that

Lincoln actually visited the house, but research workers have found that Trumbull did not acquire this home until after Lincoln left the city for the last time.

If Lincoln did not visit here, there were many other famous personages of Civil War and later times who were guests at the Trumbull home. Among these was President Grant. A later visitor was William Jennings Bryan, who had been a student in Trumbull's Chicago law office after the senator had finished his last term in Washington in 1873.

Just when this house was built is undetermined, but the present owner, Dr. C. M. Matter, believes the original portion was erected sometime in the 1850's and that subsequent owners altered and enlarged it. Senator Trumbull acquired the property in 1864, according to Dr. Matter. That would have made the senator a resident of what was then known as Cleaverville, an early community in the township of Hyde Park.

Here Trumbull lived in quiet suburban surroundings, far from the turmoil of the downtown district. He was still a senator when he moved into this house, having been first elected in 1855. He served continuously in the Senate for eighteen years. Prior to being elected to this office he had been a member of the state legislature, secretary of state for Illinois, and a justice of the Illinois Supreme Court.

This was the home of Senator Trumbull at the time he introduced the Fourteenth Amendment to the Constitution in the stormy days after the Civil War. To this unpretentious but comfortable place he returned following his refusal in the Senate to vote for the impeachment of President Andrew Johnson—a refusal that brought down much criticism on his head. Trumbull claimed there was insufficient evidence against Johnson.

It was while he was owner of this house that the idea came

to Senator Trumbull of bolting the regular Republican organization and joining a new group known as the "liberal Republicans." This he did in 1870 or thereabouts. The new group was defeated in a subsequent election, and Senator Trumbull's official career was ended. He returned to Chicago, took up the private practice of law, and lived the remainder of his days in the frame dwelling on Lake Park Avenue.

Here he died in 1896. He was buried in Oakwoods Cemetery. Sometime later his widow, Mary Ingraham Trumbull, sold the house and went East to live at Saybrook Point, Connecticut, where she had been married to Senator Trumbull in 1877. She died in 1914 at the age of eighty-three.

On seeing the Trumbull House today, the visitor who knows of the career of Senator Trumbull is somewhat surprised that such a great man, one who certainly must have been a man of means, should have occupied such an unostentatious dwelling. But it very likely suited Senator Trumbull, as he was not a pretentious man and cared little for worldly display.

Except for a front porch, which has been removed, and a veneer of stucco over the old wooden siding, the house remains much the same today as when Senator Trumbull lived under its roof. The original porch on the south side of the building is still intact. In its simple design the dwelling was not greatly different from thousands of other frame dwellings of the post–Civil War era.

The house is set back on a spacious lawn. Both the lawn and the house are kept in good condition by the present occupants, Dr. Matter and his wife. The interior is interesting, as Dr. Matter and his wife have outfitted each room with "period" furniture in keeping with the era of Lyman Trumbull.

This, then, was the house of a great Chicagoan—a man of whom, after his death, Joseph Medill, famous editor, said: "If he had remained true to his party, Judge Trumbull, I believe, would have died with his name in the roll of presidents of the United States. I have always thought that he could have been the successor of Grant. He stood so high in the estimation of his party and nation that nothing was beyond his reach."

The Abode of Colonel Jacobs

~~~~~~

ONE of the show spots of this suburb of Chicago in the early days was the home and grounds of Colonel William V. Jacobs at Seventy-second Street between Evans and Cottage Grove avenues. Colonel Jacobs maintained a palatial home here and entertained extensively." These words, taken from *Chicago's Great South Shore*, historical booklet published in 1930, refer to one of the best-known houses of Brookline, pioneer residential suburb of Chicago. The house still stands on its original site at the northwest corner of Seventy-second Street and Cottage Grove Avenue and for years has been a familiar landmark to South Siders.

The booklet tells more of the Jacobs' abode. "His [Colonel Jacobs'] stables, in which always were quartered many fine polo ponies, covered a half block fronting on the railroad. His guests came from far and wide to play polo on the great stretch of flat prairie south of Seventy-fifth Street and west of Langley Avenue in the section known as Wakeford."

The man who conducted such an abode obviously must have been a person of consequence in his community. So Colonel Jacobs was. At the time he lived in his Brookline home, he was widely known as the "father" of the streetcar system that later embraced most of the South Side. He is said to have built more than fifty miles of street railways in that section.

"As president of the Calumet Electric Street Railway Company, Colonel Jacobs did much, through his transporta-

WILLIAM V. JACOBS HOUSE
750 East Seventy-second Street

tion line, to build up this part of the city," said Miss Marie Antoinette De Roulet, who, as librarian at the Chatham Branch of the Chicago Public Library, has looked into the early history of Brookline and Grand Crossing. "His street railway served such communities as Grand Crossing, Brookline, Pullman, and South Chicago."

We learn that Colonel Jacobs, who earned his military title

in the old First Cavalry, Illinois National Guard, came to Chicago in 1873 when the city was rebuilding itself after the great fire. He was born at West Chester, Chester County, Pennsylvania, on June 19, 1853. His father's ancestors were English Quakers. His maternal great-grandfather was Jesse Duncan Elliott, quartermaster general in the Revolutionary Army under Washington.

Several months after his arrival in Chicago, William Vaughan Jacobs met Paul Cornell, real estate operator and founder of the suburb and township of Hyde Park. This meeting resulted in Jacobs' becoming secretary of the Cornell Watch Company, which occupied a factory built by Cornell at Grand Crossing. Because several railroads intersected at this point, Cornell was sure that an industrial center could be established here.

Meanwhile, Cornell went about developing various real estate subdivisions in the vicinity of Grand Crossing, one of these being Brookline. William Jacobs continued to serve in Cornell's employ until 1876, when the watch factory was sold to the Wilson Sewing Machine Company. Jacobs then went into the mortgage loan business and in time became Chicago representative of several leading New York insurance companies.

It was sometime in the late 1880's that Colonel Jacobs, now a successful businessman, erected the large rambling frame house in Brookline that was afterward to become a show place of the suburb. Here he conceived the idea of a street railway system that would serve the various isolated communities around him. He knew that, with the annexation of the township of Hyde Park to Chicago in 1889, that region would grow rapidly and be in urgent need of a transportation system.

In 1892 he organized the Calumet Electric Street Railway

Company and immediately began laying tracks on the Far South Side. Not long afterward he organized the Englewood and Chicago Electric Railway. Both of these systems have since been absorbed by the Chicago Surface Lines.

During the period Colonel Jacobs was active as a business-man and street-railway promoter he devoted part of his time to military duties. In 1878 he joined the old First Cavalry. Seven years later he was appointed lieutenant colonel and subsequently became commander of the regiment.

It was largely through his efforts that the First Cavalry brought about the erection of a large brick armory on the lake front near Madison Street. The building was put up in 1882 at a cost of $40,000. During the 1880's and 1890's it was a familiar landmark on the lake front.

Not only was Colonel Jacobs active as a business and military man but he was also a leader in social and religious affairs. In 1884 he served as treasurer of the Union League Club. Other organizations he belonged to were the Washington Park Club, Tolleston Shooting and Fishing Club, and the Skokie Country Club. For years he had been a well-known and devout member of St. James Episcopal Church.

In 1897 Colonel Jacobs gave up his South Side home and moved with his family to Glencoe. Here he won the esteem of residents and was elected a member of the village council in 1903. He died in 1923 at the age of seventy.

Today the old Jacobs' home on the South Side, standing in a triangle formed by Cottage Grove Avenue, Evans Avenue, and the embankment of the New York Central Railroad, survives as a curious reminder of a now almost forgotten suburb. It is a long odd-shaped frame dwelling with numerous gables and a square tower surmounting its façade.

An Oakland Mansion

~~~~~~

UILT more than half a century ago, the great man-sarded house of red brick with white stone trim at 3949 Lake Park Avenue, in old Oakland, is of interest today for four reasons: it was the home of a prominent citizen of the 1880's, it was designed by one of America's foremost architects, it is now being used as living-quarters for young men on a W.P.A. project, and it is noteworthy as an example of American residential architecture highly esteemed during the late Victorian era.

The man who built this huge three-story town house, whose mansard roof, dormers, tall chimneys, and other exterior details express the "grand style" of architecture of a bygone day, was John Borden, pioneer Chicago settler, leading lawyer, and founder of a family here that produced many notable personages in various fields, including the present John Borden, capitalist, sportsman, and Arctic explorer. The house was completed in 1880. This was eight years before Oakland, part of the old township of Hyde Park, was annexed to Chicago.

In its heyday this house was often the gathering-place of national and local dignitaries and social leaders. Here came President William McKinley while on a visit to Chicago, and here, more than once, came Marshall Field, Levi Z. Leiter,

Potter Palmer, and other influential Chicagoans with whom John Borden was associated in the days before the World's Fair of 1893.

Before becoming successful and amassing a fortune, John Borden had been an obscure attorney in the early days of Chicago. He came here from New Providence, Indiana—now called Borden—two years before Chicago was incorporated as a city and while Fort Dearborn was still the center of life in the little pioneer community at the mouth of the river. One of his brothers, William, remained at New Providence and set up a sawmill.

The big mansion in Oakland, then an exclusive suburb, was erected by John Borden after he and Marshall Field, as well as Levi Z. Leiter, had promoted and developed a mining project at Leadville, Colorado. It was a successful enterprise, and the three men, together with Borden's son, William, who was then a young mining engineer in charge of the project, had amassed more than a million dollars each in the Leadville venture.

In planning his mansion on Lake Park avenue, John Borden secured the services of Louis Sullivan, now internationally famous as the father of "modernism" in architecture. The Borden residence was designed, however, before Sullivan had launched his original style of architecture—a style that brought about the skyscraper and that nurtured America's best-known modernist architect of today, Frank Lloyd Wright. When the Borden house was created, Sullivan was a partner of Dankmar Adler, another Chicago architect.

"The first residence by the firm was built for John Borden on Lake Park Avenue in Chicago in 1880," writes Hugh Morrison in his excellent biography, *Louis Sullivan: Prophet of Modern Architecture*, published in 1935. "This is probably the 'large substantial residence' mentioned by Sullivan [in his

The Autobiography of an Idea] as one of the three commissions which came into the office shortly after his arrival [in Chicago]. The house is a three-story structure, soundly built, and is still standing."

JOHN BORDEN MANSION
3949 Lake Park Avenue

Morrison continues: "It might be almost any solid residence of the day, with the tall, narrow windows, the prominent chimneys, the color contrast of red brick and white stone trim, and the mansard roof popular in Chicago in 1880. But the inset panels above the second-story windows, and an astonishing efflorescence of Sullivanesque ornament on a pavilion roof in the middle of the south side, betray the individuality of the architect."

Morrison adds that "the slight projection and simple treatment of the dormers, and the subtly tapered tops of the high chimneys, do much to create a feeling of compact density in the mass as a whole." Elsewhere the author refers to the Borden house as having "dignified solidity." The house remains intact today, both exterior and interior, and is in an unusually good state of preservation. Here, also, is the brick coach house and the wide plot of ground where old John Borden maintained a vegetable garden which he used to spade himself.

His son, William, was born in this mansion. William grew up here and, after his marriage, became the father of the present John Borden, as well as of Mary Borden Spears, wife of Brigadier General Edward L. Spears of the British Army, and herself a widely known Anglo-American novelist. He was also the father of the late William Whiting Borden, who in 1912 startled Chicago by renouncing a business and social career and becoming a foreign missionary.

The first John Borden lived in his big Lake Park Avenue residence until his death in 1918 at the age of ninety-three. The dwelling then fell to his grandson, John, and subsequently was purchased by the late Mrs. Eliza J. Jenkinson, who operated it as an exclusive home for well-to-do elderly people. It is now owned by J. Herbert Cline, a Chicago real estate man.

In the last several years this old landmark of Oakland has housed about sixty-five boys and young men of the Illinois unit of the National Youth Administration. The house was chosen for this purpose by Mary Stuart Anderson, state N.Y.A. director, because of its twenty-six rooms, substantial construction, spacious grounds, and convenient location. An American flag hangs over the great stone entrance of the dwelling. The boys are in charge of Harold Dash, resident director.

The interior of the big mansion is well preserved. There are twenty-two fireplaces scattered among the twenty-six rooms. These fireplaces, in the main rooms on the first floor, are of many varieties of marble and are simply, but beautifully, designed. Over them hang great mirrors. The fine mahogany interior trim is noticeable for the leaf design that characterized Louis Sullivan's ornamental style.

The Charles L. Hutchinson Home

~~~~~~

O NE of Chicago's noted citizens, a man who was active in civic, cultural, and philanthropic enterprises
during the first quarter of the present century, was
Charles L. Hutchinson. His name is remembered today in
Hutchinson Commons at the University of Chicago and the
Hutchinson Gallery in the Art Institute. He was a man who
achieved great wealth in the banking field, but he gave back
much of this wealth to the city from which he obtained it.
Numerous hospitals, museums, asylums, and educational institutions were recipients of his benefactions.

Because of his status and achievements, the house in which
this man began his career is of interest to the entire city. This
dwelling still stands on its original site. It is located at 5115
Cornell Avenue. Prim and old fashioned, it is now numbered
among the most familiar of the ancient residences of Hyde
Park. Aside from its association with Charles Hutchinson,
this house is noteworthy today as the abode of the niece of
Paul Cornell, known as the "Father of Hyde Park."

When Charles Hutchinson lived in the Cornell Avenue
house, he was only at the beginning of his career. He was
then but a young clerk in his father's bank. Almost every-

body knew his father. In fact, the elder Hutchinson was famous in financial circles throughout America and Europe.
Whenever B. P. Hutchinson, or "Old Hutch" as he was
known, succeeded in cornering the wheat market on the Chi-

CHARLES L. HUTCHINSON HOME
5115 Cornell Avenue

cago Board of Trade, it was a matter of concern to financiers
in New York, London, and Buenos Aires.

At the time "Old Hutch" was most active on the Board of
Trade he lived in a handsome residence in Hyde Park. It
overlooked a small square on the shore of the lake known today as East End Park. A wedding celebration was held in

this mansion when "Old Hutch's" son, Charles, was married to Miss Frances Kinsley, daughter of H. M. Kinsley, of Chicago. Wanting to give the newly married couple a good start in life, and wanting them to live near him, the elder Hutchinson ordered a house built for his son and daughter-in-law. It was located but a block from his own home. "Old Hutch" presented it to the couple as a wedding gift.

This is the house still standing today at 5115 Cornell Avenue. It has been kept in good condition by its successive owners. Observing the wide grounds around it, the trim hedges, and the tall trees that shade it, one has the feeling that this was the way homes looked in Hyde Park back in the 1870's and 1880's.

This dwelling, then, was the "honeymoon house" of Charles Hutchinson and his bride. Here the couple lived in the years before the World's Fair of 1893, and here they took part in the social life of Hyde Park. When his fortune increased, however, and when he became more active in affairs of the city, Charles Hutchinson gave up the little Hyde Park home and moved into a more elegant residence near the fashionable Prairie Avenue section.

Mr. Hutchinson became one of Chicago's notable citizens. In addition to being a banker and engaging in many other business enterprises, he took part in numerous cultural, artistic, and philanthropic movements. He was a trustee of the University of Chicago, beginning with its establishment, and he was one of the founders of the Art Institute.

His collection of rare paintings is hung in the Hutchinson Gallery of the Art Institute. Evidences of his numerous financial gifts can be seen today in the Field Museum of Natural History. He was a president of the Chicago Orphan Asylum, a trustee of Hull-House, and a director of the Presbyterian Hospital. He died in 1924 at the age of seventy.

After the Hutchinsons left it, the frame house on Cornell Avenue was taken over by a number of successive owners, including Mr. and Mrs. Eugene Amory, who lived in it for more than twenty years. Among numerous residents of Hyde Park who always admired the house, as well as the trim lawns and flower beds around it, was Alice Manning, whose mother was a half-sister of Paul Cornell.

When Alice Manning went to New York and became editor of *McCall's* magazine she frequently thought of the little frame house on Cornell Avenue back in Chicago. After her marriage to Roy Dickey, an advertising executive, and the couple's return to Chicago, Mrs. Dickey found that her "dream house" was for sale. She and her husband lost no time in acquiring it. The Dickeys moved into it in 1919.

Today, under the care of Mr. and Mrs. Dickey, the house is as attractive as any to be found in Hyde Park. The interior has been little altered and has been outfitted with furniture and decorations in keeping with the period that the house represents.

If Charles L. Hutchinson were alive today and visited his early home, it is certain his artistic soul would be pleased with the way both its interior and its exterior have been preserved; and he would undoubtedly be pleased, too, by the "period" furniture, the glassware, the mantel clocks, the crystal chandeliers, and other articles with which Mrs. Dickey has furnished the house.

"The Treasure House"

ALTHOUGH the stately Victorian mansion at 4853 Lake Park Avenue is notable architecturally and as the home of a famous Chicagoan, it is also of great interest as a repository of the rare and curious. No other house in Chicago, and, indeed, few houses in America, contain such collections as are to be found in this South Side landmark.

So costly and historic are the articles and objects in this dwelling that it has come to be known as Chicago's "Treasure House." When its owner was alive only his friends saw the fabulous inside of "the Treasure House," but now, through a generous move made by the owner before he died, the mansion and its adjoining castle-like museum will be thrown open to the public.

Here for the first time will be displayed the five-million-dollar collection of medieval armor, historic articles, and curios, as well as old masterpieces, antiques, and other art objects, of the late George F. Harding, Harvard football player, pioneer aviation enthusiast, real estate operator, veteran Chicago political leader, and Republican national committeeman for Illinois.

The armor collection is one of the largest in this country. Started by Mr. Harding's father more than fifty years ago, it is composed of sixty-five complete suits of armor, most of

285

them having been worn by famous knights and princes. One suit of armor cost $75,000. Included in the collection is a small armorial suit presented by Queen Victoria to former Kaiser Wilhelm when he was ten years old.

GEORGE F. HARDING RESIDENCE
4853 Lake Park Avenue

The metal garments are worn by life-size dummy figures, some of which are mounted on wooden horses. The figures brandish lances, spears, and other knightly weapons. In addition to the armor collection, there are hundreds of shields, bucklers, swords, daggers, and lances. Included also are crossbows dating from the fifteenth century. Here, too, are pistols and blunderbusses inlaid with ivory and gold.

Many of the armor suits and articles in the later collections were purchased by Mr. Harding in 1931 when he made a tour of Europe in his own airplane, piloted by William S. Brock, a transatlantic flier. Upon landing in New York on his return home, there were some Gothamites who wisecracked that Mr. Harding, being a Chicagoan, would need armor-plate protection—which made Mr. Harding laugh heartily.

So big did Mr. Harding's collection of armor, relics, paintings, and curios become that it was necessary for him, in 1927, to erect a small two-story edifice next door to his mansion in order properly to house the articles. The two buildings are connected by an elevated inclosed passage. In this new building the Chicago political leader was able to arrange his exhibits more conveniently. The interior is laid out with secret stairways, passages, a dungeon, and other features of a medieval keep.

Here the visitor may see other interesting and unique items. Paintings by French, Spanish, and English old masters; a high-backed pew from the castle where Richard the Lionhearted was imprisoned; the bed carried by Napoleon on his Egyptian campaign and a banner carried at his funeral; pianos that belonged to Liszt and Chopin—all these are here in bewildering array.

Here, too, is a harp used by Marie Antoinette, boots worn by Louis XVI of France, a field kitchen that served Frederick the Great during the Thirty Years' War, a piano given to Sarah Bernhardt by Czar Nicholas of Russia, a rug woven by order of the Shah of Persia as a present for the Grand Duke Alexis of Russia, a stone carving supposed to be a self-portrait by an Assyrian king, canes from all over the world, ship models, rare jades, tapestries, and Egyptian mummies.

There are also American items—the black-satin-covered chaise longue upon which Abraham Lincoln reclined in his home at Springfield, the capstan of the ill-fated "U.S.S. Maine," highly carved figureheads from famous American clipper ships, paintings and other art objects by American artists, and old flintlocks used by pioneers.

Before he died Mr. Harding formed the George F. Harding Collection for the purpose of maintaining his vast collection in the Harding mansion and castle on Lake Park Avenue and conducting it as a museum. It is now open to the public by appointment.

Serving as president of the museum corporation is Miss Jessie Katz, secretary to Mr. Harding for more than twenty years. The secretary and treasurer is Arthur J. Murphy, who was Mr. Harding's attorney. Other directors of the corporation are Mr. Harding's daughter, Mrs. Mary Thompson of Milwaukee, and Gregory T. Van Meter, former collector of internal revenue and long-time associate of Mr. Harding's father, the late George F. Harding, Sr.

The origin of the residence is somewhat obscured by its present glamour. It was built in 1890 by Brenton R. Wells, member of the firm of M. D. Wells and Company, pioneer wholesale boot and shoe house of Chicago. The firm was founded in 1866 by Moses D. Wells. His daughter, Frances, in later years became the wife of Howard Van Doren Shaw, Chicago architect.

Mr. Harding purchased the residence from the Wells estate in 1916 and moved his collection into the South Side dwelling soon afterward. Here, in later years when he took less interest in politics and more in his collection, Mr. Harding often told friends: "My father always said that, when the time comes to retire, have something to retire to."

A French Gothic Mansion

AMONG famous old Chicago mansions now being used as private schools, few retain more of their old-time atmosphere of elegance than the commanding residence at 4515 Drexel Boulevard. To social historians this dwelling is of interest as the one-time home of a distinguished Chicagoan, and to architectural students it represents a style of residential design once fashionable in America.

The late Lorado Taft, sculptor, pronounced this mansion one of the best of the "Gothic" houses in Chicago. Behind its medieval stone façade, which is marked by such characteristics of French Gothic architecture as turrets and fleur-de-lis ornamental motifs, are ranged twenty-four great rooms decorated in the same style as the exterior. Here are beamed ceilings, richly carved wood mantels, oak-paneled walls, leaded windows, heavy doors, and stone passageways—all reminiscent of the interior of some storied château of the Loire district.

In this handsome domicile, for thirty years, lived John Graves Shedd, well known in his day as "the dean of Chicago merchants" and a philanthropist, art patron, and civic and religious leader whose influence in all these fields was widely felt. His greatest gift to the city—a gift that has added much to the fame of Chicago as a recreational center—is Shedd Aquarium in Grant Park.

Work on the Shedd residence was started in 1896. At that time John Shedd was a partner in the firm of Marshall Field and Company. The design of this Gothic abode was in the hands of Frederick W. Perkins and Edmund R. Krause, two prominent architects of the 1890's. In two years' time the house was completed and into it moved John Shedd and his wife, Mary, and their two daughters.

At the time the Shedd abode was built Drexel Boulevard was one of Chicago's fashionable streets. A wide thoroughfare, in the center of which stretches a tree-shaded parkway, it is one of the main highways from old Hyde Park, farther south, to the downtown district. The neighborhood of the Shedd home was once a part of the early township of Hyde Park.

The Drexel Boulevard mansion in which John Shedd lived was in striking contrast to the dwelling where he was born and reared. A native of Alstead, New Hampshire, where his birth occurred on July 20, 1850, he was brought up in a humble farmhouse. As he grew older, his father's rocky New England farm began to prove irksome, and at seventeen we find him working in a grocery store at Bellows Falls, Vermont, for $1.50 a week and board.

At the age of twenty he obtained a job as clerk in the dry goods store of Benjamin H. Burt at Rutland, Vermont. Shedd's new employer, says an old newspaper account, "encouraged and trained him in the study of dry goods and customers. His pupil's appreciation may be deduced from the fact that throughout his life Mr. Shedd kept a picture of B. H. Burt near him in his office."

One of John Shedd's fellow-clerks in the Burt store, James Sullivan, had come to Chicago seeking a wider field of opportunity and, finding it here, wrote to Shedd that Chicago was rich in prospects for young, ambitious men. As a result of this, John Shedd arrived in Chicago in 1872 and was soon a

JOHN G. SHEDD MANSION
4515 Drexel Boulevard

stock boy in the linen section of Field, Leiter and Company, earning ten dollars a week. Four months later he was promoted and given an increase in salary.

The store grew. With it grew the merchandising abilities

of the young New Englander. Mr. Field took notice. In 1893 John Shedd became a partner in the firm, the name being changed to Marshall Field and Company. When Marshall Field died in 1906, John Shedd became president of the firm, a position he held until 1922, when he retired to become chairman of the board. Before his death Marshall Field said that Shedd was "the best merchant in the United States."

In his Drexel Boulevard mansion John Shedd reigned as one of Chicago's most successful citizens. His wife was highly esteemed as a hostess, as a church and civic worker, and as a woman of rare cultural and intellectual attainments.

Two notable weddings occured in the Shedd home. The first, in 1911, was when Helen Shedd became the wife of Kersey Coates Reed, prominent attorney. He is now deceased. The second ceremony, in 1913, was the marriage of another daughter, Laura, to Charles H. Schweppe, a well-known banker. Mrs. Schweppe died four years ago.

After the Shedds gave up their Drexel Boulevard mansion and moved to the North Side and Lake Forest, it was acquired by Newton B. Lauren, a Chicago real estate man. Here Mr. Lauren and his wife and family lived until it was taken over by its present owners.

John Shedd died in 1926 at the age of seventy-six, widely mourned as a great business genius and as a great benefactor. His widow, Mary Roenna Porter Shedd, now eighty-seven, lives with her daughter, Mrs. Reed, on North State Parkway.

When John Shedd was still a minor official in the Field, Leiter Department Store more than a half-century ago, Mrs. Helen Ekin Starrett founded a girls' school on the South Side. Today that school, now one of the best-known private schools in the city, owns and occupies the old Shedd mansion as well as several adjoining residences. The Starrett School for Girls has occupied this place since 1924.

Here, in the midst of medieval Gothic rooms, several hundred girl students are being prepared for universities and colleges under the supervision of a faculty directed by Mr. and Mrs. Gerard T. Smith, principals. The school's dean, Mrs. Donald Decker, said that the old Shedd residence, now covered with English ivy, is evidently highly regarded as an architectural landmark.

PART IX
Along "The Ridge"

Introduction

Realizing its desirability as a likely residential locality, real estate men early began subdividing that long oak-shaded ridge southwest of Chicago known as the Blue Island Ridge. Long before this development took place, however, a ravine in the region was generally referred to as "Horse-Thief Hollow" because of a gang of horse thieves who frequented the place. An early settler of the district was Thomas Morgan, who owned a large tract of land along "The Ridge." Then came, in the 1870's, a group of men who purchased the Morgan tract, subdivided it, and established a residential village called Morgan Park. Another village was laid out and named Washington Heights. This was followed by the establishment of Beverly Hills. All these communities were later annexed to Chicago without losing their quiet, suburban atmosphere. Most of the homes along "The Ridge" have been built since the turn of the century, but a few remain from earliest pioneer days.

A Morgan Park Home

~~~~~~

ONE of the best preserved of the historic old homes in
Morgan Park is the trim, white-painted, two-story
edifice at 11118 South Artesian Avenue. Set back on
a smooth lawn, shaded in summer by a big walnut tree, this
house was built when Morgan Park was a small farming settlement known as North Blue Island and when houses were
few and widely separated.

When the original portion of this house was built by
Charles D. Iglehart, a Maryland tobacco planter who had
come West in 1856 and settled on the Blue Island Ridge, the
locality was popularly known as "Horse-Thief Hollow" because of a gang of horse stealers who had a hideaway in a
near-by ravine. But these lawless characters had long since
disappeared when Iglehart built his house in 1857.

Around him were the farms and tracts of the Morgans,
Smiths, Kaylors, Lackores, Frisbys, Colvins, Bernards, Wilcoxes, and other early settlers. After building his house and
establishing his family in it, Iglehart devoted his energies to
cultivating the land he had purchased. The records show he
laid out the second orchard in this region.

But of wider interest is the fact that the first birth to occur
in what later became Morgan Park took place in the Iglehart
homestead. This was the arrival of a baby daughter to the

Igleharts in 1857. She was named Mary. In the years following, other children were born. Today several grandchildren
of Charles Iglehart are still living in Morgan Park.

CHARLES D. IGLEHART HOME
11118 South Artesian Avenue

The original Iglehart farm extended from One Hundred
and Eleventh Street on the north to One Hundred and Fifteenth Street on the south and from Western Avenue on the
east to the present location of the Baltimore and Ohio Railroad tracks on the west. Sometime in the 1870's Charles Iglehart enlarged his farmhouse because of an increased family.

This new portion forms the two-story front part which overlooks Artesian Avenue today.

When the Blue Island Land and Building Company was formed in 1869 to lay out a subdivision to be called Morgan Park, the Iglehart farm was not included in the project. It therefore remained intact for years, while the section east of Western Avenue gradually filled up with homes. It was included, however, within the boundaries of Morgan Park when that community was incorporated as a village in 1882.

Charles Iglehart was an educated, cultured man and attracted other men of the same type to him. Among guests often seen in the parlor of the Iglehart home during the 1870's and 1880's were such influential Morgan Parkers as Professor William Rainey Harper, afterward first president of the University of Chicago, and the Reverend Justin A. Smith, one of the founders of the Chicago Baptist Theological Seminary in Morgan Park and father of the late Henry Justin Smith, managing editor of the *Chicago Daily News* from 1926 to 1936 and an author.

In the course of years, parts of the original Iglehart farm were subdivided, streets laid out, and dwelling houses built. Looking out of the bay windows of his home, Charles Iglehart saw the community grow from year to year, saw railroad tracks laid and roads constructed, saw more and more houses appear, and, as he looked, his mind went back to the days when all around him was prairie and farm land.

By the time death came to him in 1886, Morgan Park was one of the best known of Chicago's suburbs. In his day Charles Iglehart had seen it grow from a small settlement to a thriving, cultural center. He had witnessed with pride the construction of the Chicago Baptist Theological Seminary, the Morgan Park Military Academy, and the Chicago Female College, as well as numerous churches and primary schools.

After the death in this house of its master, the Iglehart family continued to occupy it for many years. His widow survived him for twenty-one years and was often the center of attention at gatherings of old-timers in the Iglehart home. In 1922 the house was sold to Arthur R. Ayers, and he and his family have occupied it since.

This was a fortunate sale, for the buyer was an instructor in architecture in one of the city's public high schools and an admirer of old homes. Ayers has kept the Iglehart home, as well as the grounds around it, in such good condition that it has become something of a show place in the South Side residential community.

The House on "The Hill"

~~~~~~

O N TOP of "The Hill" in Morgan Park, just west of the Rock Island Station, there stands an attractive old frame house, white painted, with board and batten siding and a "lookout" on its roof, that has long been revered as a landmark of Morgan Park's pioneer days. Here lived John Morgan, youngest son of an early settler for whom Morgan Park was named. It is one of the oldest dwellings in that quiet, elm-shaded community on the Far South Side.

When this house was built, there was no Morgan Park. There were only a dozen or so farmers in the vicinity whose homesteads were scattered along what was then known as the Blue Island Ridge. One of the largest landowners had been the father of the man who built this sturdy wooden house on "the Hill." That landowner was Thomas Morgan, who had settled in this region more than a hundred years ago when it was known as "Horse-Thief Hollow."

The story of the old house on "The Hill"—its address is 2041 West One Hundred and Tenth Place—was told by David Herriott, president of the Morgan Park Historical Society, in one of his series of interesting articles on early Morgan Park which appeared in the *Beverly Review* several years ago. These articles, as well as other data and exhibits pertaining to early Morgan Park, are in the care of Miss Marion

Barnes, historical society librarian at the George C. Walker Branch of the Chicago Public Library in Morgan Park.

After telling of Thomas Morgan's arrival here from Surrey, England, in 1844, Mr. Herriott writes: "His youngest son, John, built the house on the hill at One Hundred and Tenth Place, later the home of William W. Washburn and now [1939] the home of the Samuel F. Joors. It was erected about 1864. It is still a strong, sturdy house and has been remodeled in modern style."

Thomas Morgan was not the first settler of this region. That honor, it seems, goes to one John Blackstone. We learn from Mr. Herriott that Thomas Morgan "purchased the whole ridge from Ninety-first to One Hundred and Fifteenth streets from John Blackstone for $5,450. . . . . Blackstone had bought this land from the United States in 1839, following the exodus of the Indians."

Although Mr. Herriott writes that Thomas Morgan built a large stone house near the present site of the Ninety-first Street railroad station, we learn from Andreas' *History of Cook County* that Morgan, upon purchasing about three thousand acres from Blackstone, also acquired the Blackstone house "built prior to 1844 and which stood about half a mile north of what is now Ninety-fifth Street." Andreas goes on to say that many deer and fox were found on his tract by Thomas Morgan and that he hunted these with his hounds.

We learn that Morgan farmed a large part of his land and that he was the father of nine sons and two daughters. He died in 1857. His grave is in Graceland Cemetery. Not much is known of his youngest son, John, other than the fact that the latter had inherited a goodly portion of the original Morgan tract. Another son, William, planted the first orchard in the settlement. Still another son, Harry, moved to Blue Island in 1882.

Related to this family was James Morgan, who in 1873

became owner and occupant of what is today considered the oldest dwelling in Hyde Park. This is the venerable twin house at 5152 Hyde Park Boulevard. The original portion of this house was built by Dr. Jacob Bockee in 1857. The house is now owned by Mrs. George Owens Clinch, whose late husband was an executive of the Crerar-Clinch Coal Company.

JOHN MORGAN HOUSE
2041 West One Hundred and Tenth Place

When John Morgan erected his frame house on "the Hill" during the Civil War period, the region around it was known as North Blue Island. In 1869 John Morgan and his brothers sold large portions of their late father's tract to a firm incorporated by Geoge C. Walker and others and known as the Blue Island Land and Building Company. The company subdivided the land, improved it with streets, planted thousands of trees, and named their new suburb Morgan Park.

From the porch of his home or from the "lookout" on the roof, where he could command a wide view of the countryside, John Morgan saw his father's farm develop into an at-

tractive suburb, witnessed the building of notable educational institutions, such as the Morgan Park Military Academy
and the Chicago Female College, and observed residents on
their way to polling places to vote for incorporation of the
village of Morgan Park in 1882.

Just how long John Morgan lived here has not been
learned, but in 1890 the house came into the possession of
William W. Washburn, who became postmaster of Morgan
Park. Subsequently, it was bought by the Joors. Caring for
this old landmark for many years, Mrs. Nina Joor kept it in
first-class condition and surrounded it with shade trees,
shrubbery, lawns, and flower gardens.

The same appreciation of its historic value is being shown
by its present owners, Mr. and Mrs. Robert B. Weaver. Here
Mr. Weaver does some of his writing as a research worker in
the social science department of the University of Chicago
laboratory schools. Author of several books, he is at present
engaged on a historical work dealing with houses and home
life in America.

The abode in which he lives is two stories high with a
spacious front porch. The quaint, wooden-railed "lookout,"
or "captain's walk," on the peak of the roof gives it the appearance of a Nantucket dwelling. The low-ceilinged rooms
are trimmed with mahogany and have been outfitted by Mrs.
Weaver with appropriate period furniture. One of Mrs.
Weaver's choicest possessions is an old-fashioned melodeon, a
family heirloom. A large fireplace of field stone dominates the
living-room.

Of main interest to the Weaver children—Marilyn Ann,
thirteen, Douglas, nine, and Gregory, four—is, of course, the
"lookout" on the roof. They always enjoy seeing the sights
from the "lookout"—the same "lookout" from which John
Morgan saw his father's land change from a farm to a thriving, attractive, restful suburb.

The Smith Farmhouse

O F SOME renown in the years immediately after Morgan Park was laid out as a suburban village was the Smith orchard, located just west of the village in the vicinity of One Hundred and Eleventh Street and Western Avenue. Today there is no trace of the orchard. The hundreds of apple and pear trees that occupied most of the Smith forty-acre tract have been replaced by modern brick bungalows, houses, and apartment buildings. Still standing, however, is the farmhouse in which lived the man who planted and maintained the orchard that was so much admired in the 1870's.

The man who built this house, which stands at 11018 South Western Avenue, was Michael Smith. An English-born son of Irish parents, Michael Smith came to this country as a young man, moved to the Middle West, and finally settled at Monmouth, Illinois, where he set up a general store sometime in the late 1850's. After the outbreak of the Civil War he came to Chicago and entered the hotel business.

During the Civil War years Michael Smith conducted the National Hotel, which then stood in Wells Street between Washington and Randolph streets. Among the numerous family heirlooms in the possession of Michael Smith's granddaughter, who now occupies the old farmhouse, is a leather-

306

bound hotel register used by her grandfather when he operated the National Hotel.

In the year 1869—the same year Morgan Park was established by the Blue Island Land and Building Company—Michael Smith acquired forty acres of land from the government immediately west of the new suburban village. A few months afterward he built the farmhouse. Selling his hotel in

MICHAEL SMITH HOME
11018 South Western Avenue

Chicago, he brought his family to the farm and settled down as a tiller of the soil and a horticulturist.

It was a lucky move for him, for two years after becoming established here he was doing chores in his farmyard one windy October night when he saw a red glow in the sky in the direction of Chicago. "There must be a big fire in Chicago," he thought. As the night wore on, the glow became brighter. A little later he learned that most of the city was in flames.

It was the great fire of 1871. The hotel that Michael Smith had sold only two years earlier was destroyed.

In those early days of Morgan Park the closest neighbors of Michael Smith were Charles D. Iglehart and William Morgan. Morgan Park was named after Morgan's father, Thomas, who had settled in the region in 1844. William Morgan is credited with setting out the first orchard in the vicinity, and Iglehart the second. The old Iglehart home, incidentally, still stands at 11118 South Artesian Avenue, not far from the Smith farmhouse.

Each fall Michael Smith would take wagonloads of apples and pears along the old Vincennes Road to the market in Chicago. He also barreled and sold large quantities of cider. He was assisted in this work by his son, Fred. It was during these years that Smith's wife, Jane, kept a diary at odd moments between household duties. In it she told of the everyday life of the region and referred often to the passing of Indians over the dirt road before her house.

Although he had labored hard to plant his orchard and cultivate his ground, Michael Smith was destined to enjoy the results of his labor for only a short while. He died sometime in the late 1870's and was buried in the old Blue Island Cemetery. His widow continued to live in the farmhouse, and by this time her son, Fred, was a grown man and ready to assume his duties as head of the household.

Seated on the porch of her farmhouse, the widow of Michael Smith looked across Western Avenue and saw Morgan Park gradually grow into an attractive suburb. More and more she saw those new-fangled contraptions called "horseless carriages" chugging past in Western Avenue and was annoyed at the way they frightened farm horses. But she did not live to see the automobile as it is known today. She died in the farmhouse in 1903 at an advanced age.

Before her death her son had married an English-born girl, Mary Brittan, who had come to Chicago in 1889. The couple lived in the farmhouse, and Fred Smith added to the family income by working as a stonemason. He and his wife reared four children—Thomas, Marguerite, Henry, and James—in the farmhouse and continued to look after the fruit trees that stretched away to the west of the old dwelling.

Fred Smith died in 1917. Today the house is occupied by his daughter and her husband, Walter Hayden. The Haydens have three children—Betty and Jane, twins, and Mary Ann. The farmhouse is set back from Western Avenue some distance and, although now veneered with stucco, is noticeable as an old residential landmark of the neighborhood. It is two stories high, gable roofed, and is marked by a concrete-pillared porch stretching across its front, evidently an addition.

An interesting side light on the present master of this house, Walter Hayden, is that he is a tree expert who often wishes he could bring back the days when the house in which he now lives was surrounded by apple, pear, and other fruit trees as well as by distant stands of oaks, elms, and maples.

An Irish Castle

~~~~~~

ONE of the oldest and most familiar of architectural curiosities in Chicago stands in Beverly Hills, restful and attractive community of fine homes that once existed outside the city. This is the gray-stone castle on a grassy bluff at the northwest corner of One Hundred and Third Street and Longwood Drive. Known to neighbors as "the Castle," it is an authentic reproduction of an Irish medieval keep and was built more than half a century ago by a Chicago businessman of Irish descent. In an article he once wrote, Donald Culross Peattie, Chicago-born nature writer, said this dwelling was "an interesting if fantastic landmark."

The man who erected the Beverly Hills castle was Robert C. Givins, a Chicago real estate dealer of the 1880's. After serving at that time with the realty firm of E. A. Cummings and Company, he toured Ireland and the Continent and, upon his return to Chicago, set up his own company under the name of Robert C. Givins and Company. Associated with him in this enterprise were his son, Robert S., and another real estate operator, George T. Steen. The firm prospered, and soon Robert Givins was in a position to build himself a comfortable and attractive home.

The story is told that on his tour of Ireland he was greatly impressed by an ancient, ivy-covered castle on the banks of the river Dee. Being a person of some artistic abilities, he made sketches of this castle. Perhaps the idea had entered his mind of reproducing just such a stronghold for a home in Chicago. In any case, the idea remained in his mind, and, when the time came for him to erect a house, he designed it in the style of the castle on the banks of the Dee.

The site he chose was a bluff on Tracy Avenue—now Longwood Drive—not far from the One Hundred and Third Street station of the Rock Island Railroad. This neighborhood was then called Washington Heights. It was a neighborhood Robert Givins had been developing and subdividing. The nearest community was Morgan Park, which lay just to the south. Givins had seen the future residential possibilities of land along "the Ridge"—an anticipation that has since been realized.

"Mr. Givins was a very unusual man," explained Hyde W. Perce, a veteran Chicago real estate dealer. "Not only was he a successful real estate man but he was an inveterate reader of books, a world traveler, and an author. His book, *A Rich Man's Fool*, was widely read. He was best known, however, as a seller of lots in and around Chicago. Today you would call such a person a go-getter. He originated many unique schemes for the selling of lots.

"I recall an auction sale under a big tent at Sixty-seventh Street and Western Avenue where he advertised the giving-away of a lot. He did so by attaching an order for a warranty deed to one of several hundred toy balloons and then setting them adrift. The finder of the lucky balloon was to be given his choice of a residence lot. Several years after this a farmer near Summit, Illinois, uncovered a small tin container while plowing his field. In it was the Givins warranty deed. He presented it to Mr. Givins and received a nice lot."

The Irish castle erected by Robert Givins was completed in

1886. It was built of limestone blocks which were hauled from the quarries near Joliet in low, wooden wagons pulled by teams of stout horses. After it was finished, Givins moved

ROBERT C. GIVINS HOME
10244 Longwood Drive

into it with his wife and son, and here he intended to live for the remainder of his days. In such a home he would be constantly reminded of the historic castle on the river Dee. On the walls of his castle Mr. Givins hung numerous tapestries he had collected abroad.

Today, after more than half a century, this battlemented structure remains essentially the same as when Mr. Givins moved into it. But the neighborhood is now fully developed and villa-like mansions line both sides of quiet and elegant Longwood Drive.

Looking up at the old pile, one notes its most striking features—the serrated turrets at its four corners. These rise higher than the three-story edifice itself. One sees, too, that the southeast tower is even higher than the others and that it overlooks the entrance on the Longwood Drive side.

The interior reveals a medieval ranginess in keeping with the castle's exterior. There are fifteen rooms here, and the one of greatest interest is the huge living-room on the first floor. Its ceiling is twenty-four feet high. It is thirty-six feet long and twenty-four feet wide. Some of Mr. Givins' tapestries still hang on its walls.

For some reason Mr. Givins did not realize his dream of leading a quiet, retired life in his castle, for in 1908 the house was sold to John B. Burdett. Burdett moved into it with his family and lived there until the castle was sold to Dr. Miroslaw Siemens in 1920. During Mr. Burdett's occupation a few changes were made, including the erection of a stone portecochere on the north side and the laying-out of a driveway surrounding the castle.

Many Chicagoans will remember Dr. Siemens, the present occupant, as one of those who was largely instrumental in building and maintaining the Ukranian Pavilion at the Century of Progress International Exposition here in 1933. At that time Dr. Siemens was president of the Chicago Ukranian Society.

PART X
Near Lincoln Park

Introduction

Drawn by the natural attractions of Lincoln Park, with its shady walks and green vistas, many Chicago men of wealth and position built, in the 1870's and 1880's, majestic residences in streets adjoining the park. This was a natural development of the northward movement of exclusive residential districts. The choicest lots were those nearest to the lake or to Lincoln Park. As these were bought up, the movement continued northward until the whole west boundary of Lincoln Park was marked by elegant town houses. The proprietors of these Gothic and Romanesque dwellings could be seen driving through the park in their carriages or strolling under the elms and maples in top hats with bustled ladies at their sides. With the coming of the automobile and the introduction of new modes of housing, the Lincoln Park neighborhood changed. Many of the old mansions disappeared and were replaced by tall hotels, apartment houses, and business blocks.

Policeman Bellinger's Cottage

~~~~~~

ALMOST as widespread and persistent as the legend of the cow that kicked over Mrs. O'Leary's lantern and started the Chicago Fire is the story that has clung to the little frame dwelling at 2121 Hudson Avenue, often referred to by historians as "Policeman Bellinger's Cottage."

As if this cottage were not famous enough as one of the only two houses to escape the great fire on the Near North Side, its name has been spread all over the country by the story that Policeman Bellinger saved it from the flames with generous dousings of cider.

Whether or not such a thing ever happened, the true facts of what occurred at the cottage on that fateful October night in 1871 reveal a story equally interesting, if less unusual. It is a story of love, of a man's devotion to his bride, of his attachment to a home, and of how, single handed, he defied nature on a frightful rampage and won out in the end.

But the cider tale was accepted as fact by some later historians, and with each appearance it was enhanced by more vivid and more glamorous details. A. T. Andreas and J. Seymour Currey repeat the story in their monumental histories of Chicago. Perhaps typical of the way it has been treated is the account in *Chicago and the Great Conflagration*, a book by Elias Colbert and Everett Chamberlain published in 1871.

318

After explaining that the Mahlon D. Ogden residence escaped the flames on the Near North Side, the authors go on to say that the only other house to be saved "is that of a policeman named Bellinger, which had apparently little advantage of isolation, but was saved by dint of much exertion on the part of its occupant, aided by a favorable freak of the flames.

"Bellinger was fortunate enough to have a small quantity of water on hand when the supply from the waterworks gave out. He tore up a section of sidewalk and determined to shed the last drop—not of his blood, but of the water, which, in such a crisis, was still more precious—in defense of his castle. This he did to the best advantage, that is, reserving it until a spark alighted on the shingles.

"He stood his ground manfully until the red demon approached threateningly near, and then he redoubled his vigilance. Of this there was need, for now the sparks and brands fell thicker and faster, and his scant ladlefuls of water hissed and went up in puffs of steam as they struck the blistering shingles. By and by the last ladleful was gone, and the flames had not yet ceased to rage around him.

"If he only had a little more water—a bucketful merely—he thought he could save a home for his wife . . . . the home which he had been struggling so long to build. . . . . The wish did him honor, and the divine source of it sent him a thought which proved the wish's realization. In the cellar was a barrel of cider, which he had lately got in to drink with the winter's nuts and apples.

"He rightly judged that the red guest who now threatened his house with a visit wanted the cider worse than he did. To speak in plainer and more policeman-like terms, he knew that cider would quench fire as well as water and that his cider was what was wanted on the roof at that time. He called to his wife to draw and bring him all the contents of the cask. It was done. The libation was poured out (in the right spots) and the home was saved."

The cider story was even taught to children in the Chicago public schools. It appeared in a textbook used by them. And

BELLINGER HOUSE
2121 Hudson Avenue

for many years it was the custom of teachers to bring school children to the little cottage on Hudson Avenue each fire anniversary day and there explain to them how the house was saved by generous pourings-on of cider.

So the story went, and remained unquestioned, until one day in 1915 a small, white-haired, elderly lady walked slowly up the front steps of the cottage and knocked on the door. The knock was answered by the wife of the then owner, Mrs.

Joseph J. Kirschten. The elderly lady identified herself as the widow of Policeman Bellinger and said she was eager to see the little cottage once again.

"I was glad to show her the house," Mrs. Kirschten said afterward. "She looked eagerly around, felt the old-fashioned sliding doors, and went into the basement and touched the arched window frames. She appeared to be happy. The visit seemed to bring back memories of her girlhood romance. And then she told the true story of how her cottage was saved."

On the night of the fire, according to this story, Policeman Richard Bellinger—some say he was a captain of police—was more determined to save his house than were many of his distant neighbors. He was sure he had a good chance of doing so because the cottage was isolated, being the only one in that block.

He was not going to lose the house that meant so much to him, that was the realization of a dream he had shared with his bride. So, when the flames crept up to his neighborhood, when they were in fact licking the wooden steps in front and beginning to ignite the roof, Policeman Bellinger worked frantically, pouring bucketfuls of water on the roof and other parts.

When his cistern gave out, he went across the street and obtained more water from a dugout that belonged to a small truck farm there. He also had access to the water in what was then called Ten-Mile Ditch, which lay a block or two to the east, paralleling North Clark Street. After the cottage was saved from destruction, Policeman Bellinger and his wife furnished food and shelter for several days for twenty-one persons rendered homeless by the fire. They remained until they could get outside relief.

"The history books say that my husband put out the fire with cider, but that is not true," Mrs. Bellinger is quoted as saying. "We did have a barrel of cider in the basement, sure enough, but we didn't use it because we were able to get enough water from the dugout across the street."

Living in the house today is Joseph J. Kirschten, a retired postal clerk. His wife, who received Mrs. Bellinger, died several years ago. On the wall upstairs hangs a framed religious picture that Kirschten's mother had saved when the Chicago Fire completely destroyed the Kirschten home near North Avenue and Wells Street. Mr. Kirschten was three years old at the time of the holocaust.

A Congressman's Home

~~~~~~

FOR more than half a century North Siders on their way to the Loop have noticed a rambling, red-brick mansion of imposing design at the northeast corner of Belden Avenue and Clark Street, not far from Lincoln Park. As the years passed and a new generation appeared, the identity of the man who lived in this house became more and more vague until today there are few persons who know the name of its original occupant.

There was a time, however, when this was one of the leading houses of Chicago. For here lived a notable citizen of the Victorian era, George Everett Adams, scion of a pioneer Chicago family, Civil War soldier, lawyer, state senator, congressman, and patron of the arts. While a member of Congress from 1883 to 1891, he attracted wide attention as an authority on government finance.

Before entering politics and while still a lawyer here, Adams married Adele Foster, youngest daughter of Dr. John H. Foster, early Chicago settler and North Side landowner. Proud of the match, Dr. Foster presented to the newlyweds as a wedding gift the two-story brick mansion which still stands today on Belden Avenue. It was built in 1872 and was immediately occupied by George Adams and his bride.

The family roots of both husband and wife went back to

323

the beginnings of Chicago. George Adams' father, Benjamin Franklin Adams, had come to Chicago from New Hampshire in 1835, but did not take up permanent residence here until 1853. His wife's father, Dr. Foster, first came here in 1832 and bought several acres of land north of the city for $410.

GEORGE E. ADAMS HOUSE
350 Belden Avenue

At his death in 1874 this same property, bounded by Clark Street, Belden Avenue, Fullerton Parkway, and Lincoln Park West, was valued at $1,250,000.

A bronze plaque on the front of the Harris School, just north of the Adams house, explains that at this point the Chicago Fire of 1871 reached its northern limit, and that Dr. Foster's house, a frame edifice that stood at Belden Avenue and Clark Street, was the last building to be burned.

Dr. Foster's widow, Nancy Foster, afterward provided the funds for the building of Foster Hall at the University of Chicago. In the years just before he died Dr. Foster was held in high esteem as one of the founders of the Chicago Board of Education.

Soon after settling down in their big mansion on Belden Avenue, the Adams' became active in the social life of the North Side and began entertaining many celebrities. An old-time history says that "the Adams residence on Belden Avenue is one of the architectural attractions of the North Side of the city."

It was from this house that George Adams went to Springfield in 1881 as a state senator, marking his entry into politics. And it was to this house that he retired from political life in 1891, after having served four terms in Congress.

He remained active in other fields, however, for the record shows that he was a member of the board of overseers of Harvard University, his alma mater, and was a trustee both of the Newberry Library and the Field Museum, a member of the Chicago Board of Education, and president of the Chicago Orchestral Association.

In this great house, with its twenty-four rooms, the Adams' reared four children—two boys and two girls. The boys died while young, but the girls grew to womanhood and are now Mrs. Elizabeth A. Bross and Mrs. Margaret A. Clement. Mr. and Mrs. Adams died in 1917, within a few months of each other, at Peterborough, New Hampshire.

In 1921 the Adams residence was acquired by the School of Domestic Arts and Science, an institution founded in Chicago at the beginning of the century by Mrs. Lynden Evans. Some years ago the school received a gift of $90,000 from the present Mrs. Potter Palmer.

Few changes have been made in the interior of the Adams house since it was acquired by the school. The many spacious rooms, in most of which are marble fireplaces inlaid with William Morris tiles, reflect the personality of a cultured man. The long, narrow entrance hall has a beamed ceiling of hand-pegged cherry and white mahogany, no nails being used anywhere in placing this woodwork trim.

The reception room, library, and dining-room, each with their fireplaces, tall windows outfitted with folding inside shutters, and sliding doors, are also trimmed in cherry and white mahogany. On the east side is a small room with a fireplace in it. This was used by Congressman Adams as a study. It was here that he pored over Latin tomes and read from the hundreds of books which lined the walls of his study.

"Our out-of-town students live in this old mansion," explained Mrs. Mary Koll Heiner, director of the school, "and in it we attempt to carry on the spirit of gracious living that was so evidently a part of its beginning. The original dining-room, library, and lounge afford an unusual background for courses in correct formal as well as informal table service."

The Archbishop's Residence

AT THE southeast corner of North State Parkway and North Avenue, just opposite Lincoln Park, stands a dignified, old red-brick residence that is held in reverence by more than a million persons in Chicago and outlying cities and towns. It has been held in such reverence for more than half a century.

The reason for this is that the house is—and has been since the early 1880's—the abode of the Roman Catholic archbishops of Chicago. As such, it is held in awe not only by members of that faith but by Chicagoans in general. For a time this dwelling was nationally known when it was occupied by the late George Cardinal Mundelein, first cardinal in the Middle West and perhaps the most eminent of all American prelates of the Roman Catholic faith.

It was soon after the Chicago diocese was elevated to the status of an archdiocese, in 1880, that the city's first archbishop, the Most Reverend Patrick A. Feehan, had this residence built on the North Side. Before that time the bishop's home was at La Salle Street and North Avenue.

The residence appears the same today as when first erected by Archbishop Feehan. It is three stories high, of red brick, and is notable for its numerous chimneys, which indicate many fireplaces throughout the house. The front is dignified, with an unpretentious portico approached by wide stone steps. A porte-cochere stands on the north side of the house.

Archbishop Feehan lived in this mansion for some years before the World's Columbian Exposition, and here he planned the building of more and more schools and churches to take care of the educational and spiritual needs of the people of his faith in a rapidly growing city. In his later years he spent much time in his library, which contained some five thousand ecclesiastical and historical works, and among his beloved flowers in the conservatory at the rear of the house

Archbishop Feehan died here in 1902 and was succeeded by Archbishop James E. Quigley. Some alterations in the interior of the house were made by Archbishop Quigley, but the conservatory was left untouched as a memorial to the prelate who was first to occupy the house.

With the appearance of Archbishop Mundelein, the venerable red-brick house became of national and even international interest because of the greatness of its occupant and because of the distinguished religious and lay personages who visited it.

Probably no dwelling in the Western Hemisphere ever housed so many Roman Catholic prelates at one time as did this residence in 1926, when, for the first time in the history of America, a Roman Catholic Eucharistic Congress was held in Chicago. The congress was brought to the midwestern metropolis through the efforts of Cardinal Mundelein.

Many noted personages, however, had come under this roof before the congress. One of these was the late Cardinal Mercier of Belgium, an outstanding figure of the first World War, who visited Chicago in 1919. Another who was entertained here was the late Cardinal Cieplak of Poland, who played an important role in post-war European history.

A historic occasion associated with this house was the visit in 1937 of President Roosevelt as a luncheon guest of Cardinal Mundelein. The President and the Cardinal were friends of long standing, having become acquainted when Cardinal Mundelein was a lesser prelate in New York City. The luncheon followed a memorable address that President Roose-

ARCHBISHOP STRITCH RESIDENCE
1555 North State Parkway

velt had delivered that day at the dedication of Chicago's new Outer Drive Bridge—an address in which the country's chief executive said that aggressor nations should be "quarantined."

The interior of this residence has an atmosphere of dignity and quiet elegance in keeping with the high position of its occupant. On the walls of its many rooms, tastefully decorated and comfortably furnished, hang numerous oil portraits of church dignitaries, including the earlier archbishops of Chicago.

Aside from the chapel, the room in this house of most spiritual significance to Catholics is that known as the throne room. It contains, as its main piece of furniture, a beautifully carved, high-backed, gilded chair, the velvet seat of which is protected by a silk cord suspended between the arms. This chair, according to the tradition of the church, is reserved only for the Pope should he ever visit here. It is thus held sacred and is reverenced by the clergy and laity of the Roman Catholic faith in Chicago.

Since the death, in 1939, of Cardinal Mundelein, this residence has been occupied by Archbishop Samuel A. Stritch, successor to Cardinal Mundelein. As with his predecessor, Archbishop Stritch is a devout head of the church, an able administrator, a scholar, and a friendly, likable man. Since his appointment to the Chicago archdiocese, Archbishop Stritch has demonstrated that he is a worthy successor to the numerous distinguished prelates who had occupied this house since it was built more than half a century ago.

An eminent guest who visited this archepiscopal residence was later to become even more eminent. In 1936 Cardinal Mundelein welcomed here a fellow-prelate from Vatican City, Eugenio Cardinal Pacelli. Before sitting down for their visit, the two distinguished cardinals walked to the throne room and there paid spiritual homage to the then reigning head of the church, Pope Pius XI, whose likeness was imbedded in the back of the stately, gilded chair.

The visitor at that time was papal secretary of state. Today, imbedded in the back of the finely carved chair, that visitor's own likeness looks out as Pope Pius XII.

Once a Suburban Home

FOUR years before the township of Lake View was annexed to Chicago there was built at the northwest
corner of what is now Diversey Parkway and Sheridan
Road a three-story, red-brick residence that was widely admired by the township residents as they drove past in their
buggies. They regarded it with awe not only because its architecture was to them "grand" but also because of the prominence of the family who occupied it. Opposite Lincoln Park,
at the intersection of two important streets, that house from
the first was a landmark. And it so remains today.

In the more than half a century since it has been standing
there, that red-brick abode, with its fanciful exterior trim,
high-pitched roof, pointed tower, and wrought-iron fence, has
been owned and occupied, successively, by several families
of German origin who attained wealth and social prominence
in Chicago life. During the 1880's and 1890's it was one of the
best-known residences of the German-American colony centered in old Lake View—a colony that produced many men
and women who added much to the material and cultural
achievements of Chicago.

Not least among these were the man and woman for whom
the Sheridan Road dwelling was built. The story of this
couple, and of their house, has been uncovered by the

331

Ravenswood–Lake View Historical Society. The house, it has been determined, was erected in 1885, when Lake View was a township extending as far south as Fullerton Avenue.

RUDOLPH SCHLOESSER HOME
2800 Sheridan Road

"Our records show that this house was built for Rudolph Schloesser and his wife, Amelia, who had come up to Lake View to live a quite, suburban existence," explained Miss Helen Zatterberg, secretary-historian of the historical society. "The Schloessers were by then a well-to-do family. Mr. Schloesser had been for some years a banker in Chicago.

He and his wife brought with them to their new house a family of three children."

Research discloses that Rudolph Schloesser was one of the founders and first cashier of the International Mutual Trust Company, an institution established on La Salle Street in 1870 with a capital of $100,000. He continued as an official of the bank, branched out into real estate investments, and by 1885 was a man of means and position. It was then that he and his wife decided to settle in Lake View at a spot not far away from the shore of the lake and near Lincoln Park as it existed then.

The house was designed for them by an architect named H. Emil Frommann, who now lives on Hudson Avenue, not far from the Schloesser residence. Here the Schloessers lived in comfort during the late 1880's and 1890's, reared their children, entertained leading German-Americans of the city, and saw Lake View, after its annexation to Chicago in 1889, grow to become the thriving North Side of Chicago.

The chatelaine of this house, Mrs. Schloesser, was as well known and as well liked by people as her husband. She was a cultured woman, devoted to music and the arts of the home, and took active part in artistic and charitable affairs of the city. She and her husband went on a tour of Europe and brought back many antiques and art objects that embellished the Sheridan Road home. One of her prized possessions was a grand piano.

After the death of her husband, Mrs. Schloesser continued to occupy the family home. One of her daughters, Ida, had meanwhile become the wife of Julius Thomsen und von Colditz, scion of an aristocratic German family. A residence was built for the von Colditzes next door to the Schloesser home, and here the couple lived and entertained for many years. The Von Colditz home has since been torn down. A son of the

Von Colditzes is Dr. G. Thomsen von Colditz, now a resident of Merritt Island at Cocoa, Florida.

Another Schloesser daughter, Amelia, also had married. Her husband was Henry Spread, an English artist who had taken up residence in Chicago. Many of his oils were exhibited in the Art Institute.

After Mrs. Schloesser died, the family home was taken over by Mr. and Mrs. Spread, and, after occupying it for a few years, they left America and became permanent residents of England.

Mrs. Schloesser died in this house on January 5, 1906, leaving an estate estimated at $922,000, practically all of which was real estate. The estate included the Schloesser Block, an office building at the northwest corner of La Salle and Adams streets. In addition to providing for her two daughters, their husbands, and a son, Alfred G., Mrs. Schloesser also left bequests to several charitable institutions in Chicago. The will provided that her cherished grand piano should go to that granddaughter of hers who should turn out to be an accomplished pianist.

The house was subsequently purchased and occupied by another prominent Chicago family, the Friestedts. The head of this family was Luther Peter Friestedt, inventor, contractor, businessman, and one-time alderman of a West Side ward. Before acquiring the Schloesser home, Luther Friestedt had been elected alderman of the old Thirteenth Ward in 1902.

Prior to his entering politics, Luther Friestedt had founded the firm of L. P. Friestedt and Company, building raisers and movers, in 1881. He was the inventor of a type of steel piling used in cofferdams.

For a time after the death of Luther Friedstedt, in 1920, the old dwelling was occupied by his son, Luther Peter Fried-stedt, Jr.

It was then vacant for a while but was rented in 1930 to a Russian restaurateur, Colonel Vladimir Yaschenko, who opened an exotic dining-room here called the "Maisonette Russe." The interior was remodeled and redecorated. After several years, Colonel Yaschenko gave up the restaurant, and the house has been vacant a good part of the time since.

Recently, however, the Schloesser residence came back to life for a time as the campaign headquarters of Charles S. Dewey, banker and one-time financial adviser to the government of Poland. Dewey was successful in his race and is now congressman of the North Side district in which the Scholesser house stands.

Overlooking the Park

O N THE stained-glass window in the library of the old stone mansion at the northwest corner of Fullerton Parkway and Lake View Avenue, opposite Lincoln Park, there is a mosaic containing the date "1891." This is the year the house was built. Although not so old as numerous other dwellings in the city, this elegant three-story mansion was a noteworthy abode of the North Side during the 1890's and early years of the present century, and it remains so today.

As the residence of Andrew E. Leicht, pioneer Chicagoan who had amassed a considerable fortune in the brewing and lumber industries, it was often the scene of brilliant social functions, attended by prominent men and women of the World's Fair era. Here, too, in later years, lived a couple— son and daughter-in-law of Andrew Leicht—who today are well known socially and as leaders in cultural, charitable, and club activities.

When Andrew Leicht built this mansion, he had but a short time before relinquished the role of one of the city's outstanding brewers. As an associate of Philip Bartholomae in the operation of a large brewery the two had founded here in 1873, he had attained wealth and eminence and had taken his place among the city's successful citizens. For some years he

336

had served as secretary of the Chicago and Milwaukee Brewers Association.

A native of Hudson, New York, where he was born in 1842, Andrew Leicht was educated in New York City. In 1860 he went to Germany to learn the brewer's profession and, having completed his studies, traveled extensively in Germany, France, and England. He returned to his native land and came to Chicago shortly after the fire of 1871. Here he formed the brewing firm with Bartholomae, which, in 1890, became the Chicago branch of the United States Brewing Company.

Although he had retired from the brewing field at the time he built his Lincoln Park residence, Mr. Leicht was still a comparatively young men, being forty-nine. He soon afterward entered the lumber business in association with Hermann Paepcke, under the name of the Paepcke-Leicht Lumber Company. Another member of the firm at this time was Mr. Leicht's son, Edward A., who became treasurer.

In the same year the elder Leicht completed his mansion— its address then was 5 Lake View Avenue—a wedding reception was held there which marked the joining of two pioneer Chicago families. This was in celebration of the marriage of the younger Leicht to Miss Angelina Madlener, daughter of Fridolin Madlener, founder of an old Chicago distilling firm. A handsome residence just north of the Leicht home was presented to the newly married couple as a wedding gift.

During the time Andrew Leicht and his wife, Louise, lived in the Lake View Avenue mansion, they entertained frequently and carried on the civic and cultural activities that made their names widely known in the Chicago of that day. They varied this program with numerous trips abroad, during which they collected antiques and objects of art. These went to the enhancement of their Chicago home.

Mr. Leicht died in 1904 while attending the St. Louis Fair. He was then sixty-two years old. His son and daughter-in-law afterward came to live with the widowed Mrs. Leicht in the big Lake View Avenue residence. She died in 1929 at the

ANDREW E. LEICHT MANSION
2400 Lake View Avenue

age of eighty-one. In her will Mrs. Leicht left generous bequests to Grant Hospital and to the German Old People's Home.

In the years since their wedding reception in the stately North Side mansion, Mr. and Mrs. Edward A. Leight—the name "Leicht" was changed to "Leight"—have been active in Chicago society. As a hostess Mrs. Leight has entertained numerous distinguished visitors from Europe and different parts of America. In 1928 she was presented at the Court of St. James, then reigned over by King George V and Queen Mary. Their son, Albert E. Leight, was in the real estate investment business for some years.

For the last seven years the old Leicht residence has been occupied by the Harris School, a private, nonprofit preparatory school founded in 1921 by Miss Lilian I. Harris and a group of prominent Chicago women. Miss Harris is director of the school and is assisted by Miss Ada M. Sitterly. Composed of two departments—the boys' school and the girls' school—this institution prepares the sons and daughters of Chicago and suburban families for eastern colleges and universities.

Although some alterations have been made in it, the interior of the Leicht home remains largely as it was when occupied by Andrew Leicht. It is an interior befitting a man of wealth and social position. Of particular note are the stained-glass windows, all of them the work of H. Beiler of Heidelberg.

The large entrance hall is paneled in oak and contains an ornamental fireplace. There are seventeen rooms in the house, including a ballroom on the third floor. The main rooms on the first floor are notable for their highly polished ebony trim, parquet flooring, tile and marble fireplaces, inlaid mahogany woodwork, and bay windows of leaded glass.

In keeping with this atmosphere, Miss Harris, whose hobby is the collecting of period furniture and glassware, has outfitted some of the rooms of the Leicht residence with appropriate chairs and tables. Here, too, she has on display a large collection of etchings by T. F. Simon, a French artist, as well as a notable collection of rare glass of the star and dewdrop pattern.

Baroque Style

W HAT some architects consider an unusual example of the baroque style in residential architecture is the three-story mansion at 503 Wrightwood Avenue, not far from Lincoln Park. Although gradually being encroached upon by modern apartment houses and hotels, this residence has so far withstood neighborhood changes and remains today as a type of dwelling that was fashionable in the Chicago of half a century ago. Both its exterior and its interior are, aside from the ravages of time, in practically their original state.

Judged by modern standards, this mansion seems highly decorative, even grandiose. But in its day it was widely admired. It was built by a pioneer Chicagoan who had achieved success in business and, at the time he dwelt in this house, was rated among Chicago's outstanding citizens. His descendants are today socially prominent and active in cultural and club activities.

Embellished with statuary (two caryatids support the balcony over the main entrance), intricately carved stonework, ornamental cornices and lintels, bas-reliefs, wrought-iron balconies, and a mansard roof, the exterior of this gray-stone residence shows to the full the lavish detail of the baroque style as developed in France during the reign of Louis XV, a style which later spread to all the capitals of Europe.

The interior is equally elegant. Here are many great rooms designed in various styles—a Flemish dining-room, a Gothic library, a French Renaissance drawing-room, and a Louis XVI ballroom. In these magnificent rooms, with their fire-

FRANCIS J. DEWES MANSION
503 Wrightwood Avenue

places of veined marble, parquetry and mosaic floors, wrought-brass and copper chandeliers, fanciful rosettes on frescoed ceilings, mahogany and oak paneling, damask walls, and leaded windows—in these surroundings the visitor feels as though he were walking through some palace of the Bourbons or the Hapsburgs.

This mansion of authentic eighteenth-century grandeur is of a type rarely created except by Europeans, and investigation reveals that its architects were Adolph Cudell, son of Aix la Chapelle, and Arthur Hercz, who was reared in Hungary. Both, however, were practicing their profession in Chicago at the time they designed this house. In fact, Adolph Cudell was, at that time, one of the best-known architects in the city. Some twenty years earlier he had designed a great French-style mansion on Rush Street for Cyrus Hall Mc-Cormick. That mansion still stands.

After the Wrightwood Avenue residence planned by Cudell and Hercz was completed early in 1896, it became the home of the man who commissioned it, Francis J. Dewes. At that time he was a wealthy and successful man, having made a fortune as head of a brewing company he had established some twelve years earlier. With him when he took up his abode in the new house near Lincoln Park were his wife, Hedwig, and his son, Edwin.

Study of his origin and training indicates that Francis Dewes was an educated man, one who appreciated the refinements of civilized living. Born at Losheim, Rhenish Prussia, in 1845, he was the son of a brewer who became a member of the German parliament. After finishing his studies at Cologne University, Francis Dewes entered his father's business and soon became proficient in it. In 1868 he arrived in Chicago and engaged as a bookkeeper in the brewing firm of Rehm and Bartholomae.

Two years later he became bookkeeper of the Busch and Brand Brewing Company. Soon he bought stock in the company and later was elected secretary and treasurer. In 1876 he married Hedwig Busch. By 1882 he was ready to establish a firm of his own. This was done that year, and in time he took his place alongside Frederick Wacker, Jacob Birk,

Michael Brand, and Valentine Busch, all of whom were among the foremost Chicago brewers at that time.

It was then that Francis Dewes decided to erect a home on the North Side that would reflect his tastes in Old World art and culture. As has been seen, he attained his goal. He lived in his Wrightwood Avenue mansion until the end of the first World War. After his death, the residence was acquired by the Swedish Engineers Society of Chicago. Here the society established its headquarters without much alteration of the interior.

PART XI

The Township of Jefferson

Introduction

The city's Northwest Side now embraces the major part of the original township of Jefferson, until 1889 outside the limits of Chicago. Served by the early Milwaukee Plank Road—now Milwaukee Avenue—this region was mostly farm and prairie land in the 1850's and 1860's. When the Chicago and North Western Railroad established service through this territory, however, it began to develop, and soon numerous "suburbs" grew up along the road's right-of-way. Among these were Avondale, Irving Park, Mayfair, Jefferson Park, Norward Park, and Edison Park. In 1889—along with Lake View and Hyde Park— the township of Jefferson was annexed to Chicago. Streetcar service on Milwaukee Avenue, as well as on Elston Avenue and on numerous east-west streets, aided in building up that part of the city. On some of these streets one often encounters an old Jefferson Township house, with its windowed cupola and roomy porch and its mellowed aspect of great age.

The Falconer Farmhouse

~~~~~~

ON THE northwest corner of Cicero and Wellington avenues, just beyond a row of modern shops and stores, stands a little old white-painted frame house in a grove of ancient cottonwoods. It was there as far back as the memory of the oldest regular rider on the Cicero Avenue car line can go. It was even standing there when this section of the city, now completely built up, was prairie and farm land and an occasional Indian could be seen going past on horseback.

This squat, gable-roofed edifice, so small among towering, gnarled trees, has been an object of curiosity to passers-by for years, but there is no mystery about it to the neighborhood housewives. They know that the grammar school their children attend is named after the man who built this house and that his son is living there today.

When Laughlin Falconer bought an eighty-acre tract here and erected this little house in 1848, he had no fear of any roving bands of Indians. His faithful old flintlock musket, once carried by an ancestor in George III's army, would afford him protection. This weapon was among the few worldly possessions he brought with him to America from Inverness, Scotland, his birthplace.

It is supposed, too, that the flintlock supplied protection

348

to Falconer's brother, David, who also bought an eighty-acre tract adjoining his brother's place.

David, who was ten years older than Laughlin, had come to Chicago in 1832. Laughlin arrived a few years later. At that time Chicago was a settlement of log and frame houses clustered around Fort Dearborn. As the Falconer brothers preferred rural life to town life, they went in search of land and

LAUGHLIN FALCONER HOME
4830 Wellington Avenue

soon located a tract out on the prairies some six miles north-west of Chicago. There were only a few settlers in the vicinity, and the township of Jefferson had not yet been organized.

It happened that a low ridge went north and south across Laughlin Falconer's land, and on this he built the farmhouse which is still standing today. This ridge is known in the early history of Jefferson Township as Sand Ridge.

The brothers paid the government $1.25 an acre for their land, or a total of $200 for the hundred and sixty acres.

Laughlin Falconer afterward inherited his brother's tract, and on April 7, 1917, on his one hundredth birthday, he announced that the deed to his one-hundred-and-sixty-acre tract had been turned over to new owners. He had received $2,500 an acre, or a total of $400,000.

There was quite a celebration in the little farmhouse on the ridge that day. With the old farmer were his two children, several grandchildren, and many friends. Laughlin told his guests that he felt as spry and frisky as when he was fifty, said he had not had a sick day in his life, and attributed his good health to the chores he had performed daily around his farm.

He felt more pride, however, in showing off the electric lights installed in his farmhouse the year before. Up to then, he had been using kerosene lamps. Sharing this pride over the new improvement was his son, William, who was then sixty-four years old and was called "Willie" by the father.

In the early days the Falconer homestead was located in what was then known as Grayland, named after a pioneer of the section, John Gray. Later the name was changed to Kelvyn Grove. Meanwhile, the prairie began to fill up with settlers, farms became lots, the name of Jefferson Avenue was changed to Cicero Avenue, and in the course of years the little Falconer home was surrounded by bungalows and two-story flat buildings.

Today this section is called Belmont Park, after Belmont Avenue to the north. It is solidly built up. Most of the residents own their own homes. There are thriving shops and stores along Cicero Avenue, and just a block west of the old-fashioned dwelling in the cottonwood grove stands an imposing two-story public school—the Laughlin Falconer School.

But before this area was built up, before streetcar tracks were laid on Jefferson Avenue, Laughlin Falconer and his sons worked hard as farmers. They sold much of their produce in old South Water Street Market, driving their wagon down Milwaukee Avenue. But the city crept up to their farm, and in time they gave up tilling the soil.

Sole occupant of the old Northwest Side landmark today is Laughlin's son, William. He lives a quiet existence here, smoking his pipe, reading the papers, or talking over old times with John E. Van Natta and other descendants of early Jefferson Township settlers. William is now eighty-nine years old. There are few, if any, Chicago persons of such advanced years still living in the houses in which they were born.

An Early Homestead

AMONG numerous old houses listed in the records of the West Side Historical Society one of the most interesting is the little green-painted, gable-roofed dwelling at 4618 Armitage Avenue. For here lived an early settler and leader of the old township of Jefferson, once a rural section outside the city but now almost completely built up and known today as the Northwest Side.

That this small frame house is a survivor of the days when the area around it was open, windy country, and cabbage patches were on all sides, is evidenced by its architecture. It is a typical homestead of the Civil War era. Few of these remain within the metropolitan limits of Chicago, but any number can be found in surrounding Cook and near-by counties.

It was in this farmhouse that the largest branch of the Van Natta clan of Chicago was founded. Descendants of this pioneer Dutch family now live in all sections of the city. One of the best known today is John E. Van Natta, lawyer, soldier, and one-time candidate for Congress. He was born in the tiny Armitage Avenue farmhouse in 1872, and his present home at 5319 Agatite Avenue stands within the boundaries of what was formerly Jefferson Township.

The man who built the small Armitage Avenue farmhouse

was Attorney Van Natta's father, James, who had arrived in
this section a few years after it was organized as a township
in 1850. This pioneer's father, John, had come to Chicago in
1836 from his birthplace on the Hudson River, but he did not
remain here long, moving westward to a small farm near
Aurora.

JAMES VAN NATTA HOME
4618 Armitage Avenue

Here James was born in 1838. On reaching maturity he
drifted away from the family farm to Chicago and then went
to live in Jefferson Township. There he became acquainted
with Mary Jane Merrill, daughter of George M. Merrill,
proprietor of a tavern at Whiskey Point—as the intersection
of Grand and Armitage avenues was called in early days.

The two were married in 1858 and were presented with
eighty acres of land by the bride's father. Upon this their
farmhouse was erected—the house that still stands today on
Armitage Avenue. It is now eighty-two years old.

The Van Nattas were the parents of four children when Mrs. Van Natta died. A few years later James brought a new wife into the farmhouse, Martha Eleanor Allen of Griggsville, Illinois.

Four more children were born of this second marriage, including John, now the leading member of the Van Natta clan in Chicago. Additions had to be built to the farmhouse to take care of this large family.

Meanwhile, the township was filling up with more farmers and home-seekers, improvements were made, and many new roads and streets laid out. After the township was changed to a village in 1872, James Van Natta was elected commissioner of village streets. In the 1880's he was elected a justice of the peace and a trustee of the village board. Even after the township was annexed to Chicago by popular vote in 1889, James continued to be active in community affairs.

By 1909, when most of the early farms were subdivided into lots and new homes were appearing on all sides, James Van Natta gave up the farmhouse and moved away. His children were now grown up and living in other sections of the city. Subsequently, the farmhouse was occupied for thirteen years by Michael Fashing and his family.

The man who built this Northwest Side landmark, who founded a large family here and played a constructive role in the early history of this part of the city, died in 1924 at the Portage Park home of his son, John. How much longer this old farmhouse will stand, no one can tell.

A Link with the Past

WHEN the greater part of the present Northwest Side of Chicago was prairie and farm land outside the city limits and Indians could still be seen on the roads, there stood at what is now the busy commercial intersection of Milwaukee and Armitage avenues a well-known and hospitable inn called the Powell House. It was conducted by George N. Powell, early settler and farmer of Jefferson Township and the man after whom, until recently, Powell Avenue was named. That street, which runs through the original Powell farm, is now called Campbell Avenue.

A popular stopping-place for farmers driving their wagons to town along the muddy Milwaukee Plank Road during pioneer years, Powell House itself has long since disappeared, but a direct link to that early hostelry still remains—the home in which lived Innkeeper Powell's son, William H. Powell. This dwelling, located at 2122 North Western Avenue, stands only a few blocks north of the site of Powell House and looks quaint, prim, and old fashioned in contrast to the modern apartment houses and dwellings crowding it on all sides.

There was a time, however, when this house was in the height of architectural fashion and something of a show place

355

in old Jefferson Township. When it was built in 1868, its owner was well known in that territory not only as the son of Innkeeper Powell but as a real estate man and subdivider. In association with his brothers, John F. and Perry, he had sub-

WILLIAM H. POWELL HOUSE
2122 North Western Avenue

divided sixty-three of the original one hundred and sixty acres acquired by his father in 1832 from the government.

Several years after William Powell built his home on Western Avenue, the old Powell inn, which had stood on Milwaukee Avenue since shortly after the elder Powell had settled here, was torn down and a new three-story hotel was erected in its place by the brothers. The elder Powell died in 1851, when the brothers were still young. Upon reaching maturity the brothers entered the real estate field.

Five years after settling down in his new home, to which he brought his widowed mother, William Powell married Eliza J. Richie of Milwaukee. A son was born to the couple and was named George H. He now lives in Florida. In *Chicago and Its Suburbs*, a book written by Everett Chamberlain and published in 1874, the Powell home is described at some length and illustrated with a drawing.

"The residence illustrated," writes the author, "is a first-class frame structure costing $8,000, located on Western Avenue on a five-acre lot, which is covered with fruit and shade trees. Mr. P. sells from 500 to 600 bushels of cherries from his trees every year. The land and improvements are held worth $100,000; an offer of $75,000 was recently refused by Mr. Powell."

The author went on to say that the original Powell tract was bounded on the east by Western Avenue, on the north by Fullerton Avenue, on the west by what is now California Avenue, and on the south by Armitage Avenue.

In another and larger volume, A. T. Andreas' *History of Cook County*, we learn that William Powell's father was one of the earliest gardeners of Jefferson Township and that in this work he was associated with M. N. Kimball, another settler, and that the two employed nine men during the summer season. It was Kimball who gave the name "Jefferson" to the township when it was organized.

Andreas tells how the elder Powell became concerned one day over a party of surveyors who were straightening out Milwaukee Avenue, which had been a meandering Indian trail and wagon road. He was afraid the line of the new road would miss his hostelry. So he erected a flag over it and went down the road to meet the surveyors. He said that if they would make a beeline for the flag he would serve them the best wines and whiskies in his tavern.

His proposition, according to Andreas, was accepted, and "the boys had a good repast." They took enough on board to last them to the next tavern north, just beyond what is now Irving Park Road. "Here," says Andreas, "some scoundrel must have served crooked whisky to the surveying party, for the road runs zigzag from then on."

William Powell and his brothers continued in the real estate business for some years but gave up the second Powell Hotel, which was torn down and replaced by a business block. One of the brothers, John F., went to Waukegan and settled there. His son's widow, Mrs. George N. Powell, is living there today.

Just when William Powell gave up ownership of the Western Avenue house is not known. The edifice was later bought by a Mr. and Mrs. Frank Beck.

For the last three decades the Powell home has been owned and occupied by Herman Becker and his wife, Katharine, both of whom came to Chicago from Germany in the 1880's. In 1890 the Beckers moved to the Armitage-Milwaukee neighborhood, and Mr. Becker set up a compressed-yeast plant in the neighborhood. Today he is in the coal business.

Upon taking over the house in 1909, Mr. Becker made few alterations. The interior, with its tall, thick, paneled doors and trim of white pine, its arched door and window frames, and its ornamental fireplaces, remains much the same as when William Powell lived there.

Similarly unchanged is the exterior. Here may be seen a small ornate tower that rises over the gabled roof, bay windows, fanciful cornices, the old hickories that shade the grounds in summer, and, at the rear, a new stand of cherry and other fruit trees grown by Mr. and Mrs. Becker.

The House in Haussen Court

AT THE northwest corner of Milwaukee Avenue and Haussen Court, behind a picket fence in a spacious yard where a big frame residence is also located, stands a small gable-roofed, wooden dwelling that is of more interest than most of the other houses on the completely built-up Northwest Side of Chicago.

For this attractive little abode, with its clapboard siding, narrow porch, and brick basement, dates from the very beginning of that part of the city. Today it houses the fourth generation of a pioneer family that helped to build the Northwest Side.

The name of the man who erected this house and who settled here more than three-quarters of a century ago when this area was mostly prairie is perpetuated today in the street that adjoins the little dwelling. This man was Ferdinand F. Haussen, stone and brick contractor of the 1860's and 1870's, early settler and public official of the old township of Jefferson and in later years an alderman and civic leader.

A native of the kingdom of Prussia, where he was born on August 14, 1830, Ferdinand Haussen, after receiving an education and learning the mason's trade in his homeland, came to the United States in 1850 and for two years worked as a mason in New York City. He then came westward to Chicago and aided, as a mason, in building many brick and stone edifices of the 1850's. While doing this work he met Miss Marie Seegers, who had come to Chicago earlier from Hanover, Germany. They were married in 1856.

Soon afterward he and his brother-in-law, Charles Seegers, obtained a horse and buggy and went up the Milwaukee Plank Road in search of land. The result of this trip was the purchase of 33 acres—Haussen buying 16½ acres and his brother-in-law buying 16½ acres adjoining.

At this time the area was sparsely settled. It was in the township of Jefferson, organized only a few years earlier, and served by the old Milwaukee Plank Road, now Milwaukee Avenue. Here and there were the farms of pioneer settlers. Stagecoaches were still in use, but railroads were beginning to appear. Haussen's nearest neighbors were John Sweeney and Charles Kimball. The last named is remembered today in Kimball Avenue.

Soon after buying his land, Ferdinand Haussen, with the aid of his brother-in-law, built the frame house that still stands today. Its present address is 3146 Milwaukee Avenue. Into it he brought his wife, and here the two lived for the remainder of their lives, rearing a large family and entertaining many of the other pioneer settlers of Jefferson Township.

Gradually, more newcomers appeared and built homes around the little Haussen farmhouse. In 1873 the Chicago and North Western Railroad, which went through this area, built a station at what is now Belmont Avenue and called it "Avondale." A post office was set up at the station, and here the Haussens obtained their mail from L. B. Hull, first postmaster of the village.

Meanwhile, Ferdinand Haussen had been active as a stone and brick contractor. Hired men took care of his farm and the numerous horses and stone wagons he had by this time acquired. The little farmhouse was enlarged by an addition at the rear and was now surrounded by a great barn, well house, corncrib, and smokehouse, as well as by a large orchard and vegetable and flower gardens.

FERDINAND F. HAUSSEN HOUSE
3146 Milwaukee Avenue

During these years, according to records of the West Side Historical Society, Ferdinand Haussen helped to build many residences, factories, business blocks, and public buildings in both Jefferson Township and Chicago. One of these was the Avondale School, where his friend, John H. Stehman, was principal. Haussen later took in Frank Wilke, another mason contractor, as his partner.

Soon after arriving in Jefferson Township, "Fred" Haussen

became active in township affairs and was elected a member of the village board of trustees. Later he was elected a member of the school board and served in that capacity for twenty-three years. After Jefferson Township was annexed to Chicago in 1889, he was elected alderman of the then Twenty-seventh Ward, which embraced Avondale.

Seven children were reared by the Haussens in the little farmhouse on Milwaukee Avenue. One of these was a girl, Eda. She grew up here and, upon reaching her maturity, was married in the family farmhouse to Robert Bartels, a Chicago artist. Her father then presented a two-story frame house to the newly wedded couple. This was built next door to the farmhouse and still stands today. Here the Bartels lived and reared a family of their own. Ferdinand Haussen died in 1903.

His death was deeply mourned by his daughter, Mrs. Bartels, as she had been devoted to him. The years passed, streetcars supplanted buggies on Milwaukee Avenue, more houses were built, the old Haussen tract was subdivided, and in time the neighborhood was completely built up. But the little Haussen farmhouse, under its trees in the big yard, remained intact.

Then a movement was started to change the name of Crawford Avenue, which borders the old Haussen tract on the west, to Pulaski Road in honor of General Pulaski, a hero of the American Revolutionary War. Many opposed such a change. Two factions were formed. Mrs. Bartels was indifferent to the proposed change but became greatly alarmed when she heard that an attempt was to be made to substitute the name "Crawford Court" for "Haussen Court." This, it was believed, would satisfy the Crawford adherents and leave the Pulaski faction free to accomplish its aim.

But the Pulaski group made the mistake of ignoring Mrs. Bartels. She staged a spirited fight against the change. Others joined her. In the midst of the battle she had a paralytic stroke and died soon afterward, widely mourned as "the Little Old Lady of Haussen Court." Her fight, however, had not been in vain. The short street adjoining the little Haussen home is still "Haussen Court," and from all indications it will so remain in the future.

Survivor of Pioneer Days

IN 1859, when the township of Jefferson northwest of Chicago was a sparsely settled region of truck farmers and gardeners, and stage coaches were still in use on the Milwaukee Plank Road, there was erected for one Clarke Roberts a substantial farmhouse not far from his father's home, which stood at what is now Milwaukee and Lawrence avenues. Into this house, a year later, Clarke Roberts moved with his bride and settled down as one of the leading residents of the township.

That home is still standing, though Chicago spread outward until it engulfed the Roberts home. Located at what is now 4564 Milwaukee Avenue, this frame abode, with its low-pitched gable roof and roomy porches, is a landmark of pioneer days. The master of this house was not only the son of an early settler but was one of the best-known residents of the old village of Jefferson, which was centered at what is now Milwaukee and Lawrence avenues.

A frequent visitor to the Milwaukee Avenue house during Civil War days was the owner's father, David L. Roberts. Born at Denbigh, Wales, in 1801, David Roberts came to America as a young man, married a few years later, and settled in New York State. In this state, at Utica, Clarke was born in 1829. Seeking greater opportunities, David Roberts came West with his wife and son and took up residence at Joliet.

He became a canal contractor and, when the canal project was abandoned, set up as a merchant. Evidently he prospered, for in 1842 he is discovered in Chicago as proprietor of the Chicago Temperance House, a hotel that stood on La

CLARKE ROBERTS HOUSE
4564 Milwaukee Avenue

Salle Street near Lake Street. A few years later he was among the twenty-five Chicago residents of Welsh origin who founded the Welsh Calvinistic Methodist Episcopal Church in Chicago.

In the meantime his attention was turned to the attractiveness of land in what was later to become Jefferson Township. An early history of Cook County says: "D. L. Roberts came to the township in 1844, purchased about 320 acres of land and the tavern stand of Elijah Wentworth at the village of

Jefferson. This tavern was a blockhouse two stories high. The 320 acres included all of the original village of Jefferson and the balance was in the timber to the eastward on the North Branch of the Chicago River.

"Mr. Roberts kept this hotel from 1844 to 1851, when he leased it, moved to Chicago, and kept the United States Hotel until 1853, when it was burned down. He then returned to Jefferson, bought out the lease, and kept the old Wentworth Hotel for a year or two, when he closed it. In 1864 Mr. Roberts died."

Before his passing, David Roberts achieved the distinction of being one of the organizers of the township of Jefferson. He was among the twelve leading farmers of the region who met in Chester Dickinson's tavern on Milwaukee Avenue in 1850 and laid out plans for the township. He was elected the township's first clerk and was later elected a highway overseer and a justice of the peace. In association with his wife he helped found the Jefferson Congregational Church in 1861 and donated the land for the first church edifice and parsonage.

In addition to all these activities, David Roberts continued to operate his farm. He was assisted by his son Clarke. In the course of time young Clarke Roberts became interested in Miss Elizabeth Linscott, daughter of Newton Linscott, a justice of the peace in the township. In 1860 they were married and immediately took up residence in their new house on Milwaukee Avenue.

In the years during which he lived in this comfortable home, shaded by elms and oaks and surrounded by gardens and orchards, Clarke Roberts was almost as active as his father in affairs of the township. He served as a judge in the election of 1872 when eighty-two residents, the majority, voted to change from the township to the village form of government. He had also been, at different periods, a member of the village board of trustees and of the school board and a commissioner of highways.

Four sons and two daughters were born to the Roberts' in this spacious dwelling, and here they were reared in the years before Jefferson was annexed to Chicago in 1889. The first born, Charles N., became a well-known surveyor and civil engineer in Chicago. He died in 1932 in his Wilmette home at the age of seventy-one. Another son, Roscoe Linscott Roberts, became an attorney and is still practicing in Chicago today.

Active in North Shore society at present is a daughter of the late Charles N. Roberts—Mrs. Edwin C. Austin of Glencoe. Her daughter, Barbara, made her debut three years ago. Mrs. Austin's brother, Keith Roberts, is a Chicago mining engineer, now on duty in Alaska. These and other descendants of the pioneer settler of Jefferson Township often come to Chicago for a glimpse of the old Roberts home on Milwaukee Avenue.

After the death of Clarke Roberts, just before the turn of the century, the old house was occupied by his widow. When she died in 1906, it was taken over by a son, Lewis, who lived here for many years. In 1922 the house was acquired by Val Bartnick and his wife, Verna, and this couple and their family have been living in it ever since.

Surrounded by farms and prairies when first built, the old Roberts house today stands in the midst of a populous residential neighborhood. "But the house is so old and historic-looking," says Henry Tauber, automobile dealer across the street from it, "that lots of people in cars stop to look at it on Sunday afternoons and wonder who built it and what its history is."

The Brown House

NOTICEABLE for the tall, windowed cupola on its roof, the old two-story frame house at 3812 North Pulaski Road dates from the very beginning of the now solidly built-up community of Irving Park. It was built in 1869, the same year that a group of Chicago businessmen subdivided a large tract out in the country northwest of the city and named it Irving Park.

Most of the original dwellings of Irving Park have since been torn down and replaced by modern homes and apartment houses, but by some chance this Pulaski Road edifice has survived and stands today as a reminder of that section's grandiose and spacious past.

The man who built this house, Erastus Brown, was the father of one of the founders of Irving Park, John S. Brown. It was John S. Brown, in association with Charles T. Race and his sons, Richard T. Race and W. B. Race, as well as John R. Wheeler, who purchased a large tract from Major Noble, early farmer and landowner of old Jefferson Township, and subdivided it in 1869. Later additions were made to it by another son of Erastus Brown, Dr. Adelbert E. Brown.

The story goes that Major Noble paid $2.50 an acre when he first settled in this region in 1833. At the time Dr. Brown made his purchases the prices varied from $500 to $1,000 an acre. Soon after Erastus Brown and others built their homes in Irving Park, the Chicago and North Western Railroad,

ERASTUS BROWN HOME
3812 North Pulaski Road

which ran diagonally through the area, agreed to stop trains at the new village if the founders would build a depot there. This was done, and from then on Irving Park grew into a major suburb of Chicago.

According to records of the West Side Historical Society, the first marriage in Irving Park occurred in the Brown house. This was when a daughter of Erastus Brown became the wife of a man named Juliand. The marriage took place in 1874. Another daughter, Emma, was living in the house at that time.

A native of New York State, where in his maturity he became a prosperous farmer and afterward sold his holdings, Erastus Brown arrived in Chicago shortly before taking up residence in his new dwelling out in Irving Park. His house and the landscaped grounds around it soon became a show place of the community and were greatly admired, according to old settlers, by passengers going by in the trains of the North Western road.

At that time there were "some sixty houses of unexceptionally neat pattern, and almost endless variety" in Irving Park, according to an early history, *Chicago and Its Suburbs*, written by Everett Chamberlin. He goes on to say that Irving Park "ranks very high among Chicago's suburbs, both with respect to the natural advantages of its site, and the extent and character of the improvements already achieved."

Among the sixty houses, in addition to the Erastus Brown abode, were the homes of John S. Brown and Dr. Brown. From the Chamberlin book we learn that the John Brown dwelling was a large red-brick edifice designed in the Italian villa style of architecture at a cost of $15,000. It stood on Irving Park Road, and not far from it stood the home of Dr. Brown. Both of these houses have since disappeared.

"My paternal grandfather, Erastus Brown, died about 1888, or just before the village of Jefferson was annexed to Chicago," said Miss Eleanor M. Brown, daughter of Dr. Adelbert Brown and a resident of Chicago in 1940. "After his death the house was occupied by my aunt, Emma Brown, an artist, and she continued to live there until her death a few years ago."

During the years when Miss Emma Brown presided over this dwelling it was something of a community art center, for Miss Brown conducted an art class here for the young women of the neighborhood and showed them how to do landscapes and still lifes. One of her pupils was the present Mrs. Alice Ropp, daughter of William Spikings, early settler of Jefferson Township.

Unaltered since the year it was built but always kept in good condition, the Brown house stands today as an interesting example of post–Civil War residential architecture. The cupola dominating the low-pitched roof is characteristic of that period. So, also, are the tall windows and doors with their arched frames. The interior rooms are spacious, and the main ones contain the usual adornments of a house of that era.

An interesting side light on the house is that the cupola is closed to the present occupants, as it contains many of the paintings and other personal belongings of Emma Brown. It was in this cupola, with its view over the rooftops of Irving Park, that she maintained her studio and taught her art classes. On the night of the Chicago Fire in 1871 the Brown family crowded the cupola to view the burning city to the south.

In summertime the house is still shaded by some of the cottonwoods planted by Erastus Brown almost three-quarters of a century ago. The lawn in front is bordered by lilac and snowball bushes. Still standing at the rear of the grounds is the old Brown stable. Today the dwelling is occupied by Gordon F. Purtell and his family. Mr. Purtell is connected with the American National Bank and Trust Company.

Norwood Park's First House

SHORTLY after the Chicago and North Western Railroad had built, in 1869, a small wooden station at Norwood Park, there was erected near the station a large two-story frame house with many tall, narrow windows and a big square cupola. That house is still standing on its original site and is now widely known as the first dwelling to be built in the village of Norwood Park. It also enjoys some distinction as the home of the "father" of that attractive, elm-shaded, residential suburb on the Far Northwest Side of Chicago.

The man who built this house, who first dreamed of establishing a village in this region, was George Dunlap, pioneer Illinois settler, early resident of Cook County, state representative, and founder of a leading Chicago real estate firm of the 1880's. Today the village he nurtured is a residential section of Chicago, with neat, comfortable homes on all sides, and the house in which he lived stands as a venerable shrine of the community's pioneer days.

When Dunlap built this dwelling, Norwood Park consisted of a scattered settlement of farmhouses on the prairie northwest of the city. He had come to this region after having lived, since 1840, on his father's place in near-by Leyden Township. The elder Dunlap, William, had acquired 640

372

acres in the township, and this was known in those days as
Dunlap Prairie. The family had come west to Illinois in 1836
from Jefferson County, New York, where George Dunlap was
born in 1825.

From Andreas' *History of Cook County* we learn that
George Dunlap, while still living in Leyden, had served at
various times as supervisor of that township as well as justice
of the peace and postmaster. Seeing possibilities for developing the region on both sides of the Wisconsin division of the
North Western Railroad, Dunlap moved to the spot which
became Norwood Park in 1864.

This region was then in the township of Jefferson. Upon
his election to the state legislature at Springfield, Dunlap, in
1874, introduced a bill calling for the establishment of a new
township to be known as Norwood Park. The bill was passed,
and Norwood Park came into being, having been formed from
parts of four other townships—Jefferson, Leyden, Niles, and
Maine.

Andreas goes on to tell us that the name of the new township was obtained from *Norwood*, a novel by the Reverend
Henry Ward Beecher, and that the word "park" was added
when it was discovered that another village existed named
"Norwood." Andreas says that the "first house on the plat of
the village was the Dunlap house." Note that Andreas refers
to the "village" and not the "township" of Norwood Park.

For the first two months after the North Western built a
station here, the only person to get on or off the train at Norwood Park was George Dunlap. Next to become a passenger
was Thomas H. Seymour, first postmaster of the village. As
the years went by, Dunlap saw more and more businessmen
coming with their families to settle in Norwood Park and
watched with interest the steady growth of his community.

The Dunlap house, whose address now is 5845 East Circle

Avenue, was presided over by Mrs. Dunlap, who was the former Almeda Pierce, daughter of John and Hannah Pierce. She and her husband reared a family of six children—De Clermont, Hettie, Clifton, Alice, Jessie, and Mira. A few

GEORGE DUNLAP HOME
5845 East Circle Avenue

years after settling down in his Norwood Park residence, Dunlap set up the real estate firm of Dunlap and Swift in Chicago and carried on this business during the 1880's and 1890's.

After the death of George Dunlap, the house on Circle Avenue was occupied by a son, Clifton, and his family. It was subsequently occupied by two of Clifton's sisters, Hettie and Alice. They in turn sold the house to August Ramar, who lived in it with his family for some years. Thirteen years ago Mr. and Mrs. Carl Dette moved into the old landmark and have been living in it since. Mr. Dette has been in the grocery business in Chicago for more than forty years.

The Dettes have kept the historic dwelling in shipshape condition. Set back on spacious grounds, shaded by great elms, its porch extending clear across the front, this old white-painted house has the appearance of a stately New England dwelling of the pre–Civil War era.

It is an interesting example of a style of residential architecture popular in those early days. Here, for instance, is that distinguishing appurtenance of the era, the cupola. Here, too, is a large roomy porch, indicative of a time when people lived more leisurely.

The interior of the house, consisting of about ten rooms, has been preserved in its original state. All the rooms are large and lofty, reflecting a more spacious era than ours, and the woodwork and trim are pleasing to the eye. It is a house, in short, where the Dunlap family, with six sons and daughters, had plenty of room in which to live, and from the porch of which they saw Norwood Park grow into a restful, parklike residential suburb.

*Association House**

THEY call it the "Gray House." Of frame construction with high windows and doors, its exterior painted pigeon-gray, this dwelling, which stands at North Avenue and Leavitt Street, is easily recognized as a neighborhood landmark. And so it is—as some of the oldest of the old-timers on the Northwest Side will tell you.

Built about three-quarters of a century ago when this section was mostly prairie and farm land, the house is of interest today as the original Association House, earliest of social settlements in that part of Chicago. It is still part of the settlement, housing residents and university students connected with the social center.

In the days when it was a private dwelling, however, the few scattered settlers around it called it "the House on the Hill." They say that it stood on a small, natural hill and could be seen for miles around. Today you can still see traces of this hill, for the house rests on a mound slightly higher than the level of North Avenue. And in front of it are several gnarled old trees surviving from the grove that once shaded the hilltop residence.

Before Association House was established here in 1899, the dwelling had been for many years the home of William T.

* Demolished since this book went to press.

Johnson, a political figure and businessman of the 1880's, according to information from the West Side Historical Society. Johnson, a Republican, was a state senator in 1879 and was, in 1882, elected treasurer of Cook County. He had also served as a member of the State Warehouse Commission.

WILLIAM T. JOHNSON HOME
2150 West North Avenue

But before this time Johnson was in the hardware and cutlery business with Harlan P. Kellogg and George E. Bliss.

"From what we can find, the property on which the house is located was conveyed to Katherine A. E. Johnson, wife of William T. Johnson, in 1864," said Miss Pearl I. Field, honorary life-president of the West Side Historical Society and librarian of the Legler Branch of the Chicago Public Library on South Crawford Avenue. "It is reasonable to suppose that Johnson and his wife built the house around that time. In any case, the Johnsons lived here until a few years before Association House was established in it."

Further research shows that Mrs. Johnson was a daughter of Nathan Allen, early settler of the Northwest Side and one of the first police magistrates to be elected in what was then called West Town.

When the Johnsons lived in their "House on the Hill"— which stands on a site said to have been a meeting place of Indians—a large truck garden and cabbage patch operated by a tenant farmer named Krebs lay to the north of it. After the death of his wife, Johnson moved out of the house, and for a number of years it was occupied by one Henry Seep, who had worked for Johnson.

Meanwhile, the section around it was filling up with homes, a business district grew up at Milwaukee and North Avenues, and Wicker Park was established near by as a closely knit residential community. By the time Association House was founded here the neighborhood was pretty well built up. Immigrants from Central Europe, most of them Polish, occupied homes and tenements on all sides, and the need for a social settlement arose.

In looking about for suitable quarters, the founders of Association House settled on the old Johnson home as being the most suitable for their purpose. Here many poverty-stricken foreign families, irrespective of creed, were aided in getting a foothold in the New World. The scope of the work increased so greatly that by 1905 it was found necessary to erect a large brick building next door to the "Gray House." But the staff that operates the institution, which directs recreational activities for hundreds of neighborhood boys and girls, lives in the "Gray House." The director of Association House is the

Reverend Mr. Edwin Eells. He has been head for many years.

Standing on its sandy knoll beyond the sidewalk, above the noise of streetcars, automobiles, and trucks in North Avenue, "Gray House" looks down with the dignity of age and seems proud of the fact that it is still doing its work of providing shelter for human beings. The edifice has been kept in good repair, and very few alterations have been made in its interior.

The house remains as an example of typical residential architecture during the Civil War era. The windows are very tall and narrow, as are the doors with their ornamental bronze doorknobs. All main rooms are equipped with marble fireplaces, sliding doors, and high, decorated ceilings.

The Spikings Homestead*

WHEN the present intersection of Lawrence Avenue and Pulaski Road, now a busy shopping and commercial center, was a muddy country crossroad, there was built, just north of this point, a comfortable brick farmhouse. It attracted attention then as the home of the grandson of one of the first settlers of the region.

That house is still standing. But, instead of farms and prairies, it is now surrounded by rows of apartment houses, two-story flat buildings, stores, schools, and churches. Only a few blocks to the north are located the Chicago Municipal Sanitarium and the Bohemian National Cemetery. Streetcars, busses, and automobiles have supplanted the buggies and hay wagons that once creaked and rumbled in front of this house.

Of greater interest than the age of the house, however, is the man who lives in it today. He is the same man who built it with his own hands, brick by brick, seventy years ago, or at the time of the Chicago Fire. Now ninety-two years old, he enjoys the distinction of having spent his entire life on the property originally acquired by his grandfather.

This man is William Harding Spikings, a retired building contractor and head of a Chicago family that includes three sons, two daughters, six grandchildren, and five great-grand-

* Demolished since this book went to press.

children. His wife, Minnie, died in the old brick homestead in 1936 at the age of eighty-six. She had been brought to it as a bride in 1874. When she was ten years old, her parents brought her to Chicago from their native land, Sweden.

Two years before the area was incorporated as the township of Jefferson—and forty-one years before the township

WILLIAM H. SPIKINGS HOME
4853 North Pulaski Road

was annexed to Chicago—William Spikings came into the world in a log cabin acquired by his grandfather from an Indian chief and which stood on his grandfather's original tract near what is now Avers and Argyle avenues. As a child William Spikings often saw Indians going by on the muddy roads of Jefferson Township.

The father of the boy was Richard Young Spikings, who had quit the little wooden frontier city of Chicago in 1840, gone up the north branch of the Chicago River, and had got work on a farm in the vicinity of the present Spikings homestead. Here he became acquainted with Cornelia Harding, daughter of a farmer, married her, and was presented a large tract of land by his father-in-law. He later became a trustee of the village of Jefferson.

This marriage would not have occurred and there would probably have been no Spikings homestead today if, according to a family legend, William Harding, father of Mrs. Spikings, had not had a lucky break earlier in his career.

On his way over from England, he and other passengers were cast adrift on a raft when their vessel foundered. After several days of starvation they were reduced to such straits that they even ate the leather of their shoes. Finally, in utter desperation, so the story goes, they cast lots to select one from among them who was to be killed for food. William Harding was the unlucky man, but just before he was to be sacrificed they sighted the coast of Maine.

"With all his possessions gone, my great-grandfather did odd jobs in Maine and then drifted down to New York," explained Mrs. Alice Ropp, daughter of William Spikings, with whom she lives, and widow of Silas Ropp, member of an old Irving Park family. "In New York he set up a hog farm at what is now Central Park. Then he came to Chicago and by 1836 had acquired a section of land out in the country northwest of Chicago."

This land purchase begins the story of the present Spikings homestead, which is located at 4853 North Pulaski Road. William Harding is said to have acquired his 640 acres at eight dollars an acre. Today this tract would be roughly bounded by Lawrence Avenue on the south, Kedzie Avenue on the east, the north branch of the Chicago River (which runs east and west at this point) on the north, and Pulaski Road on the west.

After marrying Harding's daughter, Richard Y. Spikings

came into possession of sixty acres of the original Harding tract at the northeast corner of what is now LawrenceAvenue and Pulaski Road. These sixty acres were left to his son, William, and it was here the latter built his brick farmhouse and reared his family. Harding Avenue, which runs north and south through the sixty-acre portion, was named after William Harding.

What enabled William Spikings to build his homestead of brick was the fact that he operated a brickyard not far from the spot where his birthplace stood. As the years went by, Mr. Spikings worked hard, reared his family, held on to his property, and saw the city slowly creeping up.

By 1912 the real estate development he had waited for so long was about to get under way, and in that year he sold half an acre at the northeast corner of Lawrence Avenue and what was then Crawford Avenue (now Pulaski Road) for $8,000— or two thousand times the price his grandfather had paid seventy-six years before.

Today the Spikings homestead, a two-story, gable-roofed dwelling with wide porches on two sides and set back on tree-shaded grounds, presents an odd appearance as it stands there among tall, modern apartment houses. In the summer it is a restful and attractively rustic spot. The rooms still retain their old-fashioned atmosphere.

And on the porch, seated in a rocker, a cane by his side, Mr. Spikings often sits of a summer's evening. His daughter said that on these occasions he frequently talks of the days when the region around his brick house was mostly grassy prairies and truck farms.

$\mathcal{A}$ $\mathcal{P}$olish-$\mathcal{A}$merican $\mathcal{L}$andmark

〰〰〰〰〰〰〰〰〰〰〰〰〰〰〰〰〰〰〰〰〰〰〰〰

SURVIVING as something of a memorial to a noted Chicagoan of Polish birth, a man who established one of the first Polish-language newspapers in the United States and who played a leading role in the Chicago of the 1890's, is the big, three-story frame dwelling at 5917 Diversey Avenue, on the Far Northwest Side. It was originally built as a country home on a ten-acre estate, but today the house is surrounded on all sides by modern bungalows, two-story flat buildings, and apartment houses.

Although this abode has become a landmark of the new Hanson Park section, few residents of the neighborhood knew its story until it was uncovered recently by Miss Lois Bergh, member of the West Side Historical Society and a resident of Hanson Park.

It was back in the middle 1880's, when this section was prairie land dotted by farms, that Wladislaus Dyniewicz, editor of the first Polish newspaper in the city, the *Gazeta Polska*, went there, bought ten acres of ground, and erected a sixteen-room house. It was to be his country house, similar to the country house of his ancestors in Poland.

He realized his dream. For more than a quarter of a century this big white house, set in a grove of linden trees on landscaped grounds, was the summer home of the Dyniewicz family. The house was purposely built large because there were eight Dyniewicz children, and Mr. Dyniewicz, in keep-

WLADISLAUS DYNIEWICZ HOME
5917 Diversey Avenue

ing with the hospitable traditions of his race, liked to entertain week-end guests, many of whom were notable Chicagoans.

Before this house was built, he had established his newspaper, aided in founding the Art Institute of Chicago, the Polish National Alliance, St. Stanislaus and Holy Trinity churches, and had helped to organize several workingmen's groups and building and loan associations. He had also sponsored numerous editions of Polish books.

Among his intimate friends were Joseph Medill, editor; John J. Mitchell, banker; J. Ogden Armour, meat packer; and Victor F. Lawson, founder and publisher of the *Chicago Daily News*. In later years one of his intimates was Anthony Czarnecki, former collector of customs for Chicago and now a member of the editorial staff of the *Chicago Daily News*.

Born in Poland and educated there, Dyniewicz fled his native land in 1863 to escape persecution during his country's struggle for freedom. He came to America, went first to Chatsworth, Illinois, and then, in 1867, arrived in Chicago and obtained employment with the McCormick Harvester Company and, later, with the Chicago and North Western Railroad. He established his newspaper in 1873.

It was in the large library on the first floor of his country house that Dyniewicz pursued his scholarly hobbies and originated the policies that made his paper widely read among the ever growing population of Polish-Americans in Chicago. The *Gazeta Polska* was subsequently merged with the *Gazeta Katolicka*, and in 1911 Mr. Dyniewicz joined the Smulski Publishing Company.

"When I was a young girl," says Mrs. Stanley J. Kuflewski, one of the Dyniewicz daughters, "my father's house could be seen for several miles around. It was white, with green shutters and a red roof, and stood across the street from where it is now located. There were porches on the front and sides and the foundation was made of field stone."

An indication of the hospitality offered in this mansion during its heyday comes from the story told by Mrs. Catherine Gryczewski, who now conducts a grocery across the street from the house. Her father, Joseph Babicz, was a chum of Mr. Dyniewicz, and she was a guest there numerous times.

She says that on Sunday afternoons there were always many friends of the Dyniewicz family present who had driven out from the city in their buggies.

"There used to be a small observation tower on the roof of the house, and from there Mr. Dyniewicz could keep a sharp outlook along Diversey Avenue, then a prairie road," says Mrs. Gryczewski. "If he spotted guests coming in a buggy or on foot, he would rush downstairs and order some chickens prepared for cooking."

The many rooms of this great house were large and comfortable. On cold days they were heated by two furnaces. The front windows were decorated with leaded glass. The interior stairway, with its cherry-wood balusters, was wide and impressive and led to numerous guest rooms on the second floor. Here the Dyniewicz family lived until 1917. In that year the estate was sold, and the land subdivided and improved with streets and new homes.

The chatelaine of this notable house during its great days, Mrs. Albertyna Dyniewicz, died in 1921 at the age of seventy-eight, and her husband passed away seven years later at the age of eighty-five. They were survived by six children, twenty grandchildren, and eighteen great-grandchildren.

PART XII

Englewood and Vicinity

Introduction

On the Southwest Side of Chicago, far beyond the Stock Yards, lies the old and thriving community of Englewood. Its shopping and business district at Sixty-third and Halsted streets is one of the most active and crowded of such districts in the city. Beyond the stores, shops, and office buildings of this business area, in many quiet streets lined with trees and shrubbery, stand rows and rows of frame and brick dwellings, some few of them built in the days when Englewood was a village outside the city and was called Chicago Junction. This early name arose from the fact that several railroads intersected here. When a number of fine homes were built at Chicago Junction and the community showed signs of developing into a residential area, the name "Englewood" was substituted for Chicago Junction. In 1869 the Cook County Normal School was established in Englewood. The community grew and in 1889 was annexed to Chicago.

A Country Estate

ONE of the show places of suburban Chicago during the Civil War years and for some time afterward, according to local historians and old settlers, was the John Raber estate on the outskirts of what was then the village of Englewood. Consisting of a two-story, English basement residence and several acres of attractively landscaped grounds, the place was widely known as the most magnificent estate to be found anywhere "out in the country" south of Chicago.

In an old volume, *Chicago and Its Suburbs*, published in 1874 and written by Everett Chamberlin, the Raber place is described, and the description is accompanied by a full-page artist's conception of the house and grounds. "It is located," wrote the author, "on State Street, directly opposite Fifty-eighth Street, fronting eastwards toward the south parks, and is the most attractive and homelike residence in the village [Englewood].

"As will be seen, the house stands in the center of handsomely arranged grounds, consisting of six acres, and, although the building itself is not remarkable for its beauty, its surroundings are such as to render the general view very inviting. Within the enclosure are finely graveled walks and drives, bordered with beautiful arbor vitae hedges. Miniature lakes, filled with goldfishes, and other pleasing features are to be met with on every hand."

JOHN RABER HOUSE
5760 Lafayette Avenue

Some idea of the rapid rise of land values in those years may be gained from the fact that John Raber, as disclosed by the author of the book, purchased the house and grounds in

1862 for $17,000 and twelve years later the same place, diminished to six acres, was considered worth $75,000.

As to the identity of John Raber, the author gives us no clue. Our own investigation shows that at about the time Raber purchased this place he was serving as city collector for Chicago and that previously he had conducted a tavern in Archey Road, later called Archer Avenue. He was a son of Philip Raber, who had come to Chicago in 1839 and had become one of the leaders of the little group of German-Americans then living in the city.

It appears that John Raber and his family occupied the Englewood estate until the year 1876, at which time it was purchased by John W. Rumsey, one of Chicago's most successful commission merchants and Board of Trade operators of that day. He had come to Chicago in 1855, served as a lieutenant in the Civil War, and, after being associated with his brother, I. P. Rumsey, in the commission business, founded a commission house in partnership with J. W. Conley.

As with its previous owner, the estate's new owner took pains to preserve it in the best possible condition as a show place. What it looked like in the years when the Rumseys, with their large brood of children, lived here, is told by Mrs. Henry J. Seiter, who, as the daughter of John C. Teufel, pioneer Chicago meat packer, lived next door to the estate.

"It was perfectly beautiful, and many people driving by in their buggies in State Street used to stop and admire it," she said. "The grounds, with the main gate on State Street, were landscaped like a formal European garden. There were rows of elms, artistic flowerpots, statues, evergreen trees, stone walks, a big round fountain, arbor vitae hedges, and many little artificial lakes with goldfish in them."

If this estate attracted so much attention in the early village of Englewood and was the home of two important Chicagoans, what of the man who created it and was its original
owner? Research discloses that the man who laid out this
place and built the house was one Dr. Rudolph Walenta, who
came from Germany about 1850.

It seems that soon after his arrival here he became associated with Fred and Emma Rosenmerkel in an apothecary
shop on Wells Street, near Madison, and that he afterward
prospered. The records show that Dr. Walenta and his wife,
Francisca, purchased the ten acres in Englewood in 1853 from
the Rosenmerkels. Just when the house was built, the records
do not show.

Today all that is left of this country show place of the
1860's is the house, its present address being 5760 Lafayette
Avenue (formerly South Dearborn Street). Much remodeled
and grown old and shabby with the years, it stands in the midst
of the Black Belt, tall, ancient, its cupola still dominating the
neighborhood. Numerous Negro families occupy its three
floors and basement. All around it, where once was an attractive estate, crowd the ramshackle cottages and houses and
the barren, dusty streets of the city's Negro section.

An Englewood Show Place

ONE of the oldest and historically most interesting houses in Englewood, a section which celebrated the fiftieth anniversary of its annexation to Chicago in 1939, is the ancient frame dwelling, topped by a highly ornamental cupola, at 214 West Sixty-first Place. A show place of the 1860's and 1870's because of its imposing architecture, this house was built and occupied by an early settler of the community, and here, in the parlor, was organized one of the first churches in Englewood.

The man who erected the house, according to the Englewood Historical Association, was Ira J. Nichols, a successful Chicago lawyer of the pre–Civil War era and one of Englewood's first settlers. He had come to Chicago in 1854 and soon had made rapid progress in the practice of law. By 1860 he had acquired sufficient means to join his brother in the purchase of eighty acres of land "out in the country" south of Chicago at a place called Chicago Junction—afterward the site of Englewood.

A native of the Lake George region of New York, where he was born in 1824, Ira Nichols had come to Chicago during the great westward movement of the first half of the nineteenth century. With him came his brother, Daniel C., who also was a member of the legal profession. While practicing law in the city, Ira Nichols lived with his family in a small frame house where the Dearborn Street Station now stands.

Having become successful, Ira Nichols looked about and decided to settle to the south at Chicago Junction. This place was so named because it was a "junction" of several railroads

IRA J. NICHOLS HOME
214 West Sixty-first Place

entering Chicago. The land he and his brother bought was then unimproved, and scattered around it were the modest homes of a few early settlers—the Wilcoxes, Gerbers, Patricks, Burkeys, Clarks, and Crockers.

It is said that the Nichols brothers paid $1,800 for the eighty acres they bought at Chicago Junction. Today this tract is bounded by Fifty-ninth Street on the north, Wallace

Street on the west, Sixty-third Street on the south, and Wentworth Avenue on the east. Within it is a part of the thriving Sixty-third Street business area as well as Englewood High School and a solidly built-up residential section. A well-known street running through this tract, Princeton Avenue, was formerly called Nichols Avenue, after Ira Nichols.

The big residence on Sixty-first Place, now a residential landmark of Englewood, was built by Ira Nichols in 1861. It is said to have cost $40,000. Not only was it occupied by Ira Nichols and his family but here also lived his brother-in-law, John Hastings. The big house then stood on a knoll a little west of its present site and faced the road that was to become Wentworth Avenue.

"From data we have gathered, the Nichols house in those early days was something of a show place," explained Miss Minnie S. Clark, librarian of the Hiram Kelly Branch of the Chicago Public Library on Normal Boulevard, where the Englewood Historical Association has its headquarters. "Standing on its knoll, it was surrounded by a white picket fence, landscaped grounds, and a garden and orchard. People going by in buggies, we are told, used to admire its impressive architecture and the setting in which the house stood."

Although he had settled outside the city, Ira Nichols was a farsighted man and knew that some day Englewood would grow and develop. In *The Story of Englewood*, edited by Gerald L. Sullivan, we read: "Ira Nichols caused much amusement in those days by his oft-repeated prophecy that streetcars would some day be running from the city to Englewood and that its streets would also some day be lighted by gas. Although he was a substantial businessman, a good many people thought he had bats in his belfry because he harbored such absurd and unreasonable ideas."

During the late 1860's, Ira Nichols and his wife, Eleanor, sponsored Sunday services of the Baptist faith in the parlor of their home. This led to talk of founding a Baptist church. At a meeting in the Nichols house on January 31, 1872, it was decided to establish a church, and thus came into being the Englewood Baptist Church. Today this church, at Englewood and Stewart avenues, has one of the largest congregations in the community.

Six children were either born or reared in the Nichols home. The youngest of these was Daniel H. Nichols, now sixty-eight years old, retired and living at 312 West Sixty-first Place, a block west of the old Nichols residence. He was for years an electrical contractor. When he was a boy, he and his brothers and sisters often played in the cupola of their home, from where they could see Lake Michigan. Daniel Nichols' father died in this house about 1880, and the place was afterward possessed by various members of the family.

Some years ago the dwelling was bought by a family named Fleck. It was subsequently sold to the Gates family, and this family still owns it. The interior has been somewhat remodeled and is now occupied by three tenants. One of these, Mrs. Minnie Hamilton, who has lived here many years, says that the venerable residence has always been an object of admiration among old-time residents of Englewood.

In its prime the Nichols house was on a par with the best examples of this type of dwelling. Its rooms were typical of the era—tall, spacious, trimmed with fine woods, separated by great sliding doors, and adorned by decorative marble fireplaces and fancy gas chandeliers. As for its exterior, the windowed cupola on the low-pitched roof is one of the most ornamental to be seen in Chicago today. Similarly elaborate is the cornice with its scroll-like brackets and wide overhang.

This house, as well as many others in Englewood surviving from the days when this section was a suburban community, came in for special attention during the Englewood Golden Jubilee celebration, which was arranged by Willis E. Tower, head of the jubilee committee and president of the Englewood Historical Association.

Baronial Tastes

ALTHOUGH built by an obscure Chicago architect of foreign birth who is said to have claimed descent from European nobility, the big château-like mansion at 7614 South Union Avenue has for years been known as the "Ellsworth House." It was so called because here lived Henry Ellsworth, a well-known Chicago commission merchant during the early years of the present century and a veteran member of the Board of Trade.

This house is one of the most conspicuous of many residential landmarks in Auburn Park. It is of frame construction and designed in the grand style of the Victorian era. High-peaked gables, pointed towers, dormers, and round bay windows are noticeable. A spacious porch, approached by wide steps, sweeps across the front. On one side of the house stands a gable-roofed porte-cochere.

All of this seems to indicate that the designer of this stately residence had baronial tastes. But there is no evidence that he was actually a baron or a descendant of one. All that is known of him is that he was an architect named Jules de Horvath who practiced his profession in Chicago during the 1870's.

Judging from the magnificence of the dwelling he designed, De Horvath must have been a well-to-do architect. But there is no mention of him in any of the reference books of the 1870's that correspond to the *Who's Who* volumes of today. A city directory of the period gives his full name, his profes-

HENRY ELLSWORTH HOME
7614 South Union Avenue

sion, and the address of his home on South Union Avenue, which then was called Sherman Avenue.

It is evident, however, that he was an early settler of Auburn Park, for he built his great house soon after that suburb was subdivided in 1871. At that time it was outside the city limits on the Rock Island Railroad. Today it is part of the city and is completely built up.

So far as can be determined, De Horvath lived in his mansion for twenty-seven years, or from the infancy of Auburn Park until it was well on the way to becoming a thriving and exclusive suburb. In the year 1898, however, he sold his house to Henry Ellsworth, who had but a short time before founded the commission house of Ellsworth and Cross.

There is no available record of De Horvath's subsequent career. The story has persisted down to this day that he had claimed kinship to a noble Austrian or Hungarian family. That there might be some basis for his claim is indicated by the prefix "De" to his surname, not always, of course, a sign of noble lineage.

At the time Ellsworth came into ownership of the Union Avenue house he was fifty-two years old, a successful Chicago businessman and the father of three children. Born in McHenry County in 1846, he had come to Chicago as a young man and had found employment with the Underwood Packing Company. Soon he had charge of that company's sales department on the Board of Trade.

He left the Underwood company in 1891 to join the International Packing Company as its representative on the Board of Trade. Here he remained until the Spanish-American War, when he became president of the Ellsworth and Cross Company, commission merchants dealing in grain and other provisions.

After becoming a resident of Auburn Park, Henry Ellsworth took an interest in the affairs of the suburb. He was an active supporter of the Episcopal church in the community and a staunch Republican. As his hobby was golf, he was an enthusiastic member of the Auburn Park Golf

Club. His wife, Ada, was a popular hostess of the community.

In their huge residence the Ellsworths entertained often, reared their three children, and looked after the shrubs and flower gardens that grew under the estate's tall elms and sycamores. They sold the house in 1915. Henry Ellsworth died in 1923 at the home of his son, Huber H. Ellsworth, in Beverly Hills.

Today the Ellsworth house is owned and occupied by Mrs. Lucille Duff and her family. The dwelling remains largely unaltered since the year it was built. There are fourteen rooms in the house. The principal rooms on the main floor are paneled in oak and adorned with tiled fireplaces, stained-glass windows, and parquet floors.

On the outside not only does the porte-cochere remain but also such adjuncts of a great house of the 1870's as a wide porch with jigsaw trim, a coach house, and those two indispensable items of the horse-and-buggy days—a cast-iron hitching post and a sandstone carriage step.

Home of a Pioneer Woman

〰〰〰〰〰〰〰〰〰〰〰〰〰〰〰〰〰〰〰〰〰〰〰〰〰

SURVIVING from the days when Englewood was a gas-lit village outside of Chicago, and Wentworth Avenue was a dirt road going past truck farms and cabbage patches, is the small, two-story brick home at 5540 Wentworth Avenue. Set back on a wide lawn, shaded in summer by a row of poplar trees, decorated with old-fashioned "gingerbread" trim and a round ornamental tower, the house is readily identified as a landmark among the modern stores, garages, and shops of the neighborhood.

Although interesting in itself, the dwelling is of wider appeal to students of local history as the home of a pioneer Chicago woman. For here lived for more than half a century Mrs. Ella R. Adkinson, who was born in 1845 on the present site of the Chicago and North Western Railroad terminal at Madison and Canal streets. She had been a member of the Chicago Woman's Club since 1890 and was a life-member of the Art Institute.

Her father was Henry Magee, an early alderman and justice of the peace who came to Chicago in a prairie schooner. Her brother, Henry W. Magee, who as a boy used to water the family cow where the *Chicago Daily News* building now stands, was a Chicago lawyer for sixty-two years and in 1930 celebrated his ninetieth birthday. Before becoming a lawyer

405

he had sailed around Cape Horn in a clipper ship and had encountered adventures in all parts of the world.

It was in 1875, several years after her marriage to Elmer W. Adkinson, an Indiana attorney who had come up to Chi-

ELMER W. ADKINSON HOME
5540 Wentworth Avenue

cago to practice law, that Mrs. Adkinson and her husband moved into the comfortable brick house on Wentworth Avenue. Only a few years earlier the name of this section had been changed from Chicago Junction to Englewood. It was then a village in the township of Lake.

At the time the Adkinsons came here, however, Englewood was experiencing a boom. Not only the Adkinsons but hundreds of other Chicagoans were building homes in Englewood and other communities outside the city limits. The Chicago Fire of 1871 was still vivid in their minds, and they wanted their homes to be located as far as possible from the central section of Chicago.

After establishing himself in one of the few brick houses in Englewood, Elmer Adkinson was soon active in affairs of the village. In a little volume, *The Story of Englewood*, edited by Gerald E. Sullivan, we find Elmer Adkinson listed among "old-timers" who became prominent in the business, social, and fraternal development of Englewood. Mrs. Adkinson was just as active as her husband, especially among church and social groups.

Here the Adkinsons lived and reared a family and saw the gradual rise of Englewood around them. They were here when their village, with many other villages of the township of Lake, was annexed to Chicago by popular vote in 1889; when streetcar tracks were laid in Wentworth Avenue; and when the Elevated first came to Englewood. They saw cottages, homes, apartment houses, and hotels, as well as business and shopping communities, appear on all sides.

With all this development going on, however, the Adkinsons managed to retain something of the old-time rustic surroundings of their place. Their apple and cherry orchards, white and pink with blossoms each spring, existed until recent years, and a vestige of these orchards still stands today—a gnarled old crabapple tree on the lawn just south of the house.

A son of the Adkinsons who spent his boyhood here, Henry M. Adkinson, was a noted baseball player on the University of Chicago team in the 1890's. In later life he went West and became a successful mining engineer. His father died in the Wentworth Avenue house in 1927. Mrs. Adkinson survived her husband by seven years, dying at the age of eighty-nine.

Living in the house today are Mrs. Ruth Hampton, a daughter of the Adkinsons, and a granddaughter, Mrs. Maxwell C. Chapman. With the latter are her husband and four young children.

The interior of the house, with its marble fireplaces, inside-shuttered windows, bays, sliding doors, and winding staircase in the tower, has not been altered and still retains its old-time atmosphere.

Helping to maintain this Victorian atmosphere are many pieces of period furniture, some of them family heirlooms, which fill the rooms. Among these are a combination secretary and bookcase of walnut, an antique clock, grand piano, marble-topped table, hall tree, buffet, and numerous walnut and mahogany dressers, tables, and chairs.

PART XIII
Literary Landmarks

Introduction

Of as much interest as the mansions of Chicago's wealthy pack-
ers, merchants, and financiers are the houses associated with
some of its famous writers, poets, and literary personalities.
In a few of these dwellings widely read books have been written
or literary careers begun. One of them was the gathering-place of
well-known men and women of letters from all parts of America
and Europe. Once referred to by a prominent literary critic
as "the most thoroughly American of American cities," Chicago
has produced many writers who have influenced the course of
American literature. Such "thoroughly American" writers as
George Ade, Frank Norris, Theodore Dreiser, Hamlin Garland,
Finley Peter Dunne, Eugene Field, William Vaughn Moody,
and Henry B. Fuller all began their careers in the midwestern
metropolis during the 1890's. What has been called the city's
second Golden Age of Letters began in 1912 and produced a large
group of distinguished writers, including Carl Sandburg, Edgar
Lee Masters, Ernest Poole, Harriet Monroe, Sherwood Ander-
son, Henry Justin Smith, Ring Lardner, Lew Sarett, Floyd
Dell, Harry Hansen, Vachel Lindsay, and Ben Hecht. Later
came Ernest Hemingway, James T. Farrell, and Donald Cul-
ross Peattie.

Where Ernest Poole
Was Reared

〰〰〰〰〰〰〰〰〰〰〰〰〰〰〰〰〰〰〰〰〰〰〰〰〰〰〰〰〰〰〰〰〰

ONE afternoon some ten years ago a little elderly man walked up the stone steps of the old mansion at 645 North Michigan Avenue and rang the bell. After explaining the purpose of his call, he was admitted by the lady of the house and shown through all the spacious rooms and hallways. And, as he looked about, a sense of awe seemed to possess him. Then he began talking.

"My, how this house takes me back to my younger days!" he said. "You see, I used to teach dancing here to the children of the house and their friends. As I look up that grand stairway now I can see little Harold McCormick coming down in his velveteen knee breeches, ready to join the dancing class with the other boys and girls. And I can remember how reluctant the boys were to learn the polka, gallop, schottische, waltz, and other dances I taught them."

That little white-haired man was the late Alvar L. Bournique, dancing master to Chicago society for more than half a century. The old mansion he was visiting survives today as the last of the great houses that bordered both sides of Upper Michigan Avenue in the days when it was an elm-bordered residential thoroughfare called Pine Street.

Although this venerable residence, standing at the south-east corner of Michigan Avenue and Erie Street, is well known to an older generation of Chicagoans, its fame today rests largely on the fact that it was the boyhood home of a

ERNEST POOLE HOME
645 North Michigan Avenue

famous American author and, as such, is regarded as one of the literary landmarks of Chicago. It is also of interest as a type of mansion popular during the period after the Chicago Fire.

Here, in his youth, lived Ernest Poole, author of *The Harbor*, *His Family*, and other realistic novels of contemporary life in America that have placed him among the foremost of this country's writers. His recent autobiography, *The Bridge*, in which he tells how his life bridges two epochs, was a best seller when first published. In it he describes his childhood and boyhood in the big mansion on what is now North Michigan Avenue.

When this twenty-five-room dwelling was in its prime, however, it was widely known as the home of Ernest's father, Abram Poole, pioneer resident of Chicago, successful businessman, and active in the city's religious and social development. He and Mrs. Poole, with their family of seven children and other relatives, reigned here from the 1870's to the turn of the century as one of the city's first families.

Born on a farm near Johnstown, New York, where his father changed the family name of Vanderpool to Poole, Abram Poole came West, worked his way as a student through Beloit College in Wisconsin, enlisted in the Union Army, served under General Sherman in Georgia, and then, after being invalided home, found his way to Chicago. Securing a job as bookkeeper at the Board of Trade, he lived in a boarding-house with a roommate, George Westinghouse.

Before he was twenty-five years old, Abram Poole bought a seat on the Board of Trade, and from that time forward his fortunes rose. We learn from *The Bridge* that his Near North Side mansion was built a few years after the fire of 1871 on the ruins of "Grandfather Howe's old home," Mr. Howe being Abram's father-in-law. It was in Mr. Howe's home that the present Fourth Presbyterian Church was founded.

Writing in *The Bridge* of his home, Ernest Poole says: "Until one by one they went East to school, the girls worked with a governess in our long schoolroom downstairs. We [the boys] worked there, too, when we were small. In that same room, for the girls and their friends, an afternoon dancing class was held. Their teacher at first was old Mr. Bournique, who taught dancing to 'all Chicago,' those days. He danced holding the skirts of his long frock coat, for that was considered elegant. Later one of his sons [Alvar] took our class, and now we boys were forced to attend."

After telling of the religious devotion of his mother, the author goes on to say: "But religion brought no gloom in our home. With seven children, four girls and three boys, the big house hummed from morning to night. . . . . Our dining-room was some thirty feet square. At the large round table we seldom had less than ten at meals, and 'the big top' for twenty was constantly being put on for dinners for my sisters and their friends."

The artistic and intellectual atmosphere maintained in their home by the Abram Pooles produced practitioners and appreciators of the arts other than Ernest. His brother, Abram, is a well-known New York painter, and another brother, Ralph, a financier (of Chicago), is an outstanding connoisseur and patron of the arts. Ernest's son, Nicholas, who lives in Chicago, also carries on the family tradition of culture.

Similar tastes are shown by Ernest Poole's three sisters, Mrs. A. Rosecrans Baldwin of Chicago and Mrs. Parmalee J. McFadden and Mrs. Walter E. Weyl, both of New York.

For the last twelve years, or since it was vacated by the Celotex Corporation, the old Poole mansion has been conducted as a "studio house" for artists, writers, and musicians by Mr. and Mrs. Albert H. Allen. Some alterations have been made in the interior, but the main floor, with its great paneled dining-room and its impressive fireplace, designed in the Greek Classic style and set back in an alcove, remains largely intact. Here the Allens continue the Sunday-night suppers started by Mrs. Poole more than half a century ago.

Carl Sandburg's Home

NUMEROUS old houses in Chicago are noteworthy not so much for their great age but as the abodes of men who were famous in their day or who began their careers in them. A dwelling that combines both aspects, however, stands at 4646 North Hermitage Avenue. For this is the one-time home of a famous poet and writer of today, and it is also a house which was erected more than half a century ago by a pioneer lawyer whose descendants formed interesting associations with Chicago life.

It was in this two-story frame house in Ravenswood that Carl Sandburg, widely known today as "the Chicago poet," as a Lincoln biographer, and as a singer of American folk ballads, began his literary career. It was in this house, too, that he wrote his most widely quoted poem, a poem that not only brought him fame but gave powerful voice to the dynamic spirit of Chicago. Entitled "Chicago," its opening lines are familiar to almost everyone:

> Hog Butcher for the World,
> Tool Maker, Stacker of Wheat,
> Player with Railroads and the Na-
> tion's Freight Handler;
> Stormy, husky, brawling,
> City of the Big Shoulders . . . .

When Carl Sandburg, at the age of thirty-five, moved with his family into this North Hermitage Avenue house, he was unknown to fame. When he moved out of it, Sandburg was renowned as a poet and as a major voice in the free-verse movement that began just before the World War. While living in this house, he had helped, with a few other local writers, to make this city the "literary capital" of America.

His first book, which marked the beginning of his literary career, was written in the Ravenswood house. This was *Chicago Poems*, published in 1915. It was a volume that contained many free-verse poems about Chicago life, including "Chicago." Here were impressions of the Clark Street Bridge, Maxwell Street, skyscrapers, a boat lost in the fog, teamsters, working girls, shovel men, and picnic boats. It was a book written by a poet who looked at Chicago honestly, realistically, and hopefully.

In this house, too, Sandburg wrote part of his second book of poetry, *Cornhuskers*, published in 1918. It portrayed the other side of the coin of life in Middle West America—the rural side. Here Sandburg wrote of the cornfields, sunsets, freight trains, farms, and dusty roads of Illinois. Son of a Swedish immigrant who had settled at Galesburg, Illinois, Sandburg had educated himself by working as a milk-wagon driver, porter, and harvest hand in small towns of the Middle West.

Research by Miss Helen Zatterberg, secretary-historian of the Ravenswood–Lake View Historical Society, shows that Carl Sandburg, with his wife, Lillian, and their two-year-old daughter, Margaret, moved into the North Hermitage Avenue house in 1913. They occupied an apartment on the second floor. The house at that time was owned by Harry S. Moniger.

Before moving into this house, Sandburg and his wife had

lived in Milwaukee. After working as a newspaper reporter there, he had been appointed secretary, in 1910, to the then Socialist mayor of that city, Emil Seidel. Sandburg served in this capacity for two years and then, in 1913, came to Chi-

CARL SANDBURG HOME
4646 North Hermitage Avenue

cago. Here he got a job as associate editor of *System Magazine*, a journal devoted to business management. This job provided him with a living, but in his leisure moments, while living in the Ravenswood house, he wrote the poems that were to bring him fame.

The Hermitage Avenue flat was presided over by Mrs. Sandburg, whom the poet had married in Milwaukee in 1908. Mrs. Sandburg is a sister of Edward Steichen, famous American portrait photographer. Recently, Mrs. Sandburg, now chatelaine of a large new Sandburg house on a pine-shaded bluff overlooking the lake at Harbert, Michigan, explained that her husband, as long ago as the Ravenswood days, had been compiling notes and data for his monumental six-volume life of Lincoln, now completed and published.

While still living in the Ravenswood house, Carl Sandburg quit his job with *System Magazine* and joined the staff of the *Day Book*, a newspaper without advertising started in Chicago by N. D. Cochran. But the paper failed after a few years. Then Sandburg joined the staff of the *Chicago Daily News*. One of Sandburg's close friends during the Ravenswood years was John L. Hervey, editor of the *Horse Review*, bibliophile, and appreciator of the arts.

The Sandburgs moved out of the Hermitage Avenue house in 1916. Since that time the house has been owned by a number of different persons, including members of a family named Wehrli, and today it is owned and occupied by the Greske family. The second floor has been improved and modernized, but the exterior remains the same as when the Sandburgs lived here. It is a rangy, two-story dwelling of frame construction, shaded by tall elms and cottonwoods.

The house was built in 1875, when Ravenswood, part of the old township of Lake View, was outside the boundaries of Chicago. It was erected by Samuel B. Gookins, a well-known Chicago lawyer of the Civil War and Chicago Fire periods who had first come to this city in 1858. A native of Vermont, Gookins had come West, had studied law in Indiana and become a judge there, and then had come up to Chicago.

His son, James F. Gookins, was a prominent artist here at the time the elder Gookins built the Ravenswood house. James was one of the founders of the old Chicago Academy of Design and was active in getting the World's Columbian Exposition for Chicago, as well as in promoting many other civic enterprises. His greatest dream for Chicago, however, was to do away with surface streetcars and build a subway.

This dream he bequeathed as a legacy to his son, Shirlaw D. Gookins, who in his mature years was a city engineer. The latter almost brought his father's dream to realization in 1907, when P. D. Armour and other Chicago capitalists were ready to back a subway project proposed by Shirlaw. But the project fell through. Today, the dream of the artist, James Gookins, is being realized at last.

An Author's Boyhood Home

~~~~~~

ANY study of literary landmarks in Chicago should include some reference to the modest, old-fashioned frame house at 2204 West One Hundred and Eleventh Street, situated "on the Hill" in old Morgan Park. For this was the childhood home of a noted author and newspaper editor whose books on Chicago are standard works and whose influence as a journalist was widely felt in the newspaper field. He was also an influence in contemporary American literature through his ability to detect and encourage writing talent.

But in addition to this association, the house is distinctive in another respect, for it is, if not the birthplace, at least the cradle of a leading American educational institution, the University of Chicago. The small group of ministers and professors who founded the present "Gothic City" on the Midway formulated their plans for it in the small parlor, lighted by kerosene lamps, of this unpretentious dwelling on the Far South Side.

It was in this house, say his closest friends, that the character of the late Henry Justin Smith, author of *Deadlines* and numerous other books and for years managing editor of the *Chicago Daily News*, was formed; and here, too, was born the literary talent that carried him to success in the writing field.

He was brought to this house as a baby of four and he left it as a cub reporter of twenty-four.

In the years between these ages, Smith, an only child, grew up in the Morgan Park home and absorbed the atmosphere of a literary, cultured, and religious household. Not only was his father, Dr. Justin A. Smith, one of Morgan Park's leading ministers and widely known in the Chicago of the 1870's as editor of *The Standard*, a Baptist publication, but he was also a scholar of distinction in other fields besides religion.

As a boy in this home the future author, surrounded by books, acquired a taste for reading and was encouraged in this pursuit by his educated father. He was guided, too, by his mother, a writer herself as well as a gifted pianist. She taught him to play the piano and instilled a love of music in him that lasted throughout his life. In addition to managing her household, she edited a woman's page in her husband's magazine, wrote religious tracts, and was active in affairs of the Morgan Park Baptist Church.

Some idea of what Morgan Park was like when H. J. Smith lived in the One Hundred and Eleventh Street house as a youth may be obtained from passages in his *Chicago: A Portrait*, published in 1931. "It was a pastoral village," he wrote, "with barefoot boys, innumerable dogs, and cows in professors' pastures. The learned theologians not only milked their own cows, if necessary, but made their own butter.

". . . . The dummy line puffed slowly and good-naturedly thither, with not enough trains a day to disturb the peace of nature. . . . . There were really two strata of society, that 'on the hill' and that 'below the hill.' Whereas the intellectual and the old-settler element dwelt mainly on the highlands, some ordinary folk . . . . occupied homes close by the old white-painted general store, or along the main line of the Rock Island.

".... Amusements, as now known, did not exist. Lights went out in the village soon after nine o'clock, save where, in some cottage, an oil flame illumined the desk of a professor writing a new denominational history. Church sociables and hayrack rides varied the monotony of winter. . . . . In those frame houses furnished with relics of New England . . . . the

HENRY JUSTIN SMITH HOUSE
2204 West One Hundred and Eleventh Street

heating was by means of iron coal stoves, the lighting that of kerosene lamps, the water was from cisterns . . . . and there were only a few practicable bathtubs in the whole village."

Then Smith goes on to hint of certain conferences in a particular Morgan Park house that occurred when he was a boy. It is in this passage that the reader gets a glimpse of the beginnings of the University of Chicago.

"In a cottage so surrounded [with roses and wild flowers]," he wrote, "and dappled by the shade of the thriving maples, there were held at a certain time lengthy conferences about a vain project to establish here, in a classic suburb, the great university, which, it was said, Mr. Rockefeller wished to found. And the stout-bodied, swarthy Dr. Harper, exhausted by a dozen irons in the fire, used to come in, fling himself down on a couch, and drop to sleep. There lived in that house a gentle being nearing seventy, whose advice many a man would seek.

"But to develop that story would take too long. Another reason is that this is not a family memoir."

The "gentle being nearing seventy" was Henry J. Smith's father. In 1860 he and a few others founded in Chicago the Baptist Theological Union. This was the parent-body of the theological seminary in Morgan Park. And it was among faculty members of this seminary, including Dr. Smith, that the movement was started to found a university.

The men who met in the Smith parlor, who at first wanted the proposed university in Morgan Park but later agreed to its location in Chicago, were Dr. William Rainey Harper, afterward first president of the University of Chicago, Dr. George W. Northup, Dr. Thomas W. Goodspeed, and F. T. Gates.

Meanwhile, these meetings did not disturb the youthful Henry Smith in his studies or playtime activities. He continued to read and thus laid the foundation for a creative bent through which he afterward produced books about newspaper life, about Chicago, and about American history that are widely read. He also wrote several volumes of fiction. His historical work, *The Master of the Mayflower*, promises to become an American children's classic.

Long after Henry J. Smith departed from his boyhood home to seek a career for himself, the house was occupied by his widowed mother. And all during these years she was visited at regular intervals by her famous son. She died there in 1925, at a time when her son was serving as assistant to the president of the University of Chicago.

Today the sixty-two-year-old Smith house is occupied by Cecil Bolton, a Morgan Park businessman. This is fortunate, for not only does Mr. Bolton realize the historical significance of his house but is at pains to keep it in good condition and to maintain the garden at the rear that was the pride of Mrs. Smith and the delight of her sensitive, artistic-minded young son.

Home of
"The Poet of Nature"

~~~~~~

AT FIRST glance it seems odd that such a well-known naturalist and author as Donald Culross Peattie, whose many books express the solitude and peace of open fields, quiet gardens, and whispering woods, should be a product of Chicago, metropolis of sky-scrapers, shunting cattle trains, mansions, tenements, street-cars, and smoking factories. When the full story of Peattie's boyhood home is known, however, this contrast does not seem so great; in fact, one feels that such a dwelling, with its surroundings, could have easily produced a naturalist or a writer.

When Donald Culross Peattie was a small boy with an impressionable mind, his home was located in an undeveloped section of the Far South Side of Chicago that had been annexed to the city but a few years earlier. It was practically open country on the shore of the lake, its sandy wastes dotted with clumps of oaks and tangled underbrush. The Peattie house is standing on the same spot today, but now it is surrounded by the residences, apartment houses, and hotels of a completely built-up neighborhood called the South Shore.

This dwelling, which stands at 7660 South Shore Drive, is

426

the one-time home of one of the best-known literary and journalistic families in Chicago's recent history. It has added appeal, too, as a landmark of the South Shore's early days, of the time when this area was outside Chicago in the old township of Hyde Park.

Large and attractive when built more than half a century ago, with wide verandas and a low-pitched roof dominated by a cupola, this two-story frame house has since been remodeled to such an extent that it is hardly recognizable, according to long-time residents of the neighborhood, as the old Peattie home. The windowed cupola has been removed and the verandas have been replaced by built-in porches veneered with stucco.

The man who built the Peattie home was Donald's maternal grandfather, Frederick Wilkinson, a Kalamazoo attorney who had come to Chicago with his family shortly after the fire of 1871. Research by Miss Helen S. Babcock, secretary-historian of the South Shore Historical Society, discloses that Frederick Wilkinson built his home in what is now the South Shore area about 1880. At that time South Shore Drive was a dirt road called Bond Avenue.

The area Frederick Wilkinson had selected for his home— there were only five other homes in the vicinity—was known as Cheltenham Beach. In his *History of Cook County*, A. T. Andreas says that Cheltenham Beach "is a residence property on the lake shore nine miles south of Chicago between Seventy-fifth and Seventy-ninth streets. It was first known as White Oak Ridge, then as Westfall's Subdivision."

Here, in the midst of trees and rolling surf on the beach, Frederick Wilkinson lived with his wife, Amanda, and four daughters. At this time he was engaged in the real estate business. Later he entered the newspaper field and became publisher and owner of the *Hyde Park Herald* and, afterward, the *Oakland Call*. A man of bookish leanings, he reared his daughters in an atmosphere of learning and culture.

One of his daughters, Elia, early showed the effect of this environment and became interested in writing. Reaching her

DONALD CULROSS PEATTIE HOME
7660 South Shore Drive

maturity, she was married in the Wilkinson home to Robert Burns Peattie, a newspaperman then on the staff of the old *Chicago Daily Herald*. This marriage took place in 1883. The following year he joined the staff of the *Chicago Daily News* as dramatic critic. His wife came with him on the *Daily News* and wrote many articles and stories. Both formed a close friendship with Eugene Field, another member of the *Daily News* staff.

When Mrs. Peattie's parents gave up their South Shore home and went back to Michigan to spend the remainder of their days, the house was taken over by the Peatties. Three children were born to them here, including Donald, whose birth date is June 21, 1898. Another child, Roderick, had been born earlier when they were temporarily living in Omaha, Nebraska. Today he is one of this country's leading geographers.

In accordance with her own upbringing, Mrs. Peattie reared her children in a literary atmosphere. Meanwhile, she and her husband attended to their newspaper and writing pursuits. In addition to writing many books of her own, Mrs. Peattie was for years literary editor of the *Chicago Tribune*. Her husband, for almost as long, was Chicago correspondent of the *New York Times*.

In such a home, whose walls were lined with books, young Donald Peattie grew up. He eagerly absorbed the contents of the books, especially volumes on natural history, and combined this study with almost daily excursions in the vicinity of his home—trips along the shell-strewn beaches, into nearby woods, along the banks of Lake Calumet, and even to the distant Indiana sand dunes. On all these trips he observed birds, flowers, trees, and the minute phenomena of nature.

It is safe to say that these early trips formed the basis of his later work and determined his career as a "poet of nature."

Some of the field excursions he took as a young man still living in the South Shore Drive home were described in a series of articles in the *Daily News* during 1925. Ten years later, in another series in the *Daily News* called "A Breath of Outdoors," he told of the attractions of nature to be found in the Chicago region.

Although he had written numerous books before this time, Mr. Peattie won national attention in 1935 when he was awarded the gold medal of the Limited Editions Club for his *An Almanac for Moderns*, deemed the most likely contemporary book to become a classic. Since then, among other volumes, he wrote *A Prairie Grove*, which described the natural as well as human history of a homestead in Illinois. *Audubon's America*, which he edited, became a best seller in 1940. Like his boyhood home, his dwelling today is within sight of a wide beach. He lives near Santa Barbara, California, with his wife and children, and his home overlooks the Pacific. His wife, Louise Redfield Peattie, is also an author, specializing in fiction.

A Literary Salon

~~~~~~

IN THE years immediately before and during the first
World War, when the spirit of American literature was
becoming more indigenous and less derivative, and Chicago was regarded as the literary capital of America, one of
the best-known literary landmarks of the city was the three-
story, red-brick mansion at 2970 Ellis Avenue.

Not only was it noted as the one-time home of a distinguished Chicago poet and dramatist but it was equally
famous as a gathering-place of more writers, both American
and foreign, than any other house in Chicago. As a literary
salon, presided over by a charming and remarkable woman,
it played the same role in Chicago life that Mme Récamier's
did in Paris or Mrs. Pennell's in London.

Today this once magnificent mansion is in a dilapidated
condition and all but falling into ruin. Because of a change
of population on the South Side, it now stands in the Negro
section of the city. Living in it now are Negro families and
several Negro evangelists. The great carved wooden doors,
through which so many notable persons once passed, are
weather-beaten and ruinous, the wide steps of the portico are
sagging, and the paint on the mansard roof is peeling off.

This was the abode of William Vaughn Moody, an outstanding American poet and playwright, whose writings,

most critics agree, helped to bring about a truly American school of literature. It was in this house that many of his poems and some of his famous dramas, such as *The Great Divide* and *The Faith Healer*, were either conceived or written. The first-named play, composed in 1909, ran for two years on Broadway.

Here lived, too, the woman who was as much, if not more, responsible for making this house famous as was her husband. A frequent visitor to the house, Charles Collins, now conductor of the "A Line o' Type or Two" column in the *Chicago Tribune*, writes (in a letter to the author) that "she [Mrs. Moody] met William Vaughn Moody in 1900. They became greatly attached to one another. She was ten or fifteen years older than Moody and gray-haired, but a beautiful woman still, romantic of temperament and abundant of vitality. Moody's closest men friends, Robert Morss Lovett and Ferdinand Schevill, were also in the circle; but Moody was the white-haired boy. He was a poet, and Mrs. Brainard was Chicago's Muse of Poetry."

Before her marriage to Moody, the chatelaine of the house on Ellis Avenue—it was then called Groveland Avenue—bore the surname of her first husband, Edwin Brainard. He was the son of Dr. Daniel Brainard, an eminent Chicago surgeon. After a few years, the couple separated. Being a woman of unusual ability and gifts, Mrs. Brainard set up a catering business in her residence and called it the "Home Delicacies Association." Before that time she had taught at Hyde Park High School, and one of her pupils then was Charles Collins, from whose letter the above statements are quoted. Mrs. Brainard's maiden name was Harriet Converse Tilden. She was the daughter of a pioneer Chicago family.

As far as can be determined, Mrs. Moody first became the presiding genius of the residence on Ellis Avenue sometime during, or shortly after, the World's Fair of 1893. From the outset she attracted literary and cultivated people about her. Many of these were from the University of Chicago. Soon William Vaughn Moody, then teaching English at the uni-

WILLIAM VAUGHN MOODY HOME
2970 Ellis Avenue

versity, was drawn into the circle. His visits to the residence increased, except for intervals when he traveled in Europe, and Mrs. Brainard in time became a kind of literary god-mother of the poet. They were married on May 7, 1909.

Among the art objects that hung in the living-room and library of the Moody home were many paintings by Moody himself, for he was a talented artist in addition to being a poet.

After Moody's death in 1910 at the age of forty-two, Mrs. Moody continued to entertain native as well as visiting poets, authors, and other celebrities. On the walls of various rooms were hung autographed photographs of these notables— Vachel Lindsay, Robert Frost, Robert Nichols, John Masefield, James Stephens, Padraic Colum, Sir Rabindranath Tagore, Yone Noguchi, Alfeo Faggi, and Gustavo Arsila.

These were only a few of the many distinguished persons who came to this house in the years after William Vaughn Moody's death. One of the secondary attractions of this cultured household—an attraction that brought it much distinction—were the dinners served by Mrs. Moody. She had always been interested in the fine art of dining, and her meals were widely regarded as rare epicurean adventures. It was out of her experiences in cookery that Mrs. Moody established Le Petit Gourmet, a restaurant in North Michigan Avenue.

"Guests are served in the drawing room, in one corner of which are the shelves and desk where her distinguished husband worked," wrote Hi Simons, a Chicago poet and art critic. "A tiny table is set before each guest, and a servant who has been trained by years of service with the hostess places the food upon those tables. Comfort to a degree undreamed of and conversation of a quality unsurpassed result from this unconventionality."

Mrs. Moody continued to live in the mansard-roofed mansion on Ellis Avenue for many years, and there she died in 1932. Before her death, however, she paid high tribute to the life and work of her late husband by establishing two permanent institutions at the University of Chicago. These are the William Vaughn Moody Lecture Foundation, which regularly brings to the campus some famous author, and the William Vaughn Moody Library of American Literature, which contains a comprehensive collection of books by American authors.

If the Moody mansion is today becoming faded, not so is the picture of Mrs. Moody in the minds of many writers and poets. As one Chicago poet, Mark Turbyfill, said of her: "She was unforgettable. She was one person to whom the phrase 'radiant personality' could be applied without question. Seated on her velvet-covered 'suspended' lounge, which hung on chains attached to the ceiling, she conversed brilliantly on a wide variety of topics and reigned as the literary queen of Chicago."

PART XIV

Here and There

Introduction

Drive or walk anywhere in Chicago, outside the downtown district or the area that was destroyed in the fire of 1871, and you will come, now and then, upon old houses of the sixties and seventies whose proportions and architecture indicate that they were built by persons of affluence and position. These houses are not confined to certain sections or neighborhoods. They may be found anywhere on the North Side, West Side, or South Side. Often, while riding the elevated train, you can see their windowed cupolas above the roofs of modern apartment houses or "two flats" that surround them. Most of these venerable dwellings, with their spacious porches, tall windows, overhanging cornices, and quaint ornamentation, were built in the Civil War period. Some are still being lived in, while others have been converted into institutions of various kinds.

A Civil War Landmark

O F THE few pre–Civil War houses in Wabash Avenue below Eighth Street surviving today as faded reminders of the era when Wabash Avenue was a fashionable, tree-lined thoroughfare, none is better preserved and richer in historical associations than the three-story brick residence at 1145 South Wabash Avenue, now the headquarters of the Illinois Humane Society.

Several years ago a newspaper carried the story that Abraham Lincoln was one of the many distinguished persons entertained in this house when it was in its prime. But this story has been discounted. The daughter of the man who built the house told the present writer that the Lincoln story was untrue.

"If Abraham Lincoln ever visited our house, it would have been such a wonderful thing that my sister and brother and I would certainly have heard of it from our parents," said Mrs. Lester B. Grant, who now lives in Riverside. "It would have been our family's proudest boast. But we never heard of such a visit. There were many other distinguished visitors, however, who came to our house in the years before the Civil War and the Chicago fire."

Although the Lincoln story is shown to be unfounded, the one-time master of this dwelling, John L. Wilson, a Chicago newpaper publisher of the 1850's and 1860's, was a close friend of the Civil War president. Wilson and his brother, Charles L. Wilson, were among the Chicago group who supported Lincoln in the senatorial contest of 1858.

It was Charles Wilson, then associated with his brother in publishing the *Chicago Journal*, who first suggested the Lincoln-Douglas debates, and he was also the man who nominated Lincoln for United States senator at the Republican convention in Springfield in 1858.

After Charles was named by President Lincoln as secretary of the American legation at the Court of St. James, the publishing of the *Chicago Journal* was left in the hands of brother John, who was assisted by Andrew Shuman, editor. Charles returned to Chicago in 1864 and once more took up his duties on the newspaper.

Before all this happened, however, John Wilson had built the residence which still stands today at 1145 South Wabash Avenue. The house was erected in 1857. Although not overly pretentious, it reflected the personality of a successful man of that day. Brother Charles, then a bachelor, was a frequent visitor at the house and was much thought of by the Wilson youngsters.

John Wilson is shown by historians to be one of the actual founders of the city of Chicago. He was a supporter of the movement to get the town incorporated as a city, a movement that was successful in 1837. He first came to Chicago in 1834 and was accompanied by another brother, Richard L. Wilson. Both were natives of New York State.

The two brothers immediately entered the mercantile business. But, in addition to that, John was soon active in public life, becoming second assistant postmaster and a member of the town's first volunteer fire department. Then in 1835 the Wilsons were joined by their younger brother, Charles L., who also went into the mercantile business and who later became a friend of Lincoln.

JOHN L. WILSON HOUSE
1145 South Wabash Avenue

During the years 1839–40 we find John and Richard among the many contractors engaged in building the Illinois and Michigan Canal. Then John became a Whig candidate in

1840 for state senator of the Chicago district but was defeated by the Democratic candidate. Several years later Richard, who seems to have had literary talent, came out with two travel books, *A Trip to Santa Fé* and *Short Ravellings from a Long Yarn.*

From being author of two books it was but a step for Richard to become a newspaper publisher. He and J. W. Norris brought out the first issue of the *Chicago Journal* on April 22, 1844. The *Journal* was Chicago's oldest daily newspaper at the time of its absorption a few years ago by the *Chicago Daily News.*

By this time all three of the Wilson brothers were conducting the *Journal.* Charles joined the newspaper a year after it was founded. John was its business manager. After the death of Richard in 1856, Charles became owner of the paper. That same year John was elected sheriff of Cook County. It was during his term as sheriff that John built the South Wabash Avenue house.

In the following years many notables were entertained in the Wilson house. Richard J. Oglesby, Civil War governor of Illinois, was a frequent visitor, and here, too, came Stephen A. Douglas. A brilliant occasion was the dinner given to General Grant here in 1868. Another visitor was Ole Bull, famous Norwegian violinist.

The Wilson family continued to live in the house until 1870. Here were born and reared a son, R. L. Wilson, and two daughters, Gertrude Quintard Wilson—afterward Mrs. Lester B. Grant—and Laura, who became Mrs. Henry Farrar. A large oil portrait of Laura Wilson, painted by G. P. A. Healy after Miss Wilson had been presented at the court of Queen Victoria, hangs in the Riverside home of Mrs. Grant's daughter, Mrs. Alastair Valentine.

In 1871 the United States government rented the house as headquarters for General Sheridan and his staff at a yearly rental of $5,000, and in the fall of that year the Chicago Fire occurred—but did not touch the house. General Sheridan, who had been placed in charge of the Middle West army corps area, maintained his offices on the second floor. A tall flagpole was erected on the roof.

In 1893 a group of civic-minded men and women of Chicago—among them Marshall Field, Silas B. Cobb, Philip D. Armour, T. B. Blackstone, George Pullman, and O. S. A. Sprague—purchased the Wilson house and presented it as a gift to the Illinois Humane Society. This society, founded in 1869, is dedicated to the saving of animals and children from cruelty.

A few years ago the society granted Mrs. Grant's request for the old flagpole that stood on top of the house. She presented it to her three grandsons, Alastair, Jr., David Charles, and John Lester, and it now stands in the yard of the Valentine home at 238 North Delaplaine Road, Riverside.

A Pioneer Judge's Home

N OTICEABLE as a residential landmark obviously
dating back to a more fanciful era in domestic architecture than ours is the small, two-story dwelling
at the southwest corner of Ashland Avenue and Blackhawk
Street. For the last twenty-three years this house has been
occupied by the St. Elizabeth Day Nursery, a Roman Catholic institution devoted to the care of children of the neighborhood whose mothers are at work during the day.

When first built, more than three-quarters of a century
ago, this little old-fashioned abode stood in the center of a
sparsely settled neighborhood of German immigrants. It soon
became the most important house of the neighborhood, for
here dwelt Jacob A. Schoenewald, regarded by local historians as the "father" of Chicago's once large German-
American colony. Today, because of population changes, the
house stands in the midst of the city's crowded Polish-Ameri-
can quarter.

It was sometime in the 1840's, when Chicago was still a
frontier community, that Jacob Schoenewald came here from
his birthplace, Cologne, Germany. He had been educated at
Bonn University, where he studied law, and soon after his
graduation he married and brought his wife to America with
him. Several years after settling in Chicago, he went back to

445

Germany, told his fellow-countrymen of the opportunities to be found here, and returned with a large group of them.

Before building his homestead on Ashland Avenue, Schoenewald attracted considerable attention in Chicago as the hero of the "beer riot" of 1855. This occurred in North Clark Street when a crowd of German-Americans from the

JACOB SCHOENEWALD HOUSE
1360 North Ashland Avenue

"Nord Seite" were marching on the City Hall to protest the Sunday closing law for saloons and were dispersed by police firing revolvers. One of the marchers was killed and several were wounded.

Through quick thinking on the part of Schoenewald, who was then a justice of the peace, further bloodshed was prevented and order was restored. He was afterward officially commended by the city for his acts during the riot, the city council presenting him with a gold medal "for gallant conduct in the riot of April, 1855."

Three years later, Schoenewald built the house on North Ashland Avenue. After eighty-two years, it remains sound and looks much the same, according to Schoenewald descendants, as when its master first moved into it with his family. So sparsely settled was the section then that the family could see the white sails of ships out in the lake from the front porch of the house.

Schoenewald did clerical work, served as an interpreter in the courts, became a justice of the peace, and in 1850 was named warden of the House of Correction, which then stood at Market and Harrison streets. By this time he had reached a position of moderate affluence and was a leader in civic and political affairs.

He was a staunch supporter of Abraham Lincoln during the presidential campaign of 1860 and was personally acquainted with the candidate. When the Civil War broke out, Judge Schoenewald rallied the German-Americans of the city to the Union cause, and his home on Ashland Avenue became a headquarters for the enlistment of German-American volunteers.

Some years before settling down in his Ashland Avenue house, Jacob Schoenewald and his family lived for a time in a modest dwelling on a lot he owned at what is now Jackson Boulevard and La Salle Street. This site is now occupied by one of Chicago's tallest and most famous office buildings, the forty-five-story Board of Trade Building. Judge Schoenewald sold his lot long before moving to Ashland Avenue in 1858.

After the Civil War he was elected city judge and served in that capacity until his retirement in the late 1870's. He died in 1882. One of his sons, Frank, was afterward elected a state senator. The home was later occupied by Jacob Deutsch and his wife and family. Mrs. Deutsch was one of Judge Schoenewald's daughters.

The house afterward came into the possession of several owners outside the Schoenewald family and finally was acquired by the St. Elizabeth Day Nursery. Meanwhile, the neighborhood had changed, factories and tenements appeared, and Polish immigrants supplanted the early German settlers. The one-time Schoenewald abode today is probably the oldest dwelling in the neighborhood. Many years ago a brick basement was placed under the house when Ashland Avenue was raised to a higher level.

The front of the house is notable for its decorative trim and high-arched windows and doors. A porch stretches across the entire front, and the square columns supporting its roof are marked by highly ornamental capitals. Similarly ornate are the cornices around the edges of the gabled roof. All this is typical of pre–Civil War domestic architecture.

Scores of neighborhood children are cared for in the old Schoenewald home each day by a staff of six nuns of the Order of St. Francis. Activities are directed by a sister-superior, who has won the confidence of mothers and fathers on all sides of the institution. She and the other nuns may be seen on summer afternoons watching over dozens of youngsters as they frolic and play on the grass lawns around the old dwelling.

One day, a few years ago, a woman visited the nursery. She was Mrs. Nicholas G. Miller, wife of a Chicago coal dealer whose grandparents had come to the city in the 1840's.

"I am a granddaughter of Judge Schoenewald," she told the nuns. "I was born in that room where you now have the sanctuary. My parents were Mr. and Mrs. Deutsch. I am sure that my grandfather would be highly pleased if he knew that his home was now a Catholic institution. All his life he had been a devout Catholic."

House of the Arts

╭───╮

I F ONE of Chicago's early settlers and manufacturers, Seth P. Warner, were alive today he would no doubt be pleased at seeing the way in which his residence, now a venerable landmark of Austin, is being used. For it is now one of the liveliest and most influential cultural centers on the city's West Side.

Seth Warner would undoubtedly feel this way about his old mansion at 631 North Central Avenue because he was not only an energetic businessman but also a lover of the arts and a lifelong devotee of music in all its forms. As early as 1846 he was listed as second leader of the Choral Union, one of Chicago's first organized singing groups.

His mansion, which he built in the late 1860's, when Austin was a new residential village outside the city, today houses the Austin Academy of Fine Arts, a nonprofit institution founded by Paul Vernon, violinist. Besides being director of this school, Mr. Vernon is conductor of the Austin Symphony Orchestra, the Austin Choral Club, and the Oriana A Cappella Choir, both of which hold rehearsals in the Warner house.

That Seth Warner, before coming to Austin, was an early resident of the then young city of Chicago is evidenced by the inclusion of his name among those members of the Calumet

449

Club, fashionable organization of the 1880's, who came to Chicago before 1840. Anyway, soon after his arrival here from New England, he is found taking active part in cultural

SETH P. WARNER HOME
631 North Central Avenue

and municipal affairs and laying the foundation for his business career.

In 1846 he became associated with Charles M. Gray in the manufacture of what was then called the Virginia Reaper, a new farm machine invented by Cyrus H. McCormick. The following year McCormick entered into partnership with Gray, and thus was begun the International Harvester Company, one of Chicago's world-famous industries.

When the Civil War broke out, Warner was among the prominent citizens of Chicago who signed the call for a patriotic mass meeting in Bryan Hall. At this meeting the people of Chicago pledged their loyalty to the Union and the Union cause.

A. T. Andreas, in his *History of Cook County*, says that Seth P. Warner "was the first to erect a fine and costly residence" in the village of Austin, which was then the township of Cicero.

Here the Warners resided during the years when Austin was becoming an increasingly populous suburb. Here they reared their son, Charles, and their two daughters, Irene, afterward Mrs. Hasbrouck, and Eva, afterward Mrs. Henry Vandercook.

Warner was one of the founders of the Austin Presbyterian Church, established in 1871. His opinion was sought and respected on matters of public policy in the village, but he never held public office. A year after Austin was annexed to Chicago in 1899 he and his family gave up their home and moved to the South.

The house went into the hands of successive owners, some of whom remodeled it a bit here and there.

Today not many old Chicago houses are so well preserved and so tastefully outfitted with furniture of the era in which it was built as this residence in Austin. Glimpsing its many high-ceilinged rooms with their fine woodwork trim, one is taken back to the Victorian period—to the days of bustles, Prince Alberts, and coaches-and-four.

The exterior is of red brick with white stone trim, high

arched windows, and a wide porch across its front. This porch, incidentally, replaces the original veranda. When first built there was a cupola on the roof, but this was later removed.

All the main rooms, each one notable for veined Italian marble fireplaces, doors of solid walnut, and old-fashioned chandeliers, have been outfitted by Mrs. Vernon with furniture appropriate to the period when Seth Warner lived here.

An Educator's Home

~~~~~~

ONE of the most revered landmarks in Chicago
Lawn, a residential community on the Southwest
Side, is the Eberhart home at 3415 West Sixty-
fourth Street. Here lived the founder of Chicago Lawn, John
F. Eberhart. His fame, however, goes beyond the boundaries
of this community, for John Eberhart was an outstanding
Chicago educator of the 1860's and the founder of the Chi-
cago Teachers College.

When he built this two-story brick dwelling in 1875, John
Eberhart was one of the best-known educators in Illinois.
He had already served as Cook County's first superintendent
of schools and had retained this post continuously during the
Civil War era, or for a total of ten years. Prior to serving in
this capacity he had been editor of the *Northwestern Home
and School Journal.*

"Before his election to this office [county superintendent of
schools], the schools of the county had never had any county
supervision," says a biographical sketch of Eberhart in Andreas' *History of Chicago.* The sketch continues: "And it was
during his term of office, and through his personal effort, that
the schools were first lifted to a higher condition of excellence,
and system and method introduced. He devoted all of his
time to the duties of the office, traveling the county over

from end to end, visiting the different schools, and addressing the people, to create a greater interest in education."

John Eberhart was a native of Mercer County, Pennsylvania, where he was born January 21, 1829. The son of a

JOHN E. EBERHART HOUSE
3415 West Sixty-fourth Street

farmer, Eberhart began teaching at sixteen, worked his way through college, and attained the position of principal of Albright Seminary at Berlin, Pennsylvania. Because of ill-health, however, he resigned this position. He came to Chicago in 1855 and became a lecturer as well as editor of the *Northwestern Home and School Journal.*

"According to our records, it was John F. Eberhart who first introduced Senator Stephen A. Douglas to Abraham

Lincoln," says Mrs. Florence E. Richards, honorary life-president of the Chicago Lawn Historical Society. This historical society, incidentally, was founded by John Eberhart in 1873.

After serving as county superintendent of schools and after helping to organize the Illinois State Teachers Association as well as the State Normal School at Normal, Illinois, John Eberhart retired from the educational field and entered the real estate business. It was in this capacity that he founded Chicago Lawn. His name is perpetuated in the John F. Eberhart School at Sixty-fifth Place and Homan Avenue.

At the same time that Eberhart built his brick dwelling, four other brick houses were erected in Chicago Lawn. Also constructed then was the Chicago Lawn railroad station on the Grand Trunk Railroad. The story is told that John Eberhart and his wife and children, as well as his mother and father, lived in the railroad station while his home was being completed. It was John Eberhart who subdivided Chicago Lawn and who gave the community its name.

In its heyday the Eberhart home was an attractive dwelling, shaded by a grove of trees and surrounded by shrubs, flower gardens, and an orchard. Here were reared the Eberhart children—John J., Frank N., Mary E., and Grace. Here, also, Mr. and Mrs. Eberhart entertained some of the best-known Chicago educators and cultural leaders of their day.

One who came often to the Eberhart home was the Reverend Hiram W. Thomas, who afterward became president of the Peoples Church of America. A one-time pupil of Mr. Eberhart, the Reverend Mr. Thomas had been induced to come to Chicago by his former teacher, and a parish was "made" for him in Chicago Lawn. The present Thomas Memorial Congregational Church at Sixty-fourth Street and Homan Avenue was named after the Reverend Mr. Thomas.

After the death of John Eberhart, the house on Sixty-fourth Street was occupied by his widow, and, with her passing, it became the home of a married daughter, Grace. She was the wife of Clarence B. Herschberger, famous University of Chicago football star of the 1890's. "Herschie," as he was familiarly known to football fans, was the first of the great gridiron stars developed by Coach A. A. Stagg and was one of the all-time greats of Midway football history.

After his graduation from the University of Chicago, Herschberger taught and coached at Lake Forest College. From 1907 to 1921 he was associated with Frank A. Vanderlip, the financier, in New York. He afterward returned to Chicago to enter the real estate business. He died in the Eberhart home in 1936. His widow continued to occupy for some time the house she had lived in since she was a year old. She then moved to another part of the city.

The old landmark is at present occupied by Joseph A. Zerkel and his family. The interior has been somewhat remodeled, and a new brick porch has been added. Living on part of the old Eberhart estate is another daughter of the noted educator, Mrs. George M. Tobey, whose home is at 6420 South Homan Avenue. Her husband is secretary of the Office Building Managers' Association.

An Auburn Park Home

~~~~~~

WHEN John M. Schorling, oldest resident of Auburn Park, died in 1940, attention was centered on the house at 417 West Seventy-ninth Street. For this venerable dwelling was erected by his father, August Schorling, one of the founders of Auburn Park and an early settler of the southern region once adjacent to, but now within, Chicago. He had come here in 1857 when young Chicago was lifting itself out of the mud and beginning to assume importance as a railroad center.

In the years prior to the time he built the two-story frame dwelling on Seventy-ninth Street, just west of Vincennes Avenue, August Schorling had been proprietor of the Ten-Mile House, a well-known stopping place in the 1860's for farmers and travelers on their way to or from Chicago. It stood on old Vincennes Road at what is now Eighty-first Street and Vincennes Avenue.

Before Schorling appeared in this section the Ten-Mile House was conducted by his father-in-law, Christian Duensing.

A cabinetmaker at Michigan City, August Schorling decided that Michigan City's chances of becoming the metropolis of the West were growing less as Chicago pushed forward, acquiring more and more railroads. So he came here with his wife. He did not take up residence in the city proper but immediately went out to the country around the Ten-Mile House and acquired a tract that today is bounded by Seventy-ninth and Eighty-first streets, Vincennes Avenue, and the Rock Island tracks.

He and his wife lived in the Ten-Mile House with Christian Duensing. Soon afterward August became proprietor of the inn, and his fame as a host spread among the Hoosier farmers using the old Vincennes Road. It was eight years after August settled here that his son, John, was born.

Later another child came to the Schorlings—a daughter named Anna. In addition to his duties of conducting the Ten-Mile House, August Schorling was kept busy tending to his many horses and raising hay to feed them. He never became a farmer in the true sense of the word. In those early years the only other settlers of the district, then known as Cummorn, were the Sutherlands, Henkervilles, and Schultzes.

When the time came for Schorling to erect a dwelling of his own, he selected a site at the north end of his tract on what is now Seventy-ninth Street. The house was completed in 1871, soon after the great Chicago Fire, and a few months later August and his family moved into their new abode.

"Before all this happened, and while he was still an inn-keeper," explained his daughter, Mrs. John J. Monahan, widow of a well-known Board of Trade operator, "my father often took care of large numbers of cattle and other livestock being shipped in trains to Chicago. This happened when the trains became stalled in snowdrifts near his tract and the cattle faced starvation. He would water and feed them in his big barns until the snow melted and the trains could move on."

The Schorlings lived comfortably in the Seventy-ninth Street house, saw Auburn Park grow up around them, witnessed the subdividing of their own tract, and were present when Auburn Park and other communities of that region were annexed to Chicago in 1889. A few years later August Schorling and his wife presented the Seventy-ninth Street

AUGUST SCHORLING HOME
417 West Seventy-ninth Street

house as a wedding gift to their daughter, Anna, when she became the wife of John J. Monahan.

The elder Schorlings moved to another house on what was then called Schorling Avenue. At this time August Schorling was operating a tavern at Seventy-ninth Street and Vincennes Avenue known as Schorling's Corner. When he died in 1904 the tavern was taken over by his son, John, who had meanwhile become owner of the Auburn Park semiprofessional baseball team.

In the years when John Schorling was coming to the front as a baseball promoter, his brother-in-law, John Monahan, now master of the old Schorling homestead, was rising as a Board of Trade operator. He and his wife took good care of the venerable house in which they lived and carefully tended the flowers, lilac bushes, and other shrubs that grew under the great shady oaks and elms originally planted by the elder Schorling. The Monahans sold the old place sixteen years ago and moved to Beverly Hills.

Since that time the house has been occupied by Fred J. Wall, veteran engineer of the New York Central System and one-time outfielder of the old Auburn Park baseball team when it was owned by John Schorling.

Although set back a considerable distance from the street, the old Schorling home is easily noticeable. The general construction, the high-gabled roof, the roomy porches with spindled balustrades, and the wide steps and tall, arched windows are marks of the transition period between the Greek Revival and later forms of domestic architecture.

Not quite so old as this dwelling, but nevertheless a landmark, is the frame house a few doors west, where John Schorling lived during most of his married life and which is now occupied by his widow, Mrs. Maude Schorling.

A House in Ellis Park

STANDING in lonely and dilapidated splendor above the dusty elms of one of Chicago's little "forgotten parks" is an old-time mansion that merits the attention of the historically minded of today. For not only is this house noteworthy architecturally but it is also to be remembered as the home of a prominent Chicagoan of the 1870's and 1880's whose name lives today in the little park in front of his mansion—a park that inspired an oft-quoted poem.

More than a decade ago Miss Caroline M. M'Ilvaine, local historian, wrote of this small park: "Another square almost as ghostly, if not as grand [as the then Aldine Square], is Ellis Park between Thirty-sixth and Thirty-seventh streets, just west of Cottage Grove Avenue. Long ago the rustic two-story bandstand disappeared with its mysterious grotto on the ground level, where was an ever flowing artesian well, but lovely shrubbery and greensward still afford a pleasant outlook for the double line of small dwellings that define the east and west boundaries of the park."

Although most of the homes on both sides of Ellis Park are small, the one outstanding exception is the mansion under discussion. Located on the east side of the landscaped park, it rises to a height of two and one-half stories and is surmounted by that characteristic appurtenance of old-style residential architecture, the cupola. The façade is of red brick and is marked by fanciful bay windows and cornices, a richly ornamented stone entrance, and outward-spreading stone steps.

More than half a century ago, or in the years just after the Chicago Fire when the South Side was experiencing a residential boom, this house was built for Almon D. Ellis, afterward known as one of the largest boot and shoe commission dealers in the city.

In the year 1877, when Ellis and his family moved into their new abode, Almon Ellis had not yet entered the boot and shoe business. He was then a successful manufacturer of fine-cut tobacco. "In the early part of 1870," says an old Chicago history, "Almon Ellis formed a partnership with Charles W. Allen of this city, and engaged in the manufacture of fine-cut tobacco."

The history goes on to say that "their entire business was swept away by the fire of 1871, and although they suffered heavily, they met their fate bravely. They re-established the business on their old ground, and not only succeeded in retaining their immense trade, but in three years thereafter had increased their business till it yielded an annual product of $1,000,000." We learn that two years after settling down in his palatial abode on the South Side, Almon Ellis sold his interest in the tobacco firm and retired from active life. He was then fifty-six. Evidently he had decided to spend the rest of his days in the fine residence he had but recently built. Having always been an energetic man, however, Ellis soon tired of inactivity, and in 1881 we find him back in business, this time as a partner of A. A. Putnam in the manufacture of boots and shoes.

While meditating in the library of his mansion, Almon Ellis must have frequently thought of that day in 1867 when he first arrived in Chicago and of the trying days he went through as a private, and later as a lieutenant and captain, in the Union ranks during the Civil War.

ALMON D. ELLIS HOME
3615 Ellis Park

The records show that Almon Ellis remained owner of the South Side residence until 1888. In that year he sold it to one Charles J. Furst. Then followed a succession of owners. In the course of years the neighborhood began to change, and soon Ellis Park and the old Ellis residence were surrounded by a Negro population. Before this happened, however, Ellis Park provided the inspiration for a poem by a Chicago poet which has been reprinted in many anthologies.

The poem is entitled "Ellis Park" and was composed by Helen Hoyt. Here it is in full:

> Little park that I pass through,
> I carry off a piece of you
> Every morning hurrying down
> To my workday in the town;
> Carry you for country there
> To make the city ways more fair.
> I take your trees,
> And your breeze,
> Your greenness,
> Your cleanness,
> Some of your shade, some of your sky,
> Some of your calm as I go by;
> Your flowers to trim
> The pavements grim;
> Your space for room in the jostled street
> And grass for carpet to my feet.
> Your fountains take and sweet bird calls
> To sing me from my office walls.
> All that I can see
> I carry off with me.
> But you never miss my theft,
> So much treasure you have left,
> As I find you, fresh at morning,
> So I find you, home returning—
> Nothing lacking from your grace.
> All your riches wait in place
> For me to borrow
> On the morrow.
> Do you hear this praise of you.
> Little park that I pass through?

At the present time, standing in aloof decay, the ancient Ellis mansion is occupied by the New Bethlehem Church, an all-Negro congregation. In striking contrast to this abode, which survives as an example of housing in the 1870's, is a housing project a block away which heralds a new era in American living conditions—the Ida B. Wells low-cost housing development for Negroes, sponsored by the federal government.

Among the
Elms of Groveland Park

~~~~~~

WHEN Joy Morton, shortly after founding his salt company in Chicago in 1885, decided to build a home in keeping with his social and business standing, he selected a site in Groveland Park. This was natural, for Joy Morton, like his distinguished father, who originated Arbor Day, was a lover of trees, shrubs, and flowers. Groveland Park, that private little residential area on the South Side, provided him with the sort of environment he wanted.

Here, under the shade of friendly elms and in the midst of lawns, bushes, flower beds, and winding paths, he erected a brick residence that was destined to become one of the best-known dwellings in "the park" during the 1890's. Standing on the north side of Groveland Park at No. 638, it is of interest today both for its architecture and as the former home of one of the most prominent families in Chicago's recent history.

Perhaps another reason Joy Morton chose the small South Side park, which, together with its neighbor, Woodland Park, was laid out on land originally owned by Senator Stephen A. Douglas, is that it reminded him of his boyhood home in

Nebraska. He was reared on a rustic estate in Nebraska City called "Arbor Lodge," and it was there that his father, J. Sterling Morton, Nebraska pioneer and territorial governor, inaugurated Arbor Day. The estate, with its attractive Colonial mansion, is now set aside as a park.

After working for a bank in Nebraska City and for the Burlington Railroad at Aurora, Illinois, young Joy Morton came to Chicago with his bride and entered the salt business here. A few years later he had organized, in association with his brother Mark, the salt firm of Joy Morton and Company. The firm subsequently became the Morton Salt Company, and Joy Morton remained at its head throughout most of his mature life.

It was in 1887 or 1888, when Groveland Park was in its prime as an exclusive residential community, that the Morton home was built. As with many dwellings of the well-to-do at that time, it was designed in the prevailing Romanesque mode made popular by the noted American architect, H. H. Richardson. The two corner towers, with their conical roofs, as well as the high-pitched main roof and second-floor window arrangement of this house reveal its Romanesque origin. Instead of the rock-face stone typical of this style, however, the Morton house is constructed of brick.

Here the Mortons lived with their two children, Sterling and Jean, during the late 1880's and 1890's, and here they enjoyed the quiet, leafy charm of the little private park they had chosen for their home. Around them in "the park" lived friendly neighbors. During hot summer afternoons the Mortons lived mostly out on the shaded lawns where a cooling breeze from the lake, although it was sometimes laden with smoke from passing Illinois Central locomotives, brought them comfort.

"Those were happy days," said Joy Morton's coachman,

Jake Soleski, who now lives on East Thirty-fourth street, across from "the park." Although he is white-haired and sev-

JOY MORTON HOUSE
638 Groveland Park

enty, Jake is still active and now serves as janitor for the old Morton home, as well as other homes in Groveland Park. He began as a coachman for the Mortons shortly after their house was built and continued with them until after the Spanish-American War.

"I used to have lots of fun with the Morton children, showing them how to ride their ponies around the park," said Jake. "Then, once or twice a week, I would drive them in the family carriage to their dancing lessons at Bournique's dancing school on Prairie Avenue. And often, too, I drove Mr. Morton to his salt works downtown at the mouth of the Chicago River. But I remember him best for the keen interest he took in the trees and flowers of Groveland Park."

The scene of frequent dinners, attended by many prominent citizens of the day, the Morton home attracted widest attention for its hospitality during the World's Columbian Exposition of 1893. It was in that year that Mr. and Mrs. Joy Morton entertained President Cleveland in their Groveland Park home, as well as the elder Morton, who was then secretary of agriculture in the Cleveland cabinet. Many other distinguished guests were present on the occasion of the presidential dinner.

Among these guests, it might be added, was the host's brother, Paul, who afterward became secretary of the navy in the cabinet of President Theodore Roosevelt. While serving in this position, he often visited the Mortons in Groveland Park. After leaving the cabinet, he became president of the Equitable Life Assurance Company of New York.

The Mortons lived in "the park" until 1905 and then sold their property. Their residence was subsequently acquired by Miss Grace Reed, a schoolteacher, who lived here from 1920 until her death nine years ago. The house is now owned by her niece, Alma Van Winkle, who lives in Florida. Several families rent the premises. Except for marks of age, the old dwelling remains unchanged since the days it was occupied by the Mortons.

There is no record of whether Joy Morton ever dreamed of some day establishing a great arboretum in the Chicago area when he lived in the cream-colored brick house in Groveland Park more than half a century ago. It is certain, however, that the small park, with its elms and lilac bushes, kept alive his interest in horticulture and arboriculture—an interest that was first aroused in him, it will be recalled, as a boy on his father's estate in Nebraska.

Thanks to that interest, Chicagoans today may enjoy the pleasures of one of the largest and most beautiful arboretums in the world. This is the Morton Arboretum, southwest of the city, established in 1921 by Joy Morton. Visited by thousands annually, this four-hundred-acre sylvan tract has been made the home of every type of deciduous and coniferous tree known in the temperate climate. As an outdoor laboratory for the study of such trees it is unsurpassed in America.

Shrine of the Tons

ORTY-EIGHT years ago John Ton, one of the first
settlers of the original Dutch community which
grew into the Roseland of today, erected a two-story,
red-brick house on his prairie farm near One Hundred and
Third Street and Wentworth Avenue and moved into it with
his large family. In doing this, however, he had no idea that
the house he had built would in later years become an unusual
Chicago landmark.

For this dwelling, now old fashioned as it stands there surrounded by modern homes, is a shrine of the Ton family, one
of the largest organized families in the Middle West, its membership including the descendants of John Ton and his
brothers and sisters. There are two thousand in the family
clan, including the descendants' wives, husbands, and children. It is the only family in Illinois to be incorporated as a
nonprofit organization, and its members live in all parts of
the state and in Indiana, Wisconsin, and California.

So strong is the clan feeling of the Tons, so enthusiastic are
they over their family history and traditions, that once a year
a reunion is held in some South Side park or picnic grove, the
Tons coming from adjoining states and sometimes from Los
Angeles, where another large branch exists. Always, on the
appointed day, they gather on the poplar-shaded grounds of

the old John Ton house before starting out for the picnic grove.

These family reunions have been staged here each summer for the last forty-five years. When the first one was held, John Ton was still alive and took active part in the festivities, although he was well along in years. As the founder of the family in America he received the homage due a patriarch. Two years later, however, he died, but the annual picnics have continued and become larger each year. His house has since been occupied by his daughter, Mrs. F. W. Jansen, and her husband.

It was not until John Ton had reached a position of moderate affluence that he built the red-brick house at 316 West One Hundred and Third Street. He had sailed from Holland in 1849 with fifteen other Hollanders and their families, and the entire group, wooden shoes and all, came to Chicago the same year and settled on the prairie some twenty miles south of the city.

In a few years there was a neat, thriving community of Dutch farmers and burghers here called South Holland. How these farmers lived in this pioneer settlement, how they worked hard growing vegetables, raising cattle, making cheese, and rearing large families, is described in one of Edna Ferber's novels, So Big, which won the 1924 Pulitzer prize in fiction.

On the voyage over from Holland in a sailing vessel, an otherwise tragic voyage that lasted forty-two days and was marked by the deaths of seventeen passengers from cholera, romance blossomed for young John Ton. He became acquainted with Agnes Vandersyde, daughter of Leendert Vandersyde, one of the Holland group, and several years later, after their arrival in Chicago, they became husband and wife. That was the beginning of the Ton family in America.

After becoming established as a farmer and after helping to found the First Dutch Reformed Church and the first school in South Holland, John Ton acquired twenty acres of

JOHN TON HOME
316 West One Hundred and Third Street

land at Riverdale, just north of the Dutch settlement, took up residence there, and later became owner of forty acres on One Hundred and Third Street in what was afterward called Fernwood. He and his brother-in-law, Goris Vandersyde, were the first to make a plat of the village of Roseland, so-called because of the profusion of wild roses that grew in that section.

By this time John Ton was ready to build a brick house on his One Hundred and Third Street farm. But before doing this he and his wife went back to Holland on a pleasure trip, and while there John became interested in the domestic architecture of his native land. As a result of this, according to his daughter, the brick house he built upon his return embodies some of the exterior decorative features of a typical suburban home in the Netherlands.

Although the main part of the house, with its squat, pointed tower, numerous gables, bay windows, and Old World details of decoration, remains the same as when it was first built in 1891 by John Ton, the original porch has been replaced by an inclosed brick porch of modern design. An old photograph shows that the original porch was at the second-floor level and was highly decorated with the sort of fanciful wooden scroll work one might find on an old-style Netherlands house.

At the time John Ton was living here the house was surrounded by apple and cherry trees, and north of it lay his fertile acres of farm land. He was then the head of a large family. Four of his children were living with him and five others who had been married were living in various parts of Roseland and South Holland. By this time, too, his three brothers and three sisters, who had come from Holland at his suggestion, were residents of the vicinity and were also founding large families.

The interior of the Ton house has been slightly remodeled, a winding stairway from the basement to the second floor having been removed, but the principal rooms, each with a tiled fireplace, remain intact. On one wall hangs a pencil drawing of the first John Ton farmhouse on the banks of the Calumet River in Riverdale.

One small room of the house is a kind of office headquarters of the Ton Family, Incorporated. Here Mrs. Jansen keeps records of all the Tons, making entries of births and deaths as the occasion requires, and here she preserves old photographs, family relics, and mementos. Although she has no wooden shoes, Mrs. Jansen says she owns a fancy clothes basket brought over from Holland by her mother. She became official historian of the Ton family after the death in 1915 of her brother, Cornelius J. Ton, state legislator, lawyer, and until then historian of the Tons.

PART XV

Toward the Future

Introduction

When English Gothic and French Renaissance houses were still fashionable among the wealthy people of Chicago, a few dwellings were built which presaged the future course of architecture in America and throughout the civilized world. These "straws in the wind" were the work of original architects—men who strove to create an architecture more in keeping with the spirit of modern life than Gothic castles and Renaissance palaces. One of them, Richardson, found freedom from the strait jacket of the classical by designing houses and buildings in a simplified style that was yet dignified, strong, and artistically pleasing. He was followed by Sullivan, who said that the form of a building should be determined by its function. Then came Frank Lloyd Wright, who, benefiting by the work of Richardson and Sullivan, went beyond them and created a typical architecture of the twentieth century, often referred to as "the international style."

The Heath House

ALTHOUGH he intended it to last a long time, Ira A. Heath, contractor of the 1880's, undoubtedly had no idea when he built his residence on the South Side fifty years ago that it would survive to become an architectural landmark of Chicago. So regarded today, the house is often visited by architectural students interested in the evolution of modern American residential design. It stands on its original site at 3132 Prairie Avenue and is usually referred to as the Heath House.

Strikingly simple for a dwelling built during the gaudy late Victorian era, this house, according to experts, is of significance today as a link between an older style of architecture in America, still under the influence of European modes, and a newer development that resulted in the architecture of today as exemplified in the work of Frank Lloyd Wright and other "moderns." In this house we see a breaking-away from unnecessary ornamentation and an attempt instead at directness, simplicity, and artistic balance—all characteristics of modern architecture.

The man who designed this residence, who gave it what significance and fame it has today, was Louis Sullivan, one of America's great architects, noted throughout the world as the "prophet of modern architecture." He designed it, however, before achieving his own original style and while still under the influence of another great American architect, H. H. Richardson, who had helped pave the way for the modern movement. The house, therefore, is Richardsonian in style.

The status of this dwelling in American architectural history is indicated by Hugh Morrison in his excellent biography, *Louis Sullivan: Prophet of Modern Architecture*. After telling of the beginning of Sullivan's career in Chicago and of the partnership he formed with another architect, Dankmar Adler, Morrison says: "That Richardson exerted a strong influence on Sullivan in the late 1880's is apparent not only in the Auditorium but in the Standard Club and the Heath residence, both built before the Auditorium was finished."

Morrison goes on to say that "the Ira Heath residence, built in 1889, is much more Richardsonian and much better architecture [than the Standard Club], although totally unlike any other residence designed by Adler and Sullivan. Here the extravagant depth of voussoirs over doors and windows and the vibrant surface texture of random-coursed and quarry-face masonry endow the façade with much greater richness and force. Richardson himself could not have done better in a similar program."

But Sullivan was not an imitator. Morrison says that "the most interesting aspect of Richardson's influence on Sullivan is the rapidity with which Sullivan assimilated it [Richardson's architectural ideal] and developed it into something entirely new." In another part of the book Morrison points out: "Of course, Sullivan built creatively on what Richardson gave him, never merely imitating but assimilating and going beyond Richardson; this can be seen ever more clearly in later buildings such as the Walker Warehouse in Chicago and the Dooly Block in Salt Lake City."

What Sullivan, as a young man, admired in Richardson's architecture was its simplicity, strength, and honesty; its

IRA A. HEATH HOUSE
3132 Prairie Avenue

doing-away with "all sentimentalities and trivialities" such as characterized most houses of the late Victorian period. But if Richardson's treatment was simple, still its origin was European, for it was a modified form of the Romanesque style. After serving in this style, Sullivan went beyond it and evolved an even more simple and direct manner, a style that more truly represented life in twentieth-century America.

A comparison of the Heath residence with Richardson's most notable example of residential architecture still standing in Chicago, the Glessner House at 1800 Prairie Avenue, shows the extent to which Sullivan came under the Richardson influence. In both houses are found the rough masonry, rounded arches, and simplicity of treatment of what has become known as the Richardsonian Romanesque style of architecture.

Compare the Heath abode, however, with the Charnley residence at 1365 Astor Street, which also was designed by Sullivan, and you observe how much farther, within a few years, Sullivan had gone on the path of originality than had Richardson. And to carry the story even beyond that, compare the Charnley residence with the Robie House at 5757 Woodlawn Avenue, which was designed by Sullivan's pupil, Frank Lloyd Wright, and you obtain a step-by-step picture of the evolution of modern American residential architecture.

In the years since the Heath House was built, the neighborhood in which it is located has undergone a change, and it now stands almost in the center of the great Negro section of the South Side. It is a three-story dwelling and contains some ten or twelve rooms, those on the first floor being adorned with fireplaces and woodwork trim of simple design. The house is said to have cost $15,000 to build. For the last fourteen years the Heath House has been occupied by Mrs. Louise Montgomery and her family.

"Modernism" in the Nineties

F EW residential landmarks of the city have attracted greater attention among students of American architecture than the three-story, horizontal-looking residence at 1365 Astor Street. Situated in the midst of the Gold Coast, it has also been of interest to social historians as the abode, at different periods, of several families long prominent in Chicago life.

What brings architectural students to this dwelling is the fact that it represents one of the first attempts at "modernism" in architecture—an attempt all the more daring because the house was built in the era of eclectic ostentation. Designed for James Charnley, wealthy Chicago lumberman of the 1890's, this mansion survives today as a somewhat joint effort of those two acknowledged innovators, Louis Sullivan and Frank Lloyd Wright.

In his book, *Louis Sullivan: Prophet of Modern Architecture*, Hugh Morrison tells us that the Charnley house was built in 1892. He writes: "Frank Lloyd Wright is probably responsible for the general form, and certainly for detailing the working drawings, although the latter were traced and printed in the office of Adler and Sullivan. It is broader in conception than any of Sullivan's other residences, with more feeling for the organization of plane surfaces, skillfully punctuated by the window voids.

"The severely cubic volumes suggest the beginnings of Wright's later horizontalism. Certain features, such as the balcony and the cornice, are indeed Sullivanesque, but although Wright had completely mastered Sullivan's ornament, he tended when left free to organize it in a tighter

JAMES CHARNLEY HOUSE
1365 Astor Street

geometric fashion, eliminating much of the free-flowing efflorescence of Sullivan's leaf ornament and reducing it to a flatter plane; the difference between the detail of this balcony and Sullivan's own work is striking."

Describing the residence more in detail, Morrison writes: "The base of the building is of limestone ashlar, extending upward to form a horizontal panel around the door and two flanking windows. This is a composition of great simplicity and distinction. The walls are of long, narrow ('Roman') brick, yellow in color, the balcony is stained wood, and the cornices are a light green copper.

"Students familiar with Wright's developed 'prairie style' of the early 1900's find it hard to believe that this is one of his designs, since it has so many qualities of formal symmetry, monumentality, and sheer height that are completely lacking in his later work, together with certain undeniable Sullivanesque features. But a comparison [of this house with others] leaves little doubt that the Charnley residence may be considered as essentially a very early work of Frank Lloyd Wright."

From Morrison's book we learn that Wright, foremost living exponent of modernism, got his start in this field under Louis Sullivan. Arriving in Chicago in 1887 as a lad of eighteen, Wright was given a job in Sullivan's drafting-room where he helped in the work of designing the Auditorium—combination hotel, office building, and theater. Wright stayed with Sullivan until 1893, when he branched out on his own. Afterward he went further than Sullivan in designing buildings that were true reflections of twentieth-century life.

The man who had the daring to erect this house in an age of French roofs, Italian balconies, and Greek columns had come to Chicago in 1866 with a diploma from Yale. James Charnley was a native of Philadelphia, where his father had been a banker. Soon after arriving in Chicago, which then was in the midst of the Civil War excitement, Charnley entered the lumber business and soon was a partner in the lumber firm of Bradner, Charnley and Company. The firm prospered, and Charnley became a man of wealth.

When the time came for him to build a residence suitable to his station, Charnley was one of the best-known lumbermen in the Middle West, having expanded his business to include lumber mills in Wisconsin, Minnesota, and Mississippi. He and his wife, whom he had married in 1871, became well-known residents of the Near North Side millionaires' colony after settling down in their Astor Street residence. The architecture of their new house was then considered "odd" by neighbors on all sides of it.

The Charnleys lived and entertained here during the 1890's and for some time after the turn of the century. The house was then acquired by Redmond Stephens, attorney and socially prominent citizen. His wife, Marion, was a daughter of Norman B. Ream, railroad magnate and philanthropist.

At the close of the World War the house was bought by James B. Waller, real estate man, son of a pioneer settler of Lake View, and father of the present James B. Waller, former alderman, civic leader, and real estate operator.

James Waller had spent his younger days on the little Waller farm up in Lake View, then a township outside Chicago. It was the Waller tract, which lay near what is now Buena Park, that inspired Eugene Field, "the children's poet," to write one of his well-known poems, "The Ballad of Waller Lot." The oldest high school on the North Side is named after Robert A. Waller, brother of the man who bought the Charnley house.

But James Waller did not live long to enjoy his newly acquired residence. A year or so after its purchase he died. His son, James B. Waller III, then took over the house and has been living in it with his family ever since. Here he has carried on the activities that have made him well known in social, political, welfare, and civic circles. Mrs. John Alden Carpenter is his sister. Mrs. Carpenter's first husband was John Borden, socially prominent Chicagoan and explorer.

An occupant of the Charnley house for the last twenty

years, Mr. Waller says that architectural students often come to study his dwelling. The original exterior is intact, as is most of the interior. It is a single-family dwelling and has eleven rooms. The wood trim of the living-room, dining-room, and library on the first floor is noteworthy for the Sullivanesque leaf design that embellishes it.

Where Louis Sullivan Lived

HIDDEN away in old Kenwood, its existence all but unknown to the present generation of Chicago citizens, the house in which lived a great Chicagoan, a man whose influence was world-wide, still stands today. This is the simple but dignified gray-stone abode at 4575 Lake Park Avenue. Here, in the 1890's, when he was at the height of his career, dwelt Louis H. Sullivan, internationally famous architect and father of what is known as the "modern" movement in architecture—a movement that fostered both the skyscraper and the work of Frank Lloyd Wright.

Not only did Sullivan live here but he also designed this dwelling—a fact that makes it an architectural landmark of significance. For in the creation of this house, erected almost half a century ago, Sullivan showed some of his original ideas as an architect and pointed the way toward the modern movement. At the time he conceived this house, Sullivan was in partnership with another architect, Dankmar Adler, and this firm had already executed its greatest achievement, the Auditorium.

Although he had planned the Lake Park Avenue house and lived in it, Louis Sullivan did not own it. From a biography, *Louis Sullivan: Prophet of Modern Architecture*, by Hugh Morrison, we learn that the house had been commissioned by

Louis' older brother, Albert W. Sullivan, who at that time was an official of the Illinois Central Railroad.

"Louis himself lived in it," says the Morrison biography, "from 1892 to 1896, after which his older brother occupied it until 1905, when it passed into other hands. Wright [Frank Lloyd] also mentions having worked on this house, but his original designing must have been confined to certain details, as the general conception seems to be Sullivan's. It is perhaps the best small urban residence designed by the firm."

When plans for this house were drawn, Wright, then a young man, worked in the architectural office of Adler and Sullivan. Wright is regarded today as the leading exponent of modernism in architecture, but few people know that he was greatly influenced, while a young architect, by the original ideas of Louis Sullivan. Subsequently, of course, Wright went much farther than Sullivan in evolving a typical American style of architecture, often called "prairie" architecture.

Three years before moving into his brother's South Side dwelling, Louis Sullivan was married to a Chicago girl, Margaret Hattabough. The couple lived quietly in the Lake Park Avenue dwelling during the time of the World's Columbian Exposition. It was at this exposition that Sullivan, through his design of the great Transportation Building, introduced to the world his conception of architecture based on steel skeleton construction.

While living in this two-story house, Sullivan could recall the buildings and edifices that were to make his name immortal. "Sullivan's permanent place in the roster of great architects is assured," says the *Dictionary of American Biography*. "Chronologically, at least, he is the father of modernism in architecture—the Transportation Building at the World's Columbian Exposition anticipated by five years the Art Nouveau movement in Europe."

LOUIS H. SULLIVAN HOME
4575 Lake Park Avenue

The *Dictionary* continues: "He founded a school of architectural philosophy which has become almost universally accepted. He, more than any man, helped to make of the skyscraper America's greatest contribution to architecture. His original 'Sullivanesque' style of architectural ornament, while too personal and complicated for popular acceptance, was yet a distinct and valuable contribution to the thesaurus of architecture, and his book, *The Autobiography of an Idea*, an intensely personal revelation, is a notable addition to American literature."

In the Lake Park Avenue house, Sullivan, who was the son of an Irish immigrant, spent much time in his library reading books in all fields of thought. "He read a great deal," says the Morrison biography. "The books in his library reveal some rather esoteric interests. There were several books on Japan and Japanese art. . . . . There were a few books on the history of music, others on musical analysis, harmony, etc., and fourteen volumes of oratorios.

"Several books on psychology and psychic phenomena reveal a profound interest in this field. There were in addition well-worn copies of Walt Whitman's *Leaves of Grass* and Nietzsche's *Thus Spake Zarathustra*, especially suggestive to the student of his writings."

After moving out of the South Side house, and after being separated from his wife, Sullivan lived in various places and then, in his last years, occupied a room in the Warner Hotel on Cottage Grove Avenue. There he lived in reduced circumstances, forgotten by the city he had helped make great, and there he died in 1924 at the age of sixty-eight. He was buried next to his father and mother in Graceland Cemetery.

The house he designed and in which he lived stands as a noteworthy example of his unique architectural style. Here is the simple, honest "form follows function" creed he originated and here, too, is the famous "Sullivanesque" ornamentation. In addition to this house and a few more residences in Chicago, other edifices, monuments to his genius, remain—among others, the Auditorium, the Carson, Pirie, Scott department store, and the Garrick Building.

Although most Chicagoans know little of Sullivan, he was accorded some recognition at the Art Institute in 1940, when an exhibition of his preliminary sketches for the Auditorium was displayed. After his death in 1924, a group of Chicago architects and builders erected a monolith over his grave in Graceland Cemetery, and on it were carved these words:

"By his buildings great in influence and power; his drawings unsurpassed in originality and beauty; his writings rich in poetry and prophecy; his teachings persuasive and eloquent; his philosophy where, in 'Form Follows Function,' he summed up all truth in art, Sullivan has earned his place as one of the greatest architectural forces in America."

An "Old" Modern House

A T FIRST glance it seems odd to include, in our discussion of old Chicago houses, a dwelling built only thirty-three years ago. Most people would say such an abode is "new," not "old." But the house we have in mind is old in another sense, for it is a pioneer—and a world-famous pioneer at that—of the modern movement in architecture and design. As such, it has taken on a venerable aspect.

What makes this house, located adjacent to the University of Chicago at the northeast corner of Woodlawn Avenue and Fifty-eighth Street, an architectural shrine, a mecca for architect-pilgrims from all parts of the world, is the fact that it was designed by Frank Lloyd Wright, now generally regarded as a great American architect and as one of the founders of what is called the "international style" in architecture—that is, a modern style in tune with the twentieth century.

After discussing the work of Louis H. Sullivan, an earlier Chicago architect who is said to be the "father" of the skyscraper, the late Thomas E. Tallmadge (an architect, too), in his authoritative book, *The Story of Architecture in America*, wrote: "The most brilliant of Sullivan's disciples was Frank Lloyd Wright of Oak Park, Illinois. . . . . His book of his own work, published in Germany, 1912, is an accepted milestone in the advance of the new architecture. . . . . As one who took the mantle of Sullivan as it fell from him, and smote the waters [of convention in architecture] so that they parted hither and thither, he is venerated by modernists the world over."

In another and more recently published book, *Art in America*, edited by Holger Cahill and Alfred H. Barr and released under the auspices of the American Federation of Arts, the Woodlawn Avenue house is described. "Perhaps one of the finest [of early Frank Lloyd Wright houses]," says this book, "is one of medium size, the Robie House in Chicago (1908) with its fine brickwork, its ship-like plan, and its splendid precision of execution."

Referred to in the architectural profession as the Robie House, so named after the Chicago merchant who ordered it built, this South Side landmark was, according to authorities, a revolutionary departure from the formal, classical style in architecture that came to its greatest blossoming in America at the World's Columbian Exposition of 1893—a world's fair that was staged only a few blocks east of the present site of Robie House.

Although Robie House was a clean break with tradition, although it was an honest attempt to be modern, truly American, and in tune with the twentieth century, it made little impression on the America of thirty-three years ago. Americans still wanted their residences built in the European classical style. They would not listen to the voice of Wright crying in the architectural wilderness of 1908. So Wright turned for sympathy to old Europe, particularly to Germany.

In Germany his work was acclaimed by a small band of progressive architects. They saw his design of Robie House and earlier Wright dwellings and said to themselves that here at last was an architecture as typical of the twentieth century as Gothic was of the fourteenth century. Subsequently, modernism in architecture spread throughout Europe, came to America where it originated, and reached a peak at the Century of Progress International Exposition of 1933. And now, as a result of all this, America is at last building its homes in a native, modern style.

In designing Robie House, Wright gave full expression to the idea that the form of the house should be determined by

FREDERICK C. ROBIE HOUSE
5757 Woodlawn Avenue

its function and by its location. As he was a native middle westerner, born and reared on the prairies, he conceived the notion that a true middle western house, especially one located in open country, should be part of the prairie—that is, have long horizontal planes in harmony with the flatness of the prairie.

The man who employed Wright to design this Woodlawn Avenue house, who built it, and who lived in it with his family must have been a daring person indeed to commission what was likely to be regarded as a monstrosity. But Frederick

Carleton Robie evidently did not mind. He was a native Chicagoan with initiative in his blood. When his house was built in 1908, he was head of the Excelsior Supply Company. He was an educated man who could appreciate new things, as well as old, in the arts.

Some years later the house was sold to Marshall D. Wilber, head of the Wilber Mercantile Agency and one-time commodore of the Chicago Yacht Club. Then, in 1926, the house was acquired by the Chicago Theological Seminary. The story is told that it was the Wilber's Negro janitor, Nathan Smith, who first suggested selling the house to the Chicago Theological Seminary.

There are other stories about this unique house. A kind of neighborhood folklore has grown up about it. One story has it that Wright suggested that the chatelaine of the house should wear a dress with horizontal stripes in it so as to be in keeping with the architecture. Another story says the Robies wanted to keep fresh in memory their pleasant, sea-going honeymoon and so got Wright to design them a house in the form of a steamship.

But none of these stories can be substantiated. Today this renowned dwelling is a woman's dormitory of the Chicago Theological Seminary and is presided over by a procter, Glenn L. Utterback, and his wife, Ruth, who serves as hostess. Since taking up residence here Mr. Utterback has become something of an authority on Wright architecture.

A surprise comes to the visitor upon entering this three-story house. For here, in the long, low rooms with rows of leaded windows on either side, rooms lighted by indirect lighting and warmed by plain brick fireplaces, the visitor sees the original oak furniture, rugs, and other household articles designed by Frank Lloyd Wright. One can hardly believe that all these things, so modern, so lacking in superfluous decoration, were created a third of a century ago.

Index

Index

Adams, Annabelle, 165
Adams, Benjamin, 41
Adams, Benjamin Franklin, 324
Adams, George Everett, 323 ff.
Adams, Henry E., 165
Addams, Jane, 144, 158 ff.
Ade, George, 411
Adkinson, Mrs. Ella R., 405 ff.
Adkinson, Elmer W., 406 ff.
Adkinson, Henry M., 407
Adler, Dankmar, 72, 277, 481, 484, 489, 490
Aldine Square, 99
Aldis, Helen Lynde, 148; see also Lathrop, Mrs. Bryan
Allen, Albert H., 415
Allen, Charles W., 462
Allen, Dr. Florence, 144
Allen, Martha Eleanor, 354
Allen, Nathan, 378
American College of Surgeons, 109, 115 ff.
American Federation of Labor, 200
American Institute of Architects, 47
Amory, Eugene, 284
Anderson, Mary Stuart, 279
Anderson, Sherwood, 411
Andreas, A. T., 7, 89, 172, 198, 206, 212, 218, 254, 303, 318, 357, 358, 373, 427, 451, 453
Arbor Day, 466 ff.
Archbishop's residence, 327 ff.
Architects Club of Chicago, 52
Armour, P. D., 25, 26, 75, 420, 444
Armour, Watson, 75
Armour Institute of Technology, 47, 70; see also Illinois Institute of Technology

Arsila, Gustavo, 434
Art Institute, xi, 20, 51, 74, 131, 148, 149, 192, 262, 281, 283, 385, 405, 493
Art project, W.P.A., 83
Ascham, Roger, 264
Ascham Hall, 264, 265
Association of Arts and Industries, 38, 39
Association House, 376 ff.
Astor Street, 141 ff.
Auburn Park, 401, 402, 403, 457 ff.
Auditorium, 481, 486, 489, 493
Auditorium Theater, 71
Augustana College, 226
Austin, 449 ff.
Austin, Mrs. Edwin C., 367
Austin Academy of Fine Arts, 449 ff.
Austin Presbyterian Church, 451
Auten, Philip L., 190
Avondale, 347, 360
Ayer, Mrs. Walter, 109; see also McCormick, Phoebe
Ayers, Arthur R., 301

Babcock, Helen S., xi, 427
Babicz, Joseph, 386
Baird, Katherine Dole, 96
Baker, Julia, xi
Baldwin, Mrs. A. Rosecrans, 415
Balokovic, Zlatko, 134, 135
Balokovic, Mrs. Zlatko, 134, 135; see also Borden, Joyce
Baptist Theological Union, 424
Barnes, Marion, xi, 303
Baronial style, 401 ff.
Baroque style, 340 ff.
Barr, Alfred H., 495
Bartels, Robert, 362

[PRINTED
IN U·S·A·]